Observing Second Edition
Primary Literacy

Praise for the first edition

'This very readable book is an extremely valuable addition to current literature on becoming a teacher of literacy. Classrooms are complex environments and learning from observation is a challenging process. This book supports such learning in a highly effective way. Powerful and realistic examples of classroom practice are accompanied by commentaries and questions which support the reader in looking critically and productively at learning and teaching. The references to seminal studies and recent research woven throughout the book cleverly reinforce the interdependency of research, theory and practice and also ensure that the reader is provided with clear direction for further self-study. Perkins's book provides accessible and well-structured support for student-teachers in exploring and examining literacy teaching. It will also be valued as a resource for teacher educators exploring new ways of enabling student-teachers to engage critically with classroom practice'.

Cathy Burnett, Professor of Literacy and Education,
Sheffield Hallam University

'What I love about this book is that it is completely grounded in an understanding of how children learn to read, of what classrooms and schools are actually like, and of what students and early-career teachers need to know. Margaret Perkins writes about real children in real classrooms, where things are good, but by no means perfect, and in each context, she shows how excellent teaching makes a difference. The book covers all the big and important theoretical ideas about literacy development but explains and links them to the realities of classroom life in ways that demonstrate that "there is nothing as practical as good theory". This book's value to students and early-career teachers is without question'.

Sue Ellis, Professor of Education, University of Strathclyde

'A very clear book, helping students identify good practice. This is extremely useful as PGCE programmes move towards extended school-based training'.

Alison Baker, University of East London

'This is excellent! Beautifully written. A "must" on our PGCE programme and for teachers doing Masters work'.

Colin Mills, University of Manchester, Institute of Education

Observing Primary Literacy

Second Edition

Margaret Perkins

Los Angeles | London | New Delhi
Singapore | Washington DC | Melbourne

Los Angeles | London | New Delhi
Singapore | Washington DC | Melbourne

SAGE Publications Ltd
1 Oliver's Yard
55 City Road
London EC1Y 1SP

SAGE Publications Inc.
2455 Teller Road
Thousand Oaks, California 91320

SAGE Publications India Pvt Ltd
B 1/I 1 Mohan Cooperative Industrial Area
Mathura Road
New Delhi 110 044

SAGE Publications Asia-Pacific Pte Ltd
3 Church Street
#10-04 Samsung Hub
Singapore 049483

Editor: James Clark
Assistant editor: Rob Patterson
Production editor: Jeanette Graham
Copyeditor: Rosemary Campbell
Proofreader: Sharon Cawood
Indexer: Anne Solamito
Marketing manager: Lorna Patkai
Cover design: Sheila Tong
Typeset by: C&M Digitals (P) Ltd, Chennai, India
Printed and bound by
CPI Group (UK) Ltd, Croydon, CR0 4YY

© Margaret Perkins 2017

First edition published in 2011 and reprinted in 2012, 2013, and 2015 (twice)
This second edition first published in 2017

Library of Congress Control Number: 2016950863

British Library Cataloguing in Publication data

A catalogue record for this book is available from the British Library

ISBN 978-1-4739-6906-3
ISBN 978-1-4739-6907-0 (pbk)

At SAGE we take sustainability seriously. Most of our products are printed in the UK using FSC papers and boards. When we print overseas we ensure sustainable papers are used as measured by the PREPS grading system. We undertake an annual audit to monitor our sustainability.

For Jonathan, Hannah and Ben.

For all the trainee teachers with whom I have had the privilege of working over many years. Thank you for your energy and enthusiasm and for everything I have learned from you.

Contents

About the author

Margaret Perkins worked in initial teacher education for many years with undergraduates, postgraduates and those on employment-based routes in different provider institutions. Before that she taught in primary schools across the age ranges and throughout the United Kingdom as a class teacher and in positions of leadership. For the last ten years, she has been responsible for the primary Graduate Teacher Programme (GTP) and School Direct routes into primary teaching, at the University of Reading, working closely with schools located in more than eight different authorities. It is this experience which prompted the writing of this book. In September 2016 she is going back into school as a class teacher in Year 1 and to work with colleagues across the school to make the English curriculum exciting, relevant and rigorous. Her teaching career is finishing where it began. She will be recording her experiences online at www.back toschoolmargaret.com. Please read the blog and share your thoughts and experiences.

Acknowledgements

First edition

This book would not have been possible without all those teachers and trainee teachers who have shared their teaching with me. I am so grateful to them for allowing me to visit and observe them, to take away their plans and work, to talk with them about teaching and to intrude into their over-busy working lives. Thank you to them all. They are: Jonathan Nice, Helen Canham, Mark Dodds, Debbie Elsdon, Jo Yates, Carly Trillow, Jane Gow, Lisa Wallage, Alison Pumfrey, Chris Palmer, Vanessa Wilcher, Clare Castle, Tamalia Reeves, Lorna Anderton, Catherine Rodrigues, Paula Jenkins, Charlotte Wissett, Amy Smith, Chris Palmer, Zara Hoddle and Chrissie Brookes. I apologise to anyone who feels I have misrepresented their work and to anyone whose work I have inadvertently used without acknowledgement. Please contact me and I will put it right. Any fault is mine entirely.

I would also like to thank my friend and colleague, Prue Goodwin. She gave me her time by talking through ideas, reading drafts and continually reminding me of what lies at the heart of literacy.

Finally, thank you to Jesus for everything.

Second edition

More colleagues have contributed to the second edition and I want to record my thanks to them. They are: Claire Hendy, Claire Hughes, Matt Walkowiak,

Hannah Perkins, Philippa Croucher of Wisborough Green Primary School, Darren Matthews of Pyrgo Priory Primary School and Charlotte Hacking and Farrah Serroukh of CLPE. Again, any errors are mine alone.

Publisher acknowledgements

SAGE would like to thank the following people whose comments have helped to shape this new edition:

Professor Cathy Burnett, Sheffield Hallam University

Professor Sue Ellis, University of Strathclyde

Elaine Haywood, Nottingham Trent University

Colin Mills, University of Manchester, Institute of Education

Introduction: observation and reflection

There are so many books about teaching literacy in the primary school that it seems sensible to begin by stating what this book is not:

- It is not a book which aims to tell you how to teach literacy.
- It is not a book about current policies on teaching literacy (whenever you happen to be reading it and whatever the current policy may be).
- It does not cover everything that might be described as primary literacy.
- It does not only give examples of excellent practice.

You may now be wondering why you should bother reading this book at all! It is aimed at those who are training to be primary teachers and those who have just begun to be primary teachers. However, those who have been teaching for a while may still find something useful in it. Look at the title – *Observing Primary Literacy*. That is what this book is about.

Government policy over recent years has moved firmly towards the positioning of teacher training in schools. There has been a huge increase in SCITT (School-Centred Initial Teacher Training) and in the School Direct route into teacher training. This is where trainee teachers spend most of their time in school and their progress towards being able to address the Teachers Standards is monitored by an accredited provider, often an HEI, who then recommends trainees for the award of Qualified Teacher Status (QTS). However, the White Paper *Educational Excellence Everywhere* (DfE 2016), proposes that the award of QTS be replaced and accreditation awarded by headteachers after trainees have taught in school. The government also desires every school to become an academy, increasing its autonomy and taking away the requirement to employ qualified teachers. All these changes make it imperative that there are resources which support teachers in making sound judgements about the teaching and learning which are taking place in classrooms. A professional knowledge and understanding of the processes of teaching and learning involve much more than implementing schemes or techniques; the outstanding teacher needs to have a deep understanding of why some things work and others don't and be able to make choices based on a theoretically grounded understanding of pedagogy. This book is designed to help those in classrooms look at literacy teaching and learning in an appropriately informed way.

During any training programme, whether in a school or a university, most trainee teachers will encounter teachers who have expertise in literacy and often have a passion for the subject. They will tell trainees about good practice, will inform them of the theoretical underpinning and give trainees many practical ideas for putting theory into practice. I know that is what happens because it is what I do myself most days! Tutors will then tell trainees to go into schools and observe all these wonderful things happening. That is where the problem starts. Trainees go into schools and see lots of wonderful things but they are not the exact same wonderful things their tutors were talking about. The result is that either trainees stop observing, thinking that the teachers are hopelessly out of date, or they stop listening, thinking that their tutors are hopelessly out of touch.

In this book I hope to resolve that dilemma by turning things on their head. Instead of starting with the theory and giving examples of what it looks like in practice, I have started with what is going on in schools and considered how that relates to current understandings. My hope is that this will help trainee teachers to make their own observations more profitable. There are several consequences of this approach:

- The observations are messy. They are real – I collected them in real classrooms over many years. I did not ask teachers to do anything special – I just watched and recorded what they did. In this way, I hoped to be like a trainee teacher sent into school to observe. I did not always know what I was going to see before I saw it.
- The observations are not examples of exemplary teaching. Some of the observations are of trainee teachers and some are of very experienced teachers. Nobody put on a special performance because I was there. Some of the lessons were rather mundane and others were exciting. Some worked well and others not so well. I think they reflect everyday classroom practice. Nothing was written or done especially for this book.

- The observations do not cover every aspect of literacy teaching and learning. I think that most of the important things are covered in this book but not in as much detail as they could be. That is not the purpose of this book. I hope this book will model to you how to observe in schools and what to do with your observations.

Observation

When training to teach, a lot of emphasis is put on observing experienced teachers. This is where teacher training is not like other learning experiences. When learning to drive you were not taken to the side of the road and told to watch experienced drivers; when learning to swim you did not sit at the side and watch good swimmers go up and down the pool. However, it is claimed that observation is a valuable way of learning how to be a teacher.

The problem is that good teaching is invisible; it is like a swan who glides beautifully along the river while, unseen to the observer, there is frantic activity going on underneath the surface. Teaching is just like that. Often, when sitting in the corner of a classroom, observing an experienced teacher, it can all seem so easy. That is because you are only seeing the surface and all the activity cannot be seen on the surface. This book gives you a snorkel and helps you to go beneath the surface to see what it is that supports the visible teaching.

Secondly, this book will help you to make your observations more purposeful by showing you what is important to look at and what can be overlooked. It is easy to be so busy looking at one thing that you miss a key event which is taking place.

Thirdly, this book helps you to see classroom activity with fresh eyes. Most trainee teachers have spent some time in schools before starting their training and are familiar with day-to-day classroom life. There is much that becomes taken for granted. This will help you to 'make the familiar strange'.

Finally, this book will help you to ask questions about what is seen. It cannot and does not purport to give all the answers, but it does ask lots of questions, and in asking questions, I would argue, we are often guided towards a deeper understanding. Many very experienced teachers operate at the intuitive level and find articulating reasons for their practice either very difficult or very challenging. I hope that this book will help trainees make their own meaning from classroom life by the questions they ask and the connections they make. It could almost be said that the observations are the text and trainees are being guided towards making their own meaning from them with the support of the commentary in the book.

In this introduction I focus on three aspects which all relate to the key purpose of the book, which is to help you make sense of classroom observations. There is a section about learning, about observing and about becoming a teacher.

About learning

How do you learn best? I learn best by writing. If I need to remember something or make sense of a difficult idea, I write, covering pages and pages with notes that afterwards make little sense to me. It is the process of committing thoughts and words to paper that helps me learn. My daughter also learns by writing, but her writing is neat and orderly and she refers to it again and again. She makes mind maps and PowerPoint presentations and will return to them many times. At the end, she has a valuable resource of notes and thoughts. My son learns best by talking. If he has to learn or revise something, he will sit and explain it to me, or whoever else happens to be around. He will ask for opinions and ideas, and will discuss and argue for hours. At the end, there will be no visible final product but he will have made sense of it for himself and will 'know' what he needs to know.

What do these different ways of learning have in common? In our own way, we are making the body of knowledge, the concept or the skill our own. We are taking it and 'playing' with it until it is familiar and part of our understanding. This is what learning is about. We have not really learned something if it is just stuck onto the edge of our thinking; it needs to be assimilated until it is an integral part of our conceptual framework. Moon expresses this in a more 'academic' way: 'The process of learning is not … about the accumulation of material of learning, but about the process of changing conceptions' (2004: 17).

Learning to be a teacher happens in much the same way. At the beginning we try to emulate behaviours and language that we see, but it never really works. All trainee teachers lament the fact that an experienced teacher will walk into the classroom and the children will be quiet, but when the trainee walks in and, on the surface, does exactly the same thing, nothing happens. We can learn a long list of behaviour management strategies; we can know how to ask open questions and open up dialogue; we can be adept at organising and managing the class, but it is only when we *become* a teacher, rather than just acting like one, that we really understand the social and intellectual framework of the classroom and can make professional judgements of our own.

If we are to learn in this way, we need to explore what we see and dig deep below the surface. I hope that this book will help you to do that.

What we learn needs to be close to our current understanding before we take the next small step in understanding. Two trainees might watch the same lesson and they will each learn something different. That is to be expected. We need to ensure, however, that our understanding changes. If our observations just confirm what we already know and do not lead us to question or challenge our current position, we will not learn.

Read

Moon, J.E. (2004) *A Handbook of Reflective and Experiential Learning: Theory and Practice.* Abingdon: RoutledgeFalmer.

What it is important to remember about learning before we begin to observe:

* Before we begin we need to be sure of what we already know.
* Learning begins by asking questions.
* Everybody learns in a different way.
* We have not really learned something until it is a part of us.

About observing

Often, we think it is easy to observe and so do not give much thought to it. We walk into a classroom, notebook and pencil ready, sit in the corner and write down everything that happens. It will not be long, however, before we realise that it is not that simple. When do we start recording and when do we stop? Do we record everything? Can we join in while we are observing?

There are several principles of observation which, if remembered and observed, will help your observations to be more useful to you:

* *Focus.* Before beginning an observation, decide what you are looking at. If you want to learn about teachers' questioning skills, then just note all the events happening concerning questions. You do not need to record everything in the classroom. If you want to observe a teacher's behaviour management strategies then you need to record what he does when he uses them; you do not need to write down everything that happens all through the lesson. Be clear about the focus and purpose of your observation.
* *Set expectations for the lesson.* It is always helpful to talk with the teacher before you observe a lesson, so that you know what the purpose of the

lesson is and what the teacher hopes to achieve. If possible, ask the teacher for a copy of the plans; this will help you both to plan your observation and also to be aware of what the lesson is about.

- *Record objectively.* It is important to record exactly what you see and hear and be careful not to make an instant interpretation. Note the difference between this observation:

  > J was bored with the lesson and kept looking around to see what other children were doing.

  and this one:

  > J wriggled while sitting on the carpet. He turned around six times during the input and looked at the children immediately behind him.

  You will see that the second observation states what J did but the first one puts an interpretation on those actions. You have no way of knowing that J was bored; you have just seen what he did.

- *Reflect on what you have observed.* Earlier in the chapter I said that learning comes from asking questions of what is known so that our current understanding is challenged. After an observation it is important to read through your observations carefully and look for anything that surprises you and is unexpected. Match what you have seen against what you have known, and note those things which contradict your expectations.

- *Ask questions.* Having noticed the unusual and unexpected, ask questions. Why was J wriggling? Was it because the floor was hard? Was he bored? Did he want to go to the toilet? Was somebody behind surreptitiously poking him? Look beneath the surface. Why did the teacher ask that question to that particular child? Why did that child respond in that way?

- *Draw conclusions.* At the end of every observation, ask yourself the question, 'What have I learned?' Remember what your focus was and articulate what you have learned about that focus. How did you learn that? Can you explain your learning to somebody else? How has your understanding of that issue developed?

- *Plan future learning.* What do you need to do next? Do you need to read something to explain what you have observed? Do you need to do another observation to check it out? Do you need to ask the teacher or the children to explain something to you?

About becoming a teacher

Becoming a teacher is about becoming a professional, and that means making decisions and judgements about children and pedagogy. In order to make an informed decision, it is necessary to understand why teachers do what they do and why they choose not to do certain things. This means you need to reflect on what you have observed. What does it mean to reflect?

Schön (1983: 102–4) defined reflective practice as 'the capacity to reflect on action so as to engage in a process of continuous learning'. Teachers are continually making decisions based on what is happening in the classroom and Schön argues that this 'reflection-in-action' leads to professional knowledge gained from experience which informs that decision-making. Observing other teachers gives the trainee teachers the chance to step back and reflect on what is happening in classrooms. This can sometimes be challenging. In the immediacy of classroom activity, it can be difficult for even very experienced teachers to fully appreciate what is going on. I showed one teacher, whom I observed for the book, my comments on her lesson and her response was, 'I did not know all that was happening'.

The term 'observation' is used in the broadest sense. The observations in the book contain all those things that, in my experience, trainee teachers are asked to look at and learn from:

- lessons being taught
- lesson plans
- unit of work plans
- children's work
- conversations about practice.

How the book works

Observations, in whatever form they take, are presented in detail. A running commentary is provided which explains what is happening relates it to theory and asks questions to help you to reflect. As each chapter progresses, the commentary becomes thinner and the questions increase. The book is designed to provide a model and a scaffold for trainee teachers as they observe. As the government pursues its vision of a school-based system of initial teacher training, it becomes even more important that both teachers and trainee teachers are able to reflect on practice and ask questions of themselves which will lead to a deeper understanding of learning and how it is achieved. It is in this way that 'standards' will be raised and pupils empowered to use literacy for their own and the greater good. This means that trainee teachers must know how to make sense of what they see and be able to ask questions of it. In this way they will become critically reflective and responsive practitioners.

Understanding texts

Texts are at the heart of literacy. All the observations in this chapter explore what counts as a text in literacy teaching and learning, teachers' knowledge of texts, and the place of texts within the school and classroom.

The Office for Standards in Education, Children's Services and Skills (Ofsted) report *Reading by Six: How the Best Schools Do It* (2010) has at its heart the belief that learning to read is the most important thing that schools can teach children, and looks at 12 schools which are deemed to be successful in this. The summary of findings and recommendations attributes the success of these schools to 'a very rigorous and sequential approach … through systematic phonics' (Ofsted 2010: 4). This is clearly very important, and in Chapter 3 we consider some observations of strategies for teaching reading, including phonics. However, it is interesting that Ofsted makes no mention in the summary of findings and recommendations of what children read, and it is this which is the focus of this first chapter. I have deliberately called the first chapter 'Understanding texts' because it seems to me essential as teachers that we consider how the texts we use impact on children learning to be both readers and writers.

If I reflect on my own behaviour as a reader, I know that *what* I read greatly affects *how* I read. There are some novels which I read really quickly, skimming over descriptive passages because I only want to know what happens; yet I have just finished re-reading Jane Austen's *Persuasion* and I read that really slowly, savouring in the delights of Austen's language. If I am reading a magazine, I skim over the text to get the gist of the subject matter, but, if I am reading an academic textbook or article, I will read slowly, frequently re-reading sections and sometimes reading aloud to make sure I truly understand. Think about your own reading behaviour and note how the text you are reading affects how you read.

My knowledge of texts also affects how I write. In writing this, I am imagining I am talking to my current group of students. I have particular faces in mind and am remembering how they respond in lectures. I am also remembering other textbooks I have read for trainee teachers and am recalling their style and 'voice' as I write. Earlier today I wrote a reference for somebody and wrote in a very different style; I used a set format and thought carefully about how each word would be interpreted. I have also been working on an article for an academic journal and before writing looked at several past editions of the journal, reading other articles to see the style of writing that was acceptable. This emphasises again the centrality of the text in the processes of reading and writing.

What counts as a text?

It will be clear from the previous two paragraphs that I read and write a variety of texts, and there are even more which are an integral part of my daily life. Just this morning I have read and written emails, updated my status on a social network site and read the statuses of friends, looked for information on lots of different Internet sites, read the post and yesterday's newspaper, checked my diary and written in two new appointments, written notes on sticky pads as I took phone calls, read and sent texts on my mobile phone, looked on a spreadsheet to find information for the accountant and checked the label on the yoghurt for the sell-by date. All that happened in the space of four hours. The texts I read and wrote were all very different in their purposes, formats and audiences. My children read and create an even greater range of texts, using, among other things, pencils, keyboards, visual images, sound, photographs and film. It is now common to look on YouTube to find instructions or information rather than in a traditional book, and communication takes place through Twitter, Snapchat, etc. We are encouraged to scan QR codes to access information and coding is now a part of the National Curriculum in England. We must assume that this has huge implications for literacy teaching and learning.

The English National Curriculum (DfE 2013) puts emphasis on enabling children to develop pleasure in reading and states that this happens through encountering a wide range of poems, stories and non-fiction. It is interesting that in this curriculum there is no explicit discussion of the nature of texts and there appears to be the implicit assumption of print-based continuous text. The Scottish curriculum, *Curriculum for Excellence* (Scottish Executive 2004), specifies that children should encounter both continuous and non-continuous texts, including both traditional formal prose and oral, electronic or film texts. The curriculum document defines a text as 'the medium through which ideas, experiences, opinions and information can be communicated' (p. 23).

What is common about all these different kinds of texts is that in both reading and creating them the communication of meaning lies at the heart of all that is done. Texts may use a variety of methods or modes to convey or express meaning – words, pictures, images, photographs, video clips, sound files, hyperlinks. Some texts use several of these and they are known as multi-modal texts. Reading and creating a multi-modal text requires many more skills than reading or writing written texts, and children in the twenty-first century need to be skilled in all these modes of communication. The knowledge required to be an effective reader and writer today is very different from when I learned a long time ago and I am often conscious that I am catching up in my skill base.

Whatever the nature of a text, what we are reading or creating matters and it is through encounters with texts that children learn what it is to be a reader and writer. Over 20 years ago Margaret Meek wrote a very influential book about this very thing, and in more recent times Vivienne Smith has written about why texts matter for the way in which children become readers.

Read

Meek, M. (1988) *How Texts Teach What Readers Learn.* Stroud: Thimble Press.

Smith, V. (2008) 'Learning to be a reader: promoting good textual health', in P. Goodwin (ed.), *Understanding Children's Books: A Guide for Education Professionals.* London: SAGE.

Stone, G. (2011) *The Digital Literacy Classroom.* Leicester: UKLA.

Reflect

How does the nature of the text affect the reading process?

The observations in this chapter put texts at the centre of teaching primary literacy, and the first observation concerns a unit of work where the study of texts informed children's creation of their own texts.

OBSERVATION: The first two lessons of a Year 4 (ages 8 and 9) class unit of work with an author focus

This unit of work formed part of cross-curricular work in Design and Technology, Art and Literacy. The intention of the whole unit was for the children in the class to make their own books, hopefully inspired by a visit from the author, Paul Geraghty. He is a South African, now living in London, who writes and illustrates children's books. The illustrations capture the light of Africa with its vibrant colours; they are bright and yet soft and full of curves. The stories are a strange mix of reality and anthropomorphism – they explore human values, relationships and emotions but within the context of real animal behaviour. Many of the stories are based on observed real-life incidents from Africa.

The first lesson of the unit took place on the morning of the author's visit. There were two learning objectives:

- to be able to evaluate the work of an author
- to understand the relationship between text and images in a picture book.

The lesson began with an introduction to Paul Geraghty, giving a taster of information about him and informing the children that he was going to come and talk to them that afternoon. That generated a lot of excitement among the children.

Comment

It could be argued that the children were not given much notice of the author visit and there was limited time for preparation. The teacher would argue that the immediacy of the visit gave a sense of urgency to the lesson and the children were highly motivated and engaged. What do you think?

The teacher then read the book *Over the Steamy Swamp* to the class using a visualiser so that they could see the illustrations. This is a story bringing the food chain to life. A mosquito flies over a swamp; behind her hovers a dragonfly; behind her sits a frog; and so it continues. The strong illustrations are colourful and there is a humour to the whole text. After the reading the children were asked to talk with their partners and share first impressions of the book.

Comment

Notice how the teacher first asks the children to make a personal response to the book. It is really important that children are given the opportunity to do this before they begin any more detailed analysis of the text. Michael Rosen says: 'We read because it either gives us pleasure or because there is something we want to know. In other words, we read for the meaning' (2010: 2).

Note also that the children are asked to talk about their responses with their partners. We will see over and over again how important talk is in the learning process. It helps to clarify ideas, to extend understanding and develop thinking by engaging in debate.

An extremely useful framework for this has been established by Aiden Chambers. He suggests the following three 'sharings' as we talk about books we have read:

- *Enthusiasms* – what is it that excites you about the book? These enthusiasms can be either positive or negative and can relate to plot, setting, character, style or anything else at all.
- *Puzzles* – what questions do you have about the book? What is it you don't understand? Are there any gaps for you? Where do you want to go 'behind the scenes'?
- *Patterns* – what patterns or links do you notice as you read the book? Are there patterns in the language used, in the illustrations, in recurring elements of the plot, in characters' behaviours or in links to other texts you have read or to real-life experiences?

I have used this framework with children from age 3 upwards, with students and with my peers when discussing books we have read.

Read more about it and the importance of giving children time to talk about books in:

Chambers, A. (2011) *Tell Me (Children, Reading and Talk)* with *The Reading Environment*. Stroud: Thimble Press.

You might also want to look at the work Pie Corbett has done on 'Book-talk' (Corbett 2008a), which will give practical ideas on how to implement Chambers's approach.

After the pair talk, the class were asked to get into their well-established literacy groups to evaluate the book. First, as a class they discussed what it meant to evaluate a book and what they needed to look for when reading. Their discussion yielded a list which included such questions as:

- Is the story exciting?
- Is it funny?
- Is the language good? Does it help me to make pictures in my mind?
- Do the illustrations add anything to the words? Do they tell a different story?
- Do the characters seem real? Can we believe what they say and do?
- What are the best and worst bits?
- Would I recommend this book to a friend?

Comment

The questions generated by this class would indicate that they have had a lot of experience in talking about and evaluating texts. A class is unlikely to come up with such questions without these experiences. Consider how this helps the children develop their reading skills and behaviour as readers.

The children then worked in their groups. Each group produced a written evaluation of the text. They worked together; one child was elected as scribe. The groups were of mixed ability and so those less confident in writing were able to make as much contribution as others without the pressure of having to write all their thoughts down.

Comment

It is important to remember that because a child struggles with recording ideas this does not mean that their ideas are not as powerful as those of other children. This teacher used mixed-ability groups with a more able child as scribe. What other strategies can you think of?

The children were given just 20 minutes to complete their evaluations. They were written in note form and were not particularly neat! In this instance that did not matter because the purpose of the writing was to record discussion in order to remember it. This was writing used for an authentic purpose.

At the end of the lesson, the class came together and shared key points. The teacher recorded these and ensured the children were able to give concrete examples from the text for each point that was made. There then followed a short discussion on any questions or comments the children might want to put to Paul Geraghty in the afternoon.

Reflect

How well prepared do you think the children were for the author visit? What knowledge and understanding had the morning's lesson given them?

Paul Geraghty visited in the afternoon and this further stimulated the children's interest in his work. Among other things, he talked about how some ideas became books and how some did not! He showed actual examples of idea doodle-sheets, presentation thumbnails (a kind of cartoon-strip miniature of the story used to show to editors), rough drawings, finished illustrations, proof prints, the book as a large running sheet – prior to cutting – bound proofs and, finally, the finished book, which was then read to the group, who afterwards asked questions.

The next day the children began to plan their own books. The lesson began by looking at the structure and characteristics of a story. The teacher started by asking the children to remember stories they had particularly enjoyed and to tell their partners a simple outline of the plot. The class then came back together and the teacher showed them the story hill pro forma.

Comment

This activity worked for several reasons. First, it began with the children's own experiences; they were talking about books they knew well and so were confident enough to share ideas. Secondly, they were telling the story to one other person; this gave them the confidence to 'have a go' as mistakes would be relatively private. Thirdly, the 'theory' came out of the children's analysis and discussion of well-known stories and so they were able to make it their own. Deep learning is not about repeating what you have been told, it is about transforming knowledge into personal understanding.

All stories have basically the same structure:

opening → build up → climax/conflict → resolution → ending

Many resources are available to help with this, and the story hill is just one of them. It can be found on www.primaryresources.co.uk. Another idea is to take each part of a story and match it to one finger on your hand; you can then hold your story in your hand.

The teacher then read the class another Paul Geraghty book, *Solo*. This is about Solo the penguin chick who is left alone in the Antarctic when her mother leaves to search for food. The tension of the book comes from the uncertainty of Solo's survival.

The children shared their personal responses as before but this time focused more closely on the relationship between the illustrations and the written text. The teacher asked them to consider how Paul Geraghty had told the story through the different elements of the book. As a whole class they then matched the narrative of *Solo* to the story hill pro forma.

The children were then sent off to plan a story they were going to tell in the book they would make. They were given the options of brainstorming on their own, of talking about it with a friend or of drafting it out on the story hill. They could choose any or all of these strategies as long as they had firmly fixed in their minds the story they wanted to tell.

Comment

Note how the teacher allowed the children to choose how they planned their story. He offered them different ways of working, and in reality allowed other ways he had not offered. All he wanted was that, at the end of the allotted time, each child had the outline of a story in their head. He did not even worry if they had not written it down, as long as the children were sure they could remember it and were able

(Continued)

(Continued)

to tell it to somebody else. Reflecting on your own learning will remind you that learners do best when they are allowed to work in the ways which suit them. For teachers it is important to keep focused on the learning objective, and that will enable you to realise what is important and what is not.

There were several more lessons during that week in which the children worked on their story and each created their own book. They were then able to share their books with each other and eventually put them in the class library.

What can we learn from this observation?

- The first thing that needs to be said is that real texts are central to all the work. If we want children to be readers and writers they need to understand the purposes of reading and writing. By using real books as models for understanding and analysing what authors do to make a book successful, children come to understand what literacy is all about. Reading and talking about multi-layered texts and listening to authors talk is a more powerful teaching strategy for effective writing than lots of exercises adding in 'wow' words and fronted adverbials to sentences.
- Secondly, this lesson reminds us that children learn in different ways and lessons need to cater for this and be flexible in the opportunities offered to children. Teachers need to be clear about the purpose of a lesson or a sequence of lessons and allow children the time to move towards it in the way which suits them best. One approach will not suit all children.
- Thirdly, working with texts means looking at every aspect of the text and not just decoding the printed word. The illustrations in Paul Geraghty's books contribute to the meaning of the whole – the style, colour, shapes and light all evoke atmosphere and help the reader to make sense of the story. The choice of words and the order in which they are written also matter. The size of the pages, the arrangement of words and pictures and the font used, all contribute to the whole. As pupils talk about books they will come to understand this, and these children, as they created their books, were doing much more than just writing a story – they were composing a whole text.

Teachers choosing books

If teachers are going to make texts the centre of their literacy teaching, they need to have an extensive knowledge of children's texts themselves. If they are going to choose texts which will demonstrate to children the power of the written word, they need to have read, thought about and discussed these texts. It is clear, therefore, that teachers need to have a strong knowledge of children's books. The Teachers as Readers project (Cremin, Bearne, Mottram and Goodwin 2007–10) looked at this very issue and one of the main aims of the project was to discover the extent of teachers' knowledge of children's literature. They found that this knowledge was 'severely limited'. The research team suggested that the requirement of the National Literacy Strategy to focus on 'significant authors' has limited the number of authors which teachers use in their teaching.

The teachers in the sample knew such a narrow range of authors that they were unlikely to be able to make recommendations to their pupils beyond the limited selection that teachers already used in their classroom. Most of the authors named by the teachers in the sample were extremely well known.

How extensive is your knowledge of children's books?

Read

Cremin, T., Mottram, M., Bearne, E. and Goodwin, P. (2008) 'Exploring teachers' knowledge of children's literature', *Cambridge Journal of Education*, 38(4): 449–64.

OBSERVATION: Talking to teachers about reading aloud to children

A few years ago a colleague and I (Goodwin and Perkins 2009, 2010) did some small-scale research on reading aloud to children. We did this because, although reading aloud to children was a definite expectation within the Literacy Framework, anecdotal evidence suggested that it was not happening frequently. Our underpinning belief was that reading aloud is much more than an enjoyable experience, although one hopes it is that; it is also an important lesson in any teaching of reading programme. We wanted to find out if teachers did read aloud to their classes, and the reasons they had for doing this if they did. We found that teachers did read aloud to their classes but saw it mainly as a good way to establish social cohesion in a class. It was not something which was planned and it happened most often at the very end of the day. It tended not to feature in planning.

Reasons given for reading aloud included the introduction of different types of authors, books and texts to children. However, it seemed that the choice of texts read was mainly made by the children themselves, with teachers sometimes selecting their own favourite texts.

Comment

Can you see any contradiction in these statements?

There were no surprises in the types of texts read to children: short stories, poetry, picture books, comics and magazines, and a few others including newspapers, e-books, charts, song words, non-fiction and a joke book. Our sample named 220 books, including fiction texts, children's novels and single stories, collections of short stories (five), picture books (mostly younger readers), traditional tales (myths, folk tales, legends), five poetry books (two classic poems) and three non-fiction (all in narrative form).

Comment

Imagine you are the teacher of a class in a particular year group. Can you list the key authors and/or texts you would want to be absolutely sure the children in your class encountered?

If we accept the view that the texts that children encounter are important in the learning process, as teachers we need to ensure we know the best texts to introduce them to. How can teachers do that? The Teachers as Readers project (United Kingdom Literacy Association 2007–10) claims that teachers should be readers who model reading behaviours and create communities of readers. This means that they will provide children with time to get totally absorbed in a book, they will read aloud to them and offer books the children can read with ease. In order to do this, teachers need to be fully confident to make decisions about all the different texts used to teach literacy in their classrooms.

Read

Go onto the website of the United Kingdom Literacy Association (https://ukla.org/). In the research section look for the report on the Teachers as Readers project in the Previous UKLA Funded Research section.
   What are the implications of this for you as a reader?

Finding your way through the hundreds, if not thousands of children's books which are published and making an informed decision seems a daunting task unless you can turn to an expert for advice and support. Teachers urgently need librarians beside them when they set out to create confident young readers:

> The skills and knowledge offered by librarians have never been as necessary as they are now when successive governments have imposed a didactic reading curriculum and many teachers have lost confidence in their intuitive use of literature with their pupils. In education we need the support and positive input of librarians to reinvigorate the teaching of reading. (Goodwin 2011: 42)

The role of libraries

Libraries have always provided access to the worlds of information and literature for everyone. Wherever I have worked, there has always been a public library from which to borrow books, whether I have needed books for information, to learn something new or for the delight of a well-written tale. Most schools have a library – whether it be a purpose-built area with space for books, browsers and displays, or a few shelves in an old stock cupboard – a school with a library shows a commitment to literacy. There is little national support for teacher librarians in primary schools, which makes the School Library Association (SLA) well worth joining as it offers advice and support to anyone who organises a school library. Some (but increasingly fewer) local authorities fund a School Library Service (SLS) with centralised book collections and support staff. The SLS usually provides schools with collections of books to support learning. These days, most local SLSs have to charge a fee for their service. However, several hundred pounds would be nothing compared with the thousands it would cost to buy the books – not to mention the advice. Public libraries also do their best to support schools with literacy learning. Baby Bounce and Rhyme Time, storytelling for the under 5s, Summer

Reading Challenge events and book awards all invite children into the world of reading. It is unfortunate that teachers do not always make the most of these very valuable assets.

Read

Look at the website of the School Library Association and see what support they can offer you as a teacher (www.sla.org.uk). In particular download the Primary Schools Library Charter and use it to reflect on libraries in the schools where you have observed. There is more about libraries in schools in Chapter 5.

Children's views on texts

Having considered the importance of teachers' understanding of texts, the next section looks at what children think about the texts they read. I talked to groups of children in Foundation Stage 2 (age 4–5) and Year 1 (age 5–6) and Year 2 (age 6–7) about their views of the books they read. I sat with groups of children in the school library and asked them to tell me about reading. It was not possible to record the conversations but I made detailed notes immediately afterwards.

OBSERVATION: Conversations with children

1. Reception children (ages 4 and 5)

All the children said that they liked reading and their choice of favourite book seemed to be either the book they were reading at present or had read recently, or something they had seen on the television or at the cinema. All the children said reading happened a lot at home; they read to their mums and their mums read to them. They talked about going to visit the local library with their mums to choose books. They enjoyed this time of reading; it happened on the sofa or in bed and was associated with cuddles and was a cosy social time. Reading at home was all about enjoying a text together.

In contrast, they described reading at school as 'work' and they identified those in the class who were 'good readers' as those who were good at decoding. Reading in school was a serious business and not to be taken lightly; one little boy said to me: 'If we read it quickly, we might be trying to get on to another book but that's not really learning'. All their comments on reading in school were dominated by the colour of the book they were reading. One child said, 'I was the first one in our group to be on green books'.

Comment

These children had been in school for only two terms and were already making a clear distinction between reading at home and reading at school. They talked about books at home in terms of what they were about and whether they liked them or not; they talked about books in school as to how high up the scheme they were.

2. Year 1 children (ages 5 and 6)

Again, all these children said they liked reading. They had all brought their school reading book to the library with them and when I asked them what their favourite reading book was, every child chose that one. All of the children said they read at home but several said they only read school books at home to practise for reading at school. One boy told me that his mum had bought him a complete reading scheme so he could practise more at home. Reading at home was, as with the younger children, associated with a sociable comfortable time, on the sofa or in bed.

Every child knew which colour book they were on in school and, indeed, they all knew which colour book everybody in the class was on. I had no way of knowing if they were correct or not but there was a strong and confident consensus in the group!

Of the children who told me they were reading a different book at home, the books they described were significantly more challenging to read than the reading books from school they had with them; for example, one child said he was reading a book from the Horrible Histories series.

Comment

For these children, who in their reading experiences at school were beginning to decode independently, reading was measured by the success they had achieved in doing this. Reading in school was almost a competition and success was measured by how much was achieved. The children were not able to tell me what their school reading books were about; all that mattered to them about these books was their colour.

3. Year 2 children (ages 6 and 7)

Pleasure in reading was not unanimous among these children; some enjoyed reading but some did not. It tended to be that the girls said they enjoyed reading but the boys did not. When I probed deeper, however, the picture was slightly different. One boy said he only liked reading comics and magazines. He gave me a very detailed description of the magazines he read, which were all related to PlayStation 3. He told me he reads the magazines to find out about games and to help him decide which ones he wants to play. Another boy was adamant that he did not like reading at all. He went on to tell me that he supports Arsenal and every day reads the sport pages of the *Sun* newspaper. He explained to me how by doing this he can find out how Arsenal is doing and that by looking at the tables and reading the match reports he can work out if they are going to win their next game. He was describing some very sophisticated reading behaviour, but according to the colour of the reading book he had been given in school he was not a very good reader.

Comment

A lot of work has been done on boys and reading, and the observations above are very limited and small examples of the issue. They raise some important points however. The boys who said they did not like reading and did not read, actually engaged in some very demanding reading. I do not know how much help they received at home, but it was evident that this reading served a particular purpose related to the boys' interests.

The Ofsted report *English 2000-05: A Review of Inspection Survey* (2005: 32) said that, 'Boys tend to give up independent reading more easily than girls and, as they get older, seem to have greater difficulty in finding books to enjoy'. Lockwood (2008), in his research on reading for pleasure, found that 77 per cent of boys claimed to like to read a book compared with 91 per cent of girls. Seventy-two per cent of boys enjoyed non-fiction compared with 57 per cent of girls. These patterns seem to be becoming established in these young children.

All the children in this Year 2 group said they did not read much at school and only read when the teacher told them to do so.

Comment

All the children clearly read a lot in school in the course of a day's activities, but they did not recognise it as such unless they were reading from something which had been given the label 'reading book'. What are the implications of this for classroom practice?

The children seemed to think that reading in school was all about decoding. They did not mention enjoyment of the books they read at all.

They also told me that there was supposed to be a story time at school when the teacher read to them just before they went home from school but usually it was a bit late and they missed it because they had not finished their work or were still getting changed from PE.

One girl told me, 'In hard books there are more sounds which make up a word. You use up quite a lot of sounds and letters to make a word'.

Comment

The children in this school achieve highly in standard assessments and are very competent at one aspect of reading. A lot of emphasis is placed on the teaching of decoding through systematic phonics teaching and it is clearly successful. However, in one aspect of reading they are not so competent. As Dombey (2010: 5) said:

> A balanced approach means that, as well as working to master the mechanics of reading that allows them to lift the words off the page, children are encouraged and supported to focus on making sense of written text, and to see its uses in ordering, enlarging, enjoying and making sense of their lives. It means ensuring that classrooms are filled with interesting written texts – on screen as well as on paper – and that children are given rich experiences of putting these texts to use.

Read

Dombey, H. (2010) *Teaching Reading: What the Evidence Says.* Leicester: United Kingdom Literacy Association.

Task

Talk to children in a Year 5 or 6 class and see if they think differently from these Key Stage 1 children.

The attitudes reflected in the observations above pose an interesting challenge for literacy teachers and the next two observations pick up on Dombey's comment that classrooms should be full of interesting written texts. Before you read the observations, think what this means to you and consider what sort of texts you would want to put in your classroom.

Keith Topping does an annual survey on what children read through data obtained from the Accelerated Reading project. This might have a certain bias, but it does give a very interesting perspective on what motivates and excites children. The latest survey of 2016 indicates that there is a steady increase in each year group in the number of books read in a year until Year 3; after this there is a steady decline. It must be remembered that as children get older they are reading longer books so this will affect the number read, but the decline is still significant. It is interesting to look at the books read by each year group: the classic children's books tend to predominate; perhaps this relates back to teachers' knowledge of children's books, as highlighted by Cremin et al. (2008).

The classroom as a reading environment

If teachers want to encourage children to read and write, it is important that they create classrooms which are stimulating literacy environments that offer time, space and resources for reading. What might such a classroom look like?

OBSERVATION: Looking at a Year 1 classroom

The classroom is colourful, light and airy. It is one half of a very large room which is shared with the parallel class. The windows are large. There is a large book corner which has bookshelves on three sides of it and a Kinderbox (a box containing large picture books) as well. There is a rug on the floor and several large cushions. On the edge of the book corner there is an old armchair covered with a throw and filled with cushions. The teacher sits here for read-aloud sessions and children are frequently curled up here reading; it is known in the class as the 'story chair'.

On top of a unit just to the side of the book corner is a display entitled 'Our Book of the Week'. This week it is Mo Willems' book *Don't Let the Pigeon Drive the Bus*. There are several copies of the book here and children can read them at any time. There are also laminated copies of pages from the book with laminated speech bubbles, some blank and some containing the words from the text. The children are encouraged to re-create the text or to invent their own version. This book has been used in shared reading and class activities throughout the week.

On the noticeboard above the book corner is a display featuring Mo Willems. There is a picture of him with some brief facts about his life. There are also pictures of the covers of several of his books with a label which asks, 'How many books by Mo Willems have you read?' All the books are available in the book corner.

Also in the book corner is a large plastic box in which the children are encouraged to put the books they have read and really enjoyed. If children do not know what to read, they are encouraged to look in that box first. Often the teacher will put books in there too.

In the book corner is also a listening centre with earphones so children can choose a book and listen to the audio version.

The children are encouraged to re-enact the stories in the role-play area and in the small-play area. The role-play area is set up as a bus station for this week and in the small-play area are different types of vehicles and different animals. The children will often be heard saying things like, 'Don't let the cow drive the tractor'. This all relates to the overall theme for the half-term, which is Transport.

There are other examples of different kinds of texts around the classroom. All the displays are constantly used and referred to in lessons; children use them as a source of information. On the whiteboard the teacher has written the date and there are also several scribbled reminders which the teacher has written to herself to not forget to send messages home. The children know what these say and draw her attention to them at the end of the day. By the side of the whiteboard is a list of the activities of the day, in order. These are on laminated cards and at the beginning of each day the day's timetable is created with the children.

There are also opportunities for the children to create texts. There is one table for writing; it contains lots of paper of different colour, size and type, lots of different things to write with and a wire tray in which to put the finished writing. This is available for the children whenever they are free.

There is a music table which contains a few musical instruments and song books. On a stand is a copy of the song which the children have been learning that week. Children can be observed standing at this table playing the instruments and singing the song as they 'read' the musical notation.

There is also an alphabet display. Behind it is an alphabet chart with the lower case letters arranged in a rainbow shape.

Comment

This arrangement makes it easier for children, especially those with dyslexia, to find particular letters.

For other ideas look at:

Morris, M. and Smith, S. (2010) *Thirty-Three Ways to Help with Spelling: Supporting Children Who Struggle with Basic Skills*. London: Routledge.

There are also boxes of magnetic letters, arranged in sets of the letters the children have learned in phonics lessons. Some of these are joined where a grapheme consists of two or more letters. There are A4-sized magnetic boards in a box. Also available for play are wooden letters, sandpaper letters and letter-shape moulds. There are charts showing phoneme–grapheme correspondences and children are free to use these at any time.

Comment

As you read this observation and look around any classroom in which you find yourself, what are the messages that the environment is giving out? The classroom I have described above tells me:

- Books are important – there is a space for books which is furnished with care and maintained.
- Readers make choices – the box of favourite books shows that different people will like different things.
- Authors write books – the emphasis on the author teaches children that books are essentially about communication.
- Composition is important – the opportunities to re-create stories through play are teaching children compositional skills.
- I can try out different things – the writing area allows children to experiment with writing.
- Different texts are for different purposes – enjoyment, reminding, informing, asking, and so on.

OBSERVATION: Year 5 classroom (ages 9 and 10)

The classroom is one of several which go off a long corridor in a building typical of those built in the 1960s. The wall opposite the door is almost all window and the tables are arranged in groups. At the back of the room is a sink.

There is no reading area as such, but there is a clearly defined class library. This consists of two bookcases arranged in an L-shape. One contains non-fiction books. These are coded according to a very simple Dewey system and there is a chart above the bookcase explaining this. The other bookcase contains fiction. This is mainly paperback novels of various sizes and thicknesses. I did not see any poetry books. There was a variety of authors represented on the shelves and a variety of genres that would appeal to different preferences. On a table next to this bookcase was a computer which was permanently on and had a selection of book covers and titles stuck around the screen. On the screen was a form:

Title:

Author:

Why you should read this book:

If the children had particularly enjoyed a book, they were invited to go and fill in this form and log it on the database of books that had been read by the class. The comments were unedited and brief; they often were in note form and contained lots of exclamation marks and question marks. If a child did not know what to read next, they could go through the database and select a book that one of their peers had already enjoyed. They were encouraged to go and ask the other child to elaborate on what was written.

Comment

The teacher told me that he had set this up for two reasons. First, he wanted to move away from the children having to write a book review every time they had read a book. Secondly, he wanted to create an

(Continued)

(Continued)

environment where children were talking about books they had read and sharing opinions. In both respects this had worked. When I observed, he was considering making another database available of books which children had not enjoyed and had abandoned. What do you think about this? What would be the purpose of it?

This opportunity to respond to texts on screen was just one of the many types of texts evident in the classroom and a large number of them were on screen. The interactive whiteboard (IWB) was in constant use and it was an integral part of classroom activity, not just a resource for the teacher to use. The teacher used a tablet to write on as he walked around the classroom and this was recorded on the IWB; children were encouraged to record on the IWB or on one of the four computers in the room and were often flicking back and forwards between screens, some of which were created by them and some of which were from the Internet. Some of the displays consisted of these screens which had been printed out.

The whiteboard was used as a working wall and had notes and diagrams all over it. Teacher, teaching assistant and children wrote on it and, again, it was constantly referred to during lessons.

Comment

What were the children in this class learning about texts through the uses of written language in their classroom? It is a tradition in English primary classrooms that a display is always designed to look good – work is triple mounted, boards are backed with carefully chosen borders, and the font and size of print are carefully chosen. It is understandable why this is so: teachers want children to feel that their work is valued, they want to set good examples of standards of presentation and they want children to take pride in their work. I have observed the complete opposite in many primary classrooms in France. There I have seen notes made on flipcharts, the paper torn off and pinned on the wall with one drawing pin to be taken down the following day, referred to and added to. This was much the same way that the whiteboard was used in the observed classroom. Consider these two almost extremes of examples of the printed word and identify the advantages and disadvantages of each. Is there a middle way?

Anybody visiting primary classrooms will soon realise that although there are some differences, there are many more similarities. Most primary classrooms contain the same things to a greater or lesser extent, for teaching and learning literacy. Brian Cambourne (2000: 513) makes a very important point, however, when he says: 'artefacts are only valuable when students are engaged in meaningful tasks with the artefacts'. It could be said that the same argument applies to all texts used in a classroom, and so we need to be sure we understand what is meant by a 'meaningful task' in this context. How do you think Cambourne's argument relates to the views of Meek and Smith discussed earlier?

Summary

This chapter has encouraged you to think what we mean by the use of texts in the classroom. This is important because, although it is essential to teach children the skills of word recognition and language comprehension, it is imperative that teachers understand the impact that the texts which are used have on those processes.

- In reflecting on your own experiences of using and creating texts, you will have realised that texts come in many different forms. The essential characteristic of all texts is that their basic purpose is the communication of meaning. The nature of the text determines how that meaning will be created and/or accessed. Literacy teaching needs to take this into account.
- Planning for literacy teaching is best if texts are at its heart. Children will learn what makes for effective writing if they have talked about many examples of writing that have had an impact on them. Foregrounding the role of authors and writers shows children that effective writing involves many decisions which are often much more complex than the simple addition of more connectives or 'wow' words.
- Learning literacy involves knowing the purposes of different texts, and this is demonstrated by the way texts are used and displayed within the classroom. Giving children opportunities to create and read texts for authentic purposes will establish literacy as a powerful and essential tool.
- Reading aloud to children and talking with them about texts will introduce them to a range of authors and texts and will empower them to make their own choices as readers and writers.
- In order to do all this, teachers need to have a secure knowledge of texts that is relevant and up to date. This is challenging for teachers.

- There are experts in this who will help teachers, and the Schools Library Association will provide support and resources to teachers and schools.
- The text is at the heart of literacy teaching and learning and must be considered in all our observations.

Further reading

Goodwin, P. (ed.) (2008) *Understanding Children's Books: A Guide for Education Professionals*. London: SAGE.

Lockwood, M. (2008) *Promoting Reading for Pleasure in the Primary School*. London: SAGE.

Talk

Talk is an essential element of the learning process, but it is sometimes difficult to observe and to see what lies beneath the words. The observations in this chapter demonstrate talk in different contexts and how adults can help or hinder.

If you were asked to identify what is the most important thing that helps you to learn, I wonder what you would say. When we teach, it is very easy to focus on things like preparing exactly the right worksheets, thinking how we are going to explain a topic, having lots of management and organisational strategies up our sleeves and carefully differentiating all the activities. All these things are vitally important and key in becoming an effective teacher, but the most important way in which we all learn is through talk. Why do I say this? Alexander (2004: 9) says 'Children ... need to talk and experience a rich diet of spoken language, in order to think and to learn'. This is difficult to achieve and many teachers struggle to provide this rich diet of spoken language in their classrooms. Why is it important and what happens when children talk?

Research over the past few decades has convinced us of the incontrovertible link between talk and thought. Children's cognitive development is encouraged or hampered by the types of language they have encountered and the contexts in which they have encountered it. Halliday (1993) argued that learning language was about learning how to learn.

Recent research in neuroscience confirms that talk serves a powerful function in helping the brain to build connections and thus expand its capability. The primary stage of education seems to be the time in which the brain is actively developing its capacity for learning and has a strong ability to learn language. The relevance of this research for teachers is to emphasise the importance of teaching. Teachers are no longer just facilitators, providing stimulating environments, resources and activities, pressing the 'go' button and waiting for it to happen. The interactions teachers have with children are of vital importance. In other words, what you say to children and how you say it is vitally important, as are, if not more so, the opportunities you give children to talk themselves.

Read

Goswami, U. (2006) 'The brain in the classroom? The state of the art', *Developmental Science*, 8: 467-9.

One of the strongest influences on primary education in the past was the work of Piaget, a psychologist interested in the development of thinking, reasoning and understanding. His view of children as meaning-makers interacting with the environment in which they find themselves, was the prompt for much of child-centred education. Children were placed in a stimulating environment and the teacher acted as facilitator, helping the children to make connections between what they already knew and new experiences.

The thinking of the Russian psychologist, Vygotsky, challenged this idea of the child working alone to develop understanding, arguing that social interaction is at the heart of development. Language is the key tool which allows the child to understand experiences, and a child's interactions with those who are more experienced help the child to make sense of the world.

The term 'scaffolding' was first used by Bruner to describe those interactions between adult and child. Adults should provide the link between what the child can do and understand independently and what she or he can do with the support of a more experienced other. In other words, the teacher should use language in a way that challenges the child's thinking and extends understanding.

If you were to teach me how to tie my shoelaces it would be a waste of time. You might plan a superb lesson which was interactive, used resources creatively, engaged me completely and was managed smoothly, but it would all be to no avail because I am already able to tie my shoelaces and can do so independently. You might plan a similarly effective and exciting lesson to teach me the principles of nuclear physics and it would also be a waste of time – not because I already know about nuclear physics but because I have no understanding of physics at all and nuclear physics is way too advanced for me and my level of understanding. Teaching is about finding the level which is the next step forward from what is already known by the pupil. Vygotsky named this the 'zone of proximal development'.

Bruner and Vygotsky would say that providing the right context with stimulating resources would not be enough but that an effective teacher would need to be with me in my zone of proximal development, talking me through, explaining and guiding. It is the talk that is vital. This interaction has been described as 'scaffolding'; it is the verbal support which allows a child to carry out a task which they would not be able to do alone. Wood et al. (1976) described six features of effective scaffolding:

- 'recruitment' or stimulating interest in the task
- 'reduction in degrees of freedom' or simplifying the task, perhaps by breaking it down into stages
- 'direction maintenance' or focusing children by reminding them of the goal
- 'marking critical features' or pointing out key things to do and/or showing the child other ways of doing parts of the task
- 'frustration control' or managing the child's frustration during the task
- 'demonstration' or showing a way of doing the task.

Consider these characteristics as you look at the observations in this chapter.

Read

Maybin, J., Mercer, N. and Stierer, B. (1992) 'Scaffolding learning in the classroom', in K. Norman (ed.), *Thinking Voices: The Work of the National Oracy Project*. London: Hodder. pp. 186–95.

OBSERVATION: Year 1 children in free play (ages 5 and 6)

The following observation is of 5- and 6-year-old children in a free-play activity. They are working independently and talking with each other.

On two occasions different adults intervene and ask questions. Use this observation to reflect on the role of the adult in relation to what you have read about the nature of scaffolding.

In this school three parallel Year 1 classes spend 45 minutes most afternoons in free-play activities. They use a large outdoor area, the three small classrooms and a large shared area. This is known as 'Sunshine Time'. There are adults around but on the afternoon I observed they were not normally joining in the children's play but were spending their time reading with individual children.

I watched five children – four girls and a boy – working together. They were sticking coloured sheets of A4 paper together with sticky tape into a long strip. They were individually working on each piece of paper but had clearly planned it together. I started to listen when this activity had been going on for some time.

Child 1: We don't have time to stick things on. Let's just draw.

Child 2: Come on, we've got work to do. The more drawing, the more beautiful.

(Pause while the children are busily each drawing on their individual sheets of paper.)

Comment

Notice how the children are working alongside each other in what is often known as parallel play. They have planned a project together and now are individually working on their separate parts of the whole. When alone, the children do not talk much. As the adult approaches, they invite her to look at their work. What do you think of the adult's comments? What might you have said in the same circumstances?

An adult walks past.

Child 3:   Miss S, look at this. This is the longest longest city.

Miss S: Is it taller than our metre man? Is it taller than me? (Miss S lies down on the floor alongside the strips of paper. A child lies down on the other side.) Is it taller than Charlie?

Child 3:   It's taller than everything.

Comment

Notice how the adult changes the nature and focus of the talk. Previously the children were excited about their project and were discussing the process of completing it. The adult immediately turned it into a teaching situation, comparing the length of the paper with people. She did not comment on what the project was in the children's imagination but only on what she perceived she could use it for. How would you expect the children to react to this focus of questioning? Child 3 was the only child who responded here. Consider this in relation to Child's 3 talk in the following extract.

The adult then left and the children carried on talking together.

Child 2:   Seven more to go.

Child 1:   I'll do the pink one.

Child 2:   There are seven more to go. (picks it up) Look at that – all of that.

Child 3:   Who is helping?

Child 5:   Where is the Sellotape?

Child 1:   Um – where is it? There.

Child 3:   My arm is killing me. I'm doing so much drawing without a rest.

Child 2:   No more paper on this.

Child 5:   I'm going to get my own paper – not yours.

Comment

The children seem to have ignored the adult's intervention and carried on as before! Look at the different roles the children are taking and consider how what they are saying reflects these roles. For example, Child 3 is using language to draw attention to what she is doing. Her question about who is helping serves to draw attention to the fact that not many children are and her later comment emphasises her own role in the project, using language to assert this. How would you describe the roles of Children 2 and 5?

Another adult then approached.

Teacher: Is it a huge poster? A banner?

Child 3:   It's a rainbow city.

Teacher: Is each sheet a part of the city? And what's in the city? Is it an imaginary city?

(Pause. The children do not respond to the questions but carry on working.)

Teacher: That's really long.

Child 3:   Yea. Everybody helped and it's really long.

Comment

Look at the questions the teacher was asking and think how they were supporting and challenging the children's thinking. Why did the teacher ask the first question instead of asking the children directly what it was they were making? Often teachers do not like to admit that they do not recognise what children are making, and make assumptions. When she was told what the project was, the teacher then asked three questions in rapid succession without pausing for the children to answer. The children ignored her, except for Child 3, who again was the only child who responded to the teacher. Think how you could engage in conversation with the children to encourage them to talk more purposefully.

If you consider the above observation, there are some key points we can learn about what happens when young children are engaged in free-play activities:

- Children's imagination and creativity are strong and vibrant. These children were creating their own world and using the resources available for their own purposes. In his foreword to Pahl and Rowsell (2005), Allan Luke talks about the 'epistemological diversity' to be found in classrooms. What does this mean to you? It can be argued, and Luke does so, that the curriculum and pedagogy in many classrooms form a sort of 'educational fundamentalism' which reduces learning in general, and literacy learning in particular, to a much simpler and slower approach to easier and basic texts and modes of communication. In contrast, according to

Luke, 'students bring to classrooms complex, multiple and blended background knowledges, identities and discourses, constructing identity and practice from a range of scripts' (in Pahl and Roswell 2005: xiii). What does this mean in relation to the observation? It means that we need to allow the children to tell us what they are creating and how they are creating it. Both adults resorted to discussion of the measurement of length because the children were creating something long. That was not what was foremost in the children's thinking. They were using other knowledges and experiences to create their world. What are the implications for teachers in how they respond to and talk with children?

- Children think and operate in narrative. Story is the focus of Chapter 8 and we will return to consider its importance there, but, for now, consider how these children were creating their own story. Rosen (1984) describes story as a cognitive tool which helps us to understand our world. Is this what was going on here? Look again at the roles the different children took. Are they creating a shared world? Whose world is it?
- Adult interventions can open up but also close down conversations and opportunities to challenge and extend children's learning. We will return to this point later in the chapter, but, for now, reflect on the adults' questioning in the observation above and think how the questions might be modified to impact on children's learning. Consider also how a change in the way the adult talks might influence the role the adult plays in the learning episode. Try and reword the conversation according to the characteristics of scaffolding.

OBSERVATION: Year 6 children talking (ages 10 and 11)

The next observation is of children in Year 6 (ages 10 and 11). They were also talking with each other without much intervention from the teacher in a structured Philosophy for Children session. The rationale behind Philosophy for Children is an approach called 'community of enquiry'. It is designed to encourage children to think, to reason and to make sense of arguments and counter arguments. Its principles are:

- critical thinking – children are able to make distinctions, connections, comparisons and give reasons
- creative thinking – constructing alternative scenarios and explanations and making necessary links between reasons and conclusions
- caring – feeling safe to take risks and strengthening personal values
- collaborating – discussion that makes thinking a social activity.

It can be seen that this approach is Vygotskian in its underpinning and so we are justified in looking for evidence of challenge and scaffolding by the more experienced in the interaction. In this session the children were sitting on the floor in a circle – all the furniture had been pushed to one side to make space. This was the second lesson of a series. In the first lesson the teacher had read the children a story and they had identified a question which arose from it for them. This was 'Should you risk everything for your dreams?'

Each child had three opportunities to speak, signified by holding up three fingers. The child who spoke chose the next child to speak. The teacher began by reminding them of her role; she used the word 'facilitator' and said that if they lost their way she would bring them back on track. She then chose one person from the group whose question had been chosen to start.

The discussion lasted half an hour and I will give just some examples, starting with the beginning. Each paragraph is a new speaker; each speaker nominated the next speaker by name and I have left that out of the transcript.

I think it depends what your dreams are and it depends what you're risking. If it's your life, it's probably, you really shouldn't. If you can get it without really trying it really isn't a risk but if it is a really big thing that you've always really wanted it's worth the risk.

I think you shouldn't because if you're risking something like 50p there's a high chance you probably would. But if it's something where the risk is reasonably high although it could not affect you it could affect other people so in that way I think you shouldn't.

I think you shouldn't because if you say you're a thief you can get in real trouble.

I reckon you shouldn't but maybe it depends on what it is and what it's worth. If it's your life that's a different thing but if say you're risking 1p then that would, then you might want to do it if you've got a chance like of winning the lottery.

It depends on how risky it is. If someone says if you steal something from me – it depends on what they say they're going to do.

You shouldn't risk something if it affects other people because that might be causing people harm. If it only affects you, like maybe you dying, then that's the step you're taking.

I would think twice. If you do succeed then what are you going to get for it. It depends how high you're willing to go really. It depends on what you're going to get if you go to the next level.

I disagree with S. Because if it's something you really want, you shouldn't risk, for example, somebody's life or because that might be overdoing it.

Comment

This is the first time a child has made an explicit reference back to somebody else's comment. The reference back was not to the previous statement but to the first one made. The child had to wait until she was chosen to make her point. What are the implications of this for the construction of a dialogue?

I think that if it's a bad thing, like if you want to win a prize by cheating, then I don't think you should. But if you want to do something like saving red squirrels for example, then maybe you should because although you won't win anything you'll be saving something else.

Well I agree with J because he said if it affects other people I wouldn't do it but if you think about what you want to win and you want to risk your life saving your country that's good.

I agree with M because when you think about it, when you actually have a dream would you be helping somebody else? You could end up being greedy because if you're doing it just for yourself for say fame or money or things like that then it's really selfish and not very nice then if you do something to help people which could change the world, you could risk some things to help people.

Well I think that it depends on if you do succeed and it maybe makes you famous or something I would try and get benefit for other people as well, so like maybe help a charity or stuff. If you just want to be famous and not do anything about it but just earn money then I wouldn't do it.

If you had a dream and you got it by stealing you might get a worser dream like gaol.

Comment

What do you notice so far about this dialogue? You can see that the children are thinking carefully about what they are saying and are now beginning to respond to each other. Ask yourself if thinking is being challenged and if the children's understanding of the issue is growing. What are the children learning here? Why do you think the teacher intervenes at this point?

The discussion so far had taken ten minutes and the teacher then intervened. She said:

> Right, I'm just going to butt in here for a minute. Supposing you wanted something very very special in your life – a car or a football kit or jewellery – and you knew somebody who had loads of money – would you think that it would be OK – somehow – to steal from that person who had so much money to get what you would want – what you would dream of? Is it OK to do it? Or if you had somebody who didn't have any money at all, would you still do the same thing from them? Would you steal from them or … so think about that sort of thing. The rights and wrongs.

The children's discussion continued:

> I think it's wrong to steal from someone who's like rich because you never know what they're going to do with the money. Say if they give it to charity they can help more than one person.

> Well I disagree with somebody about wars, because what does it help, what does it do if you kill loads of people to make the world better, it's a smaller place really and maybe it's just making people a bit lonely if they've lost their families.

> I didn't say you'd have war. If you're in a war and your country is really poor and you're invaded like loads of times and you really want to win this war so you won't have any more problems.

Comment

What impact did the teacher's intervention have on the children's thinking? Did it change the dialogue at all? What do you think the purpose of the intervention was?

Dawes discusses the value of 'interthinking', which she defines as 'the situation that exists when two or more people achieve real communication with each other, when mental resources are pooled through the medium of talk' (2001: 128). Look at the dialogue above and see if you think it is an example of interthinking.

Barnes and Todd (1977) used the term 'exploratory talk' to describe talk where things are achieved. Mercer (1995) developed this idea and identified characteristics of this type of talk:

- Ideas are engaged with critically but encouragingly.
- Statements are considered and challenged but there are always explicit justifications and alternative proposals.
- Ideas and viewpoints are made public and the talk provides evidence of reasoning.
- The discussion moves towards joint agreement.

The discussion in the observation goes some way towards addressing these issues but there are times, maybe, when the imposed structure gets in the way of the development of thinking.

Task

Look at the following resource for other ideas for using talk to develop thinking skills:

Dawes, L., Mercer, N. and Wegerif, R. (2000) *Thinking Together: Activities for Teachers and Children at Key Stage 2*. Birmingham: Questions Publishing.

Dialogic teaching

At this point it is helpful to consider the notion of 'dialogue' and begin to focus on the role of the teacher in helping children to use talk effectively. The word 'dialogue' comes from the ancient Greek words 'dia' meaning 'through' and 'logos' meaning 'word', and so would seem to imply an interaction in which ideas are expressed and developed and thinking is visible. Bakhtin (1981) claims that dialogue is vital to an individual developing understanding, and so it would be reasonable to assume that dialogue would be a central feature of classrooms where developing understanding is a key purpose. However, Howe and Abedin (2013) have found that dialogic exchanges take place very infrequently in most classrooms and observation seems to indicate that teachers have not been good at opening up opportunities for children to talk. You will have observed many lessons, I am sure, where it seemed as though the teacher was doing most of the talking. Research backs up this impression (Bennett and Desforges 1984; Galton and Simon 1980; Mroz et al. 2000). Talk in classrooms has often been used to see if children 'know' the correct answer; rather than creating opportunities for exploration, teacher questions are testing. In real life we usually ask questions for a variety of reasons: to find out some information, to see what somebody else thinks, to question an idea or viewpoint, to request something, and so on. In classrooms teachers often ask questions to see if children remember what they have been taught and these questions can often lead to a bizarre 'guess what's in my mind' game. We can define questions by the extent to which they are open or closed. Closed questions have only one expected answer; open questions create opportunities for dialogue and thought. It is easy to identify which type of questions are generally the most effective in the classroom.

Sinclair and Coulthard (1975) described a common classroom interaction between teacher and child as IRF (Initiate, Respond, Follow-up); the teacher initiates by asking a question, the child responds and the teacher gives a brief follow-up. This is a commonly found pattern of interaction in classrooms and I am sure you will have seen, if not taken part in it yourself. It might often be that the 'response' section of this interaction is expanded so that several children respond and express different viewpoints, but, even so, little cognitive challenge takes place and the questions tend to be closed and used to check knowledge gained. When the literacy and numeracy frameworks were introduced in 1998 and 1999 respectively, there was much emphasis placed on what was described as 'whole-class interactive teaching'. Teachers were encouraged to plan lessons which were pacey, discursive and challenging. There were many teaching strategies put forward to encourage this type of teaching and to ensure that all children contribute in whole-class discussion:

- Seating arrangements – how do you think the physical layout of a class-room supports or hinders talk?
- Using props – individual whiteboards, puppets, an object to hold, counters or the hand signals used in the previous observation.

- Involving everybody – no hands up but the speaker is selected by the teacher, using a prop to choose the next speaker – named lolly sticks, talking hat, number grid.
- Alternatives to teacher–child interactions – talking partners, time to talk.
- Structures – thinking time, group spokesperson reporting back.

Task

Look for examples of these strategies when you observe lessons, and reflect on how they encourage exploratory talk in those lessons.

In 2004, however, Smith et al. found that not much had changed: 'teachers spent the majority of their time either explaining or using highly structured question and answer sequences … most of the questions were of a low cognitive level designed to funnel pupils' response[s] towards a required answer' (2004: 408). This is beginning to change as more and more teachers are using talk partners or learning partners as a way of encouraging children to express their ideas. It is important however to ensure that the talk taking place between partners is truly exploratory; exploratory talk enables children to reason and develop ideas together, challenging and evaluating viewpoints. This is difficult and needs to be modelled frequently by teachers.

Read

Smith, F., Hardman, F., Wall, K. and Mroz, M. (2004) 'Interactive whole class teaching in the National Literacy and Numeracy Strategies', *British Educational Research Journal*, 30(3): 403–19.

Robin Alexander (2008) proposes that it is, therefore, the cognitive challenge of classroom talk which needs to be addressed rather than the organisation and pace of whole-class teaching. He introduces the term 'dialogic teaching' as a way forward. His idea is grounded in the works of Bruner (1996), who argued that it is discussion and collaboration which lead to understanding, and Wells (1999), who described the learning classroom as a 'community of enquiry'. The notion also links closely with Mercer's (1995) idea of 'interthinking' discussed earlier. Alexander identifies five key principles of dialogic teaching:

- *Collective:* teacher and children addressing learning tasks together
- *Reciprocal:* teachers and children listening to each other
- *Supportive:* children free to articulate their own ideas without fear, helping each other to understand
- *Cumulative:* teachers and children building on each other's ideas to create coherent thinking
- *Purposeful:* teaching has particular educational goals in mind. (Alexander 2008: 28)

OBSERVATION: Art lesson with Year 3 class (ages 7 and 8)

The staff of this urban school were focusing on talk during the term in which this observation was made. They were looking at ways of creating opportunities for cognitively challenging talk. This lesson was part of a series in which the children had been looking at the work of graphic designers and digital artists. The overarching theme of the term's work across the curriculum was 'Extreme Environments'. The aim of the observed lesson was to design a jungle animal structure using digitally designed materials. The teacher's intention for herself was to use questions which would challenge and generate thinking. The whole-class part of the lesson involved looking at pictorial examples of sculptures made from digitally created materials, for example a table made from bottles and a parrot made from bus tickets.

Extensive use was made of 'talking partners'. The children were put into pairs by the teacher and every time there was whole-class work each child sat next to their talking partner. They worked with the same talking partner for two weeks and then the teacher changed the pairings.

Comment

The way in which talk partners are selected can make a big difference to the quality of the talk. Think about a class you know well and identify as many different ways as possible of allocating talk partners. Now think of the positive and less positive consequences of these decisions.

Do you think keeping the same partners over time is better than allocating specific partners for particular tasks?

Lancashire County Council wrote a useful pamphlet, 'Talk Partners', which you can access through Google.

The teacher asked lots of questions in the whole-class discussion and the children were engaged and clearly thinking hard. The first question came after they had looked at pictures of several very different images of graphic art.

What do all of these images have in common?

Answers varied but the class, after about five minutes' discussion, worked out that all the images had been graphically designed.

Comment

1. What enabled the children to be able to come to this conclusion together? It could be argued that the question is closed – it is asking the children to find the answer. However, it is a challenge and the children rose to it. On the surface the images were very different. The question required them to reflect critically on what they had seen and to draw on their previous experiences. While the children were making their suggestions, the teacher took a back seat, only joining in to ask for justification or clarification, and on one occasion to question a response. The children engaged with each other. We could apply all five principles of dialogic teaching to this. This happened not only because of the type of question which was asked but also due to the role the teacher adopted during the conversation. Later in the discussion she was involved in extending and challenging thinking. She was more than a facilitator but did not direct. This was a true discussion, as defined by Alexander, where there was 'the exchange of ideas with a view to sharing information and solving problems' (2008: 30).

The PowerPoint slides then looked at different examples of sculptures made from graphically generated materials. The first slide was a picture of a sculpture of a polar bear, at the Eden Project in Cornwall, made from plastic carrier bags.

There was some discussion about what the bear was made from and the teacher continually referred the children back to the picture to look for evidence to support their viewpoints. Note how she used a visual image as a 'text' in much the same way as a written text would be used.

She then asked the children the question, 'Why did they use carrier bags and not cardboard boxes to make the polar bear?' The children discussed this in their talking partners and after about five minutes the teacher asked, 'What does your talking partner think?' The children then reported back using the ideas of their partner.

Comment

Why do you think the teacher did this? If a child is shy about sharing their own ideas with the whole class, it is much easier to report on somebody else's views. This also ensured that the children listened carefully to their partners and gave them practice in identifying the key points.

Alexander identifies some characteristics of dialogic teaching and it is useful to use this as a framework for analysing the interactions we observe in classrooms. You can see them fully and read more about dialogic teaching in the following text:

Alexander, R. (2008) *Towards Dialogic Teaching: Rethinking Classroom Talk*, 4th edn. Thirsk: Dialogos.

The next image was a parrot constructed out of bus tickets. Read straight through the dialogue first; it might help to read it aloud. It went like this:

Child 1:   I think it's made of sticks.

Child 2:   No, it's too shiny for sticks. I think it's made of plastic.

Child 3:   The feathers look like they're made out of bus tickets.

Teacher: What makes you think they're made from bus tickets?

Child 3:   The yellow things that you have on bus tickets. They're long and bus tickets are long.

Child 4:   If you look closely you can see a bit of black.

Child 5:   Is it the writing on the tickets?

Child 3:   I think it must be.

Teacher: What do you notice about the ways they've used the bus tickets?

Child 2:   They've done lots of different layers.

Child 4:   That makes it look more like feathers.

Now let us look more closely at the sort of talk used and how the comments of each contributor fitted together to construct a cohesive argument. My analysis is based on Alexander's characteristics of dialogic teaching. You may not agree with me; if not, look carefully at the 'text' to justify your own viewpoint.

Child 1:   I think it's made of sticks.

Comment

This child is using talk to speculate. The comment acts as a springboard for other comments.

Child 2:   No, it's too shiny for sticks. I think it's made of plastic.

Comment

This child has clearly listened to the previous comment and is responding to it. The fact that she or he is expressing disagreement indicates confidence to express a viewpoint without the need to always be correct. The disagreement is justified; the child gives a reason for the differing viewpoint.

Child 3:   The feathers look like they're made out of bus tickets.

Comment

A clear and coherent line of argument is developing with the children collaborating to try and solve the problem of deciding what the sculpture is made from. Child 3 slightly changes the style of comment but again is speculating.

Teacher: What makes you think they're made from bus tickets?

Comment

The question asked by the teacher is firmly part of the ongoing dialogue, building on previous comments and taking them further. The question 'elicits evidence of children's understanding' and 'prompts and challenges thinking and reasoning'. The question is framed in such a way that the answer cannot be wrong; the child is asked to give reasons for an opinion which is accepted as a valid opinion.

Child 3:   The yellow things that you have on bus tickets. They're long and bus tickets are long.

Comment

The child's response is less clear without contextual clues to help understanding, but it is a definite response to the teacher's question and provides the information required to justify the expressed opinion. This child is drawing on his or her own experience of bus tickets to provide evidence and justification.

Child 4:   If you look closely you can see a bit of black.

Comment

Child 4 develops the argument further and supplies additional evidence. There is no competition in this dialogic problem-solving; the children are collaborating to find an answer. Child 4 is building on previous contributions and in turn the following statement shows another child doing the same.

Child 5:   Is it the writing on the tickets?
Child 3:   I think it must be.

Comment

Another child enters the discussion and asks a question. It is a feature of dialogic teaching that it is not just teachers who ask questions. Asking an appropriate question can be a cognitively challenging task and Child 5 shows that she or he has been following the discussion, is building on previous evidence and is fully engaged in the task. Alexander argues that in dialogic teaching, 'those who are not speaking at a given time participate no less actively by listening, looking, reflecting and evaluating' (2008: 42). This is the first contribution made by Child 5 but she or he has been an active participant in the debate. Child 3 responds; the question was addressed to the group as a whole and not necessarily to the teacher.

Teacher: What do you notice about the ways they've used the bus tickets?

Comment

Now that the materials used have been established by the group, the teacher moves the focus on by establishing a slightly different line of enquiry. Again, she focuses the children's attention on the picture and asks what they can see. This question serves a slightly different purpose from the teacher's previous one; she is bringing them back to the 'text' and challenging them to take the idea of using bus tickets even further. The responses below show that the children pick up on this and begin to discuss the method of construction rather than the materials.

Child 2:   They've done lots of different layers.

Child 4:   That makes it look more like feathers.

Comment

The first response is a direct answer to the teacher's question and the following comment by Child 4 expands on this and speculates on the outcome of the layering. This is another example of the interaction building on previous comments and collaboration in solving the problem.

One of the most significant characteristics of the interaction above was the balance of talk by the teacher and talk by the children. The children talked more than the teacher. It was also clear when observing that, although the dialogue moved forwards, there were also times of silence when the children were looking carefully at the picture and reflecting. The teacher did not feel tempted to fill that silence but allowed for thinking time.

Let us match this dialogue against the principles of dialogic teaching described above:

- *Collectivity* – the children were working together to work out what the sculpture was made from and how it was made.
- *Reciprocal* – the children were listening to each other and responding to and building on each other's comments. The teacher was also listening and played an almost equal role in the dialogue.
- *Supportive* – the children appeared to be confident in expressing their own ideas, in asking questions and in supporting each other.
- *Cumulative* – the children built on each other's comments, extending ideas and moving thinking forward. The teacher's contributions also did this without dominating or denigrating anything anybody else had said.
- *Purposeful* – this was planned with a clear purpose in mind. The teacher reviewed the comments and her own comments moved them forward according to her purpose, as evidenced in her second question.

Reflect

Do you think this is an example of dialogic teaching? If so, then what is your evidence for that claim? If not, what would you want to see to justify the description?

OBSERVATION: Conversation 1 between a teacher and a Reception child about a self-chosen book (age 5)

Let us now move on to look at interactions between a teacher and a 5-year-old little boy called Theo. The first conversation happened when the child chose a book to read and discuss with his teacher. He chose *Owl Babies* by Martin Waddell and it might help if you have the book with you as you read this dialogue.

Teacher: Why did you choose this book, Theo?

Theo: Well, my mummy always reads this to me, that's why I know it. (looking at the front cover) These are baby owls. (opens the book) This is their feathers, can you see the pattern?

Comment

Theo has chosen a well-loved book and one which he knows really well. This enables him to take control of the conversation and to initiate topics of discussion and ask questions. He is in the role of expert. What impact do you think this has on Theo's talk?

Teacher: Oh, yes, I can!

Theo: (turns to first page and compares background to previous page) See, it's the same but it's their mummy's feathers. This is Sarah, this is Percy and that one's Bill. ('reading' the words) They lived in a tree with their mummy. (turns page) Oh no, they woke up 'cause they couldn't sleep, they were hungry, their mummy had gone so they're so sad. Look at Percy's face.

Comment

Theo is half 'reading' the book by remembering the text from when his mother has read it to him and half commenting on it. This dialogue could have been in the following chapter on reading. Why do you think I chose to put it in the chapter on talk?

Teacher: Mmm. He does look a bit sad. How do you think Sarah and Bill are feeling?

Comment

Look carefully at what the teacher says. She responds to Theo's instruction to look at Percy's face and then asks Theo to look at Sarah and Bill. How do you think the teacher could have responded in a way

(Continued)

(Continued)

which would extend the child's thinking more? Look at how Theo responds to the question below. See how he is drawing on his past experiences to make his answer. How could the teacher focus his thinking to draw on evidence from the text?

Theo: Well, I think they might be a bit sad too, but they might not because they're bigger than Bill. (turns page) They're thinking about their mummy. Percy think she might get a fox. ('reads' the words) I want my mummy. (turns the page and 'reads' the words) But mummy owl didn't come. (turns the page and 'reads') A big branch for Sarah, a small branch for Percy and a bit of ivy for Bill. I want my mummy. (turns page) They snuggled together 'cause they were a little bit afraid. That's Bill in the middle 'cause he's the smallest. (turns page and 'reads') So they closed their eyes and wishes for their mummy to come. And she did. (turns two pages studying the pictures) Owls come out at night and I saw a hedgehog in my garden and it was in this pile of leaves and it stayed there all the time, I think it was a whole day. And it was sort of this big (uses hands) with lots of spiky prickles.

Comment

Here Theo is relating a real-life experience to the text. The idea of owls being nocturnal has reminded him of the hedgehog he saw in his garden. How does the teacher respond to this? What do you think about her response?

Teacher: Did it look like the one we saw this morning?

Comment

The teacher follows Theo's thoughts about the hedgehog but Theo does not seem to want to take it any further and returns to the book. Note how the teacher does not push her question but allows Theo to carry on reading the book.

Theo: Well, sort of. (returns to book) Mummy! Look, Bill almost
           jumped up and fell off and Bill he's jumping up too 'cause he's
           pleased to see his mummy! My mummy always reads this book
           to me, that's why I know it so well. (turns page and reads)
           What's all the fuss! You knew I'd come back. I love my mummy!

Teacher: Why do you like this book, Theo?

Theo: Well, I know this book 'cause my mummy picks it for me and
           reads it to me and that's why I know it.

Comment

The teacher almost repeats her first question, but this time asking why
Theo likes the book. Theo does not really answer the question and the
teacher lets it go. If you were this teacher, what question would you ask
to help Theo really think about why he likes the book? The teacher
here has let go an opportunity to challenge Theo's thinking.

This delightful conversation is about a book which Theo clearly knows very
well, and the way he makes sense of it is closely bound up with his own
emotional experiences of his mummy reading to him. Reading this book is a
very personal act and so it can be more difficult to articulate those feelings.

Let us focus on the teacher's comments and questions. At the start Theo is
very much in control and the teacher responds as an equal, sharing in the
enjoyment. From then on, however, her questions become very teacherly. She
invites him to speculate, reminds him of relevant past experiences and repeats
her question about why he chose the book. There are many ways in which
these are not bad questions and it is more a case of good questions asked at
the wrong time. If you try reading this conversation aloud, it might well feel
as though the teacher's questions do not sit easily in the natural flow of Theo's
talk. The teacher does not appear to be listening and responding to Theo and
her questions do not always build on what he is saying. This observation
reminds us of a key principle of talking with children – listen to them first!

OBSERVATION: Conversation 2 with a child in Reception class (age 5)

Theo and his class had had a visit from a member of a bat sanctuary who
gave a visual presentation on bats and then brought out two bats to show

to the children. The presentation was long (15 minutes) for the age of children; the pictures were clear and informative but a lot of the language used was subject specific and not explained to the children. After the visit, an adult had the following conversation with Theo:

Adult: Hi Theo. I wonder if you could help me. I couldn't see or hear everything that was going on in the hall with the bats and I have to write some things down about it. Can you help me please?

Theo: Well, what I found out was that bats chew off their wings or their tails sometimes when they're hungry. Well, I'm not quite sure but I think it's when they are hungry. And they live in attics and bees can live in attics. And there are bats that eat fruit and there are bats that eat insects and bats that eat moths and some nibble on birds.

Adult: What makes you think they eat their tails and wings?

Theo: Well, the man told me, but I think he got it wrong.

Adult: Maybe he meant that when the bats eat upside down, they eat off their tails and wings using them a bit like plates.

Theo: Mmmmm, yes, I think that could be right.

Adult: Did you find out anything about the noises the bats make?

Theo: Well, the lady had a machine and it had a recording of a bat and it says something and it comes back to them. And if the echo went on and on and on it wouldn't be an insect.

Adult: So what do bats do in winter?

Theo: Well, they sleep in the winter 'cause there's no food – just like the poor people don't have any food or toys or anything, but at Christmas me and mummy, we get some of my toys and an old teddy and we put it in a shoe box and then we leave it out for Father Christmas and then whoosh it goes and into the truck and off to Gambia. We also put in some tissues so the poor people can have a good blow.

Adult: So can you tell me anything about baby bats?

Theo: The baby bats when they're borned they stay with their mummies and if their mummies leave them they are all upset.

Adult: So do the babies have fur or anything when they're born?

Theo: Yes, they've got fur and they hang upside down next to their mummies.

Adult: So what do the babies eat?

Theo: Well, some eat fruit, some eat moths and some eat insects.

Adult: Can you tell me about the bats that you saw?

Theo: Well, he wanted to fly but the man had hold of him 'cause he had a poorly wing and the bat was a bit agitated. I got to stroke him and it was soft and he had tiny ears and the man was holding him by the wings so that's why it's agitated.

Comment

What is your initial response to that conversation? Do you think it was a conversation? Remember the research of Sinclair and Coulthard (1975) who described the initiation–response–feedback routine which is so common in classroom talk? Go back over this conversation and try and match the contributions to that pattern. I think you will find that as the conversation progresses there is initiation from the teacher, response from Theo but little if any feedback from the teacher. What is the purpose of this conversation? It seems to be to test Theo to see if he remembered what he had been told in the presentation. Was Theo cognitively challenged at all?

Reflect on this observation and use it to remind yourself of what you know about effective talk in the classroom.

Read

Eke, R. and Lee, J. (2009) *Using Talk Effectively in the Primary Classroom*. London: David Fulton.

Eke and Lee (2009) identify the particular characteristics of school talk as opposed to 'normal' talk; they argue that school talk is often very context bound. Other differences are:

- In normal talk speakers often skip from theme to theme whereas in school talk interactions are normally themed.
- In normal talk invitations to do something can be refused but this is not the case in school talk.

- In normal conversation speakers often overlap and interrupt each other but the rules for classroom talk tend not to allow this.
- Teacher talk often regulates and instructs; normal talk is between equals.

Teachers often claim that some children come to school familiar with the way in which language is used in school, while others operate only in the 'real world'. Eke and Lee use the term 'pedagogic communication' to describe 'the way teachers use talk to make the potential knowledge and skills actual in the classroom' (2009: 22).

It is evident that for many children the way in which language is used in the classroom is very different from the way in which it is used at home, and this provides challenge for both them and their teachers who need to model and support exploratory talk which provides cognitive challenge. There are even more barriers to learning for children for whom English is an additional language. How can teachers support them to use talk to extend and evaluate ideas? Firstly, it is important to remember that linguistic ability is not always the same as cognitive ability, and for many children the issue is not with understanding but the ability to express that understanding. NALDIC (National Association for Language Development in the Curriculum) has many useful ideas and resources on its website and also some powerful case studies of individual pupils. Children who have English as an additional language are as diverse as all other children and their individual needs must be evaluated and taken into account when planning. However, there are some key principles which can be applied to all children:

- Distinguish between the cognitive demands of an activity and its linguistic demands.
- Introduce ideas by pre-teaching key vocabulary through focused teaching and structured play.
- Provide plenty of visual support – pictures, gesture, movement and artefacts.
- Model language structures and patterns, sometimes creating a framework for talk.
- Use other pupils as learning partners who can model and support; occasionally, if you have two children who speak the same home language, allow them to discuss concepts and ideas in their home language.
- Allow plenty of listening time – do not force public speech.

Talk in the Curriculum

It is clear that there can be a tension between classroom talk which gives children chances to explore, evaluate and justify different viewpoints, and delivering curriculum goals; this can depend on where you live and which curriculum you follow! The Scottish *Curriculum for Excellence* (2004) identifies listening and talking as one of the three 'organisers' within the framework; and two of the headings under this are 'tools of listening and talking' and 'understanding, analysing and evaluating'. These give teachers in Scotland the justification to develop and promote dialogue as a tool for learning. Within the Welsh National Curriculum there is also a strand called 'oracy' which includes 'responding to others with questions' as one element of the Programme of Study. The National Curriculum in England (DfE 2013: 13) claims to reflect 'the importance of spoken language in pupils' development across the whole curriculum – cognitively, socially and linguistically'. So on the surface there would appear to be little tension, and yet within many classrooms the perceived requirement for evidence of progress dominates and excludes valuable opportunities for exploratory talk within true dialogue.

This does not have to be the case and language needs to become the action in the classroom. Nystrand emphasises this point when he says, 'what ultimately counts is the extent to which instruction requires students to think, not just report someone else's thinking' (1997: 73). It is this which must be the aim of all effective teachers.

Summary

Why is talk so important? There are many reasons:

- It is our main means of communication.
- It is used to create relationships.
- It creates and maintains cultural identity.
- It plays a key role in the development of the brain.
- It is linked to the development of thinking.
- It promotes and helps learning and raises achievement.
- It makes active citizens who can make and justify choices.

How do we help and teach children to use language in this way? As teachers, much of children's use of language in the classroom is influenced by our language. We have seen that the most effective language by teachers, whether talking with individuals or whole classes, follows the principles of dialogic teaching. It is:

- collective
- reciprocal

- supportive
- cumulative
- purposeful.

We can plan for this in all different organisational contexts, but it also means that we must listen and respond to children. Alexander argues we must also listen to other professionals and together develop our understanding of professional practice:

> The critical question concerns the impact of talk on learning … We must know where the talk is going, and do what is required to lead it there. That requires us to have a clear sense of purpose and a firm grasp of the content to be covered. (2008: 49)

Further reading

Goodwin, P. (ed.) (2001) *The Articulate Classroom: Talking and Learning in the Primary Classroom*. London: David Fulton.

Teaching reading

3

Teaching reading is a high priority and one that is politically sensitive. The observations in this chapter look at different aspects of teaching reading and consider how these fit together to support the development of 'readers'.

The first questions we need to ask ourselves when we begin to think about how to teach children to read are: 'What are we actually teaching? What is reading and how will we know when we have taught it?' These questions are not as straightforward as you might first imagine. Take a few moments to think about them and, if possible, to discuss possible answers with a friend.

What is reading?

It is helpful in answering this question to think back over all the reading experiences you have had over the last 24 hours. You will have read many different sorts of things and you will have read them for different reasons and in different ways. Sometimes you will have skimmed over a text quickly just to get the sense of what it is about, but on other occasions you will have read each word very carefully and slowly.

Task

List everything you read in the last 24 hours and note how and why you read it.

I am sure you have had the experience of reading a text to yourself and getting to the end of the page to realise that you were actually thinking about something completely different. You were able to decode the words but did not engage with the meaning at all. It would be difficult to say that you had really 'read' that text. Similarly, you may have read something and skipped over some difficult or new words, thinking you had a broad idea of the meaning. However, in discussion with somebody else you realise that you had either got the wrong end of the stick or had missed some key part of the text because you could not read an important word. These two elements of reading, the word identification and the comprehension or understanding, are both essential and need to be taught together. Knowing how that is done is a complex issue and every day in classrooms teachers are making professional judgements about the needs of children and how to address them.

The teaching of reading is a highly political issue and different governments have commissioned reports and issued policy statements on how it is to be taught. It is important that teachers understand the reading process and are able to make their own professional judgements about the teaching approaches which suit the different children in their class. It does not take long to appreciate that one approach to teaching reading does not suit all and teachers need to be able to assess and make decisions which are informed by research and experience.

There is often a tension between policy-making and classroom practice and the extent to which pedagogy is determined by research evidence. This is complicated in the teaching of reading because the sources of evidence come from different research traditions and so place different emphases on the various aspects of the reading process. It is important that you understand these perspectives as they all have something to offer you in support of those professional decisions you make in the classroom:

- If you read anything by Ken or Yetta Goodman, Don Holdaway or Margaret Meek, you will notice an emphasis on reading as a process of making meaning from the text. This psycholinguistic approach looked at how experienced readers behaved, and argued that beginning readers need to be shown how to behave in the same way. Thus, it is said that reading development does not happen in a staged way. Goodman (1992) identified three sources of information in a text that readers draw on: graphophonic (the relationship between the phonemes and the graphemes – the sounds of language and their written representation), syntactic (the grammatical structure of the written language – the way the different elements fit together) and semantic – the meaning of the text within the context. This view is echoed in the searchlights model, which was the underpinning theory of the National Literacy Strategy (2001) in England and Wales.

Many of the strategies used for teaching reading stemming from the psycholinguistic view are still in use in classrooms today and are powerful ways of helping children to become readers. They include: shared reading, guided reading, reading aloud to children, responding to texts and the importance of choosing quality texts. We will see how this works out in practice in some of the following observations.

Read

Goodman, K. (1992) 'Why whole language is today's agenda in education', *Language Arts*, 69: 354–63.

Meek, M. (1988) *How Texts Teach What Readers Learn*. Stroud: Thimble Press.

- In 2006, the Rose Review on early reading was published and moved the underpinning viewpoint in policy-making towards the perspective of cognitive psychology on reading, with a subsequent emphasis on word identification. The first appendix to the Rose Review proposed the 'simple view of reading' (Gough and Tunmer 1986) which distinguishes two elements of reading as word identification and language comprehension.

The clear distinction between the cognitive psychologists and the psycholinguists is that the former see reading development as a staged process in which there are significant differences between early and experienced readers. Word identification is seen as the key starting point and knowledge of the alphabetic system is central to learning to read. In terms of pedagogical practice, this has led to an emphasis on teaching phonics as the first step in teaching reading. It is argued that systematic phonics teaching should be the first element of a teaching reading programme.

Read

Ehri, L.C. (1995) 'Phases of development in learning to read words by sight', *Journal of Research in Reading*, 18(2): 116–25.

- A third perspective on reading comes from a view that reading is determined by the cultural context in which it takes place. Learning to read happens within a particular situation, and that will determine 'how' reading is done; for example, when I read an academic article I read it in a very different way from the way in which I read either a blockbuster novel on the beach or a page on a website from which I am trying to find particular information. I have learned how to read those very different texts for very different purposes because I have belonged to communities who read in those different ways. Some of you will find reading an academic text challenging because it is a new experience and you have never seen anybody doing that and discussed the process with them.

The pedagogical implications of this are important. We need to make sure that we understand what reading experiences the children in our class have had and so what they understand by reading. Many children are not at ease with the print- and narrative-based texts they encounter in school and so struggle because they do not know how to be a reader with these texts. Our starting point for teaching needs to be with texts and experiences that resonate with children's prior experiences.

Read

Heath, S.B. (1983) *Ways with Words*. Cambridge: Cambridge University Press.

Marsh, J. and Millard, E. (2000) *Literacy and Popular Culture: Using Children's Culture in the Classroom*. London: Paul Chapman.

Task

Look at the reading policy in your school. Can you see elements of these three approaches to reading in it? Does one view dominate?

In reality, these three approaches and others are not mutually exclusive, and you are likely to see elements of them all in classrooms. Teachers will draw on their knowledge of each child and their understanding of the reading process to use the most appropriate approach for the particular time and the particular child. This needs to be done within the statutory requirements of the National Curriculum, but a careful reading of the documentation will show that there is actually quite a lot of freedom within the programmes of study.

The English National Curriculum (DfE 2013) places strong emphasis on the decoding element of reading and prescribes phonics as the first approach. However, the importance of the pleasure of reading is much stronger in the documentation than in previous curricula and it is important that teachers of reading plan 'to develop their love of literature through widespread reading for enjoyment' (2013: 3). Similarly, *A Curriculum for Excellence* (Scottish Executive 2004) in Scotland requires pupils to be able to choose and read texts which they find interesting and enjoy. These curriculum requirements place strong demands on the subject knowledge of teachers if they are to fulfil them in the classroom.

OBSERVATION: Shared reading in a Reception class (ages 4 and 5)

The children were sitting on the carpet facing the teacher who was sitting on a very low armchair. A visualiser was on a low table next to her and the book was on this and so being shown on the screen in front of the children. A visualiser is a digital camera on an arm which enables the whole class to see a book or an object on a screen. It is an extremely useful teaching tool for shared reading. The book the class was reading together was *The Whale's Song* by Dyan Sheldon and Gary Blythe. It would be helpful if you had a copy of this book with you while you are reading this observation. It is a well-loved text and could be used in Key Stage 2 as effectively as in this Reception class.

The teacher read the title to the class and then asked them, 'Do we normally think of whales singing?'

Comment

By immediately posing a question the teacher actively involves the children in the reading. She is showing them that it is part of being a reader to question what is in a book and to relate your own experiences and current knowledge to the text. The different responses to the question were all listened to and accepted. The teacher did not indicate any answer was correct or wrong but took all as valid points of view.

The teacher then looked at the front cover. She pointed to the words and read the title again and the names of the author and illustrator. She then asked, 'From the front cover, tell the person next to you what sort of book this is'.

Comment

The teacher is using a strategy called 'pair talk'. You might well have experienced this strategy during a training session yourself. It enables children to try out ideas in a safer context than the whole group and encourages more exploratory talk (Bruner 1966). As these were very young children, the task was very focused and was developed by the teacher in the feedback time. How do you think it might be different with older children?

After a minute or two, the teacher asked one child for his idea and then said, 'Put your hand up if you agree with Matthew'. Most of the children put up their hands. The teacher then showed the class a 'big book' that they had been reading the previous week. This was a non-fiction text. Very quickly she looked at the book with the children, reminding them of the contents page, the index and the title, and drawing their attention to the characteristics which showed it was non-fiction. The teacher then focused their attention back to *The Whale's Song*, saying, 'This is a story book. The author is Dyan Sheldon and the illustrator is Gary Blythe'.

She turned to the opening pages and together she and the children looked at the pictures. She introduced them by saying, 'These give us a little taste.

They put us in the mood for the story. How do they make you feel?' The children shared the emotions that were evoked by the pictures and were very perceptive and sensitive in the suggestions they made.

Comment

In starting with an affective response to the text, the teacher was demonstrating the importance of personal response. She did not make an evaluative comment on children's responses but accepted them all; she acknowledged the differences and in her acceptance showed that it is expected that there would be different responses to a text.

She then read the first few pages of the book to the children. She pointed with a stick along the text as she read and used her hands to support the meaning of the words.

Comment

Pointing to the written text as you read aloud shows very young children the relationship that there is between the written symbols on the page and the words that are spoken. It also shows them the direction in which English print is read – left to right and top to bottom. Many children will have learned this from their experiences of being read to at home but many more children will not know this. It is something that needs to be learned and for some children it needs to be explicitly taught. It is also important to remember that for some children their experiences of print will be very different – the texts they know are not read from left to right and top to bottom. In pointing to the text smoothly underneath the print rather than pointing to each separate word in turn, the teacher was showing the importance of fluent phrased reading rather than word-by-word reading. The use of actions to support the meaning of the words makes it accessible to more children, especially those who have English as an additional language.

Attention was then turned to the illustration, which shows Lily sitting on her grandmother's lap looking up into her face. The teacher asked the children what was happening in the picture and there was a general response that Lily was listening to her grandmother. She then said, 'Could you make me a face like Lily's face – when you're really interested in what somebody's telling you?'

Comment

Through asking the children to imitate the expressions in the picture, the children were helped to identify with and so empathise with the character, Lily. The act of physically making a facial expression made concrete an abstract emotion and also focused their thinking on the fact that Lily's grandmother was telling a story to Lily, but also to them.

The teacher then went on to read the story to the children. As the shared reading continued, the teacher occasionally stopped to ask the children to talk about or respond to something: 'Talk to the person next to you and tell them what you would give them as the perfect present'. Sometimes she pointed out a word for the children to identify: 'There's a word on this page that you recognise. Can you see? There look, it says "whales"'.

There were times when the children interrupted to ask questions: 'What does silent mean?' The teacher responded, 'I'm glad you asked that question. It means it is very quiet – no sound can be heard'.

Comment

Notice how positively the teacher responds to the child's question. She first is pleased that the question is asked and then she answers it clearly and briefly. This response shows that it was a sensible and important question to ask because without understanding this word some of the meaning of the whole text might be lost. In this case, however, the teacher wanted to establish the meaning of the word quickly so that she could get on with reading the story. She made a professional judgement about a way of responding that best suited the purpose of the lesson.

When the story came to an end, there was a short moment of silence while the children absorbed and thought about what they had heard. It is important to allow these moments of reflection where children are relating new knowledge to prior experiences and understanding.

Jessica then asked, 'Is it real?' The teacher responded, 'It could be real, Jessica – a real dream. It wasn't a dream for Lily. In stories anything can happen'.

Comment

This is an interesting exchange between Jessica and the teacher, where the teacher is teaching about the characteristics of fiction. Remember how at the start of this observation she reminded the children of a non-fiction text they had been reading. After reading this very poetic imaginary tale, she is highlighting the differences between the two text types and recognising them both as valid but different reading experiences.

After finishing the discussion on the content of the book and on the children's affective responses to it, the teacher then asked, 'What helped me to read this story to you?' The answer given by several children was 'The words'. The teacher then asked, 'Did I just make the words up?' After loud responses in the negative from the class, the teacher commented, 'No, I didn't and later on we're going to do some work on sounds to show us how the sounds can help us to read the words'.

Comment

The class had read and responded to this wonderful book. They had talked about the ideas and feelings it had evoked and had related it to their own experience, knowledge and understanding. The teacher then went on to put the phonics teaching into the real and relevant context of reading and to make explicit to them the purpose of learning about phoneme and grapheme correspondences. Many years ago, Halliday (1976) wrote that those who are the most successful literacy learners are those who understand the purposes of literacy. Consider how the children in this class are being introduced to some of the purposes of literacy. Note especially that this is being made absolutely explicit to them – never assume that children will just pick things up!

The observation above is a good example of the way in which children need to be taught about what it means to be a reader as well as the mechanical skills of reading. As a reader, the most important part is to understand what the author has said and to respond to that, drawing on your own knowledge, experience and understanding. That process was being modelled to the children in the shared reading lesson. Towards the end of the lesson, however, the teacher reminded them that in order to be able to read independently they need to be able to decode the words. That is done through phonics – learning the relationship between the phonemes and the graphemes. Phonics is an important element in the teaching of reading for very young children.

In phonics teaching children are learning about the phonemes (sounds) of language and how they are written down by using graphemes. English is an alphabetic language. There are about 44 different phonemes in the English language and they are represented by graphemes. Each sound is represented by one grapheme. It would be simple if we had 44 sounds and 44 letters to represent them – life would be much easier! You know, however, that there are only 26 letters in the English alphabet and so some graphemes consist of two or more letters, for example, /th/ and /sh/. This is not straightforward and children need explicit and systematic teaching to enable them to segment (break a word down into its sounds to write) and blend (build the sounds together into words to read). The next two observations focus on phonics teaching.

OBSERVATION: Phonics teaching in a Year 1 class (ages 5 and 6)

This class used a well-known commercial scheme for their phonics teaching. It is a popular scheme which can be helpful for teaching decoding but may not always be as effective for teaching the other elements of reading shown in the previous observation. This is a 20-minute lesson with a group of 18 children and is introducing the sound /ay/. The children are set according to their ability in phonics across Years 1 and 2 and this is a middle-ability group. The lesson follows a very common pattern for phonics teaching, which you may well have observed already. The learning objective is 'to learn /ay/ and to practise reading words that contain /ay/'. The children are sat on the carpet facing the teacher.

Comment

Setting children across two year groups places an emphasis on the teaching of phonics and also on phonics as a discrete element of the curriculum. It enables the teaching of grapheme–phoneme correspondences (GPCs) to be rapid and tailored to children's needs, but clearly identifies children in terms of their ability in this small aspect of teaching reading. What do you think about this? Talk to your peers and to experienced teachers and identify the advantages and disadvantages of setting for phonics.

The first part of the lesson is called 'Revisit and Review'. The scheme produces a large wall chart with all the sounds written on it and this is displayed permanently on the classroom wall. All the children face the chart and the teacher points to each sound they have been taught in turn, using a stick with a pointing hand on the end. As she points to a grapheme, the children say the phoneme it represents and the teacher checks they are saying the sounds clearly and correctly, sometimes requiring them to repeat. When they have done the sounds in order, the teacher points to graphemes in a random order. The emphasis is on speed; the children are engaged and enjoy seeing how quickly they can respond.

Comment

This is a clear example of behaviourism in action. The stimulus is the written symbol, and when the children give the correct response they are rewarded by praise from the teacher. If they do not give the correct answer, praise is withdrawn. You might consider that this approach is appropriate for something so 'straightforward' as learning GPCs – or is it? What are the implications of this and where might problems arise? We will return to this later in this observation but meanwhile why not consider what other aspects of the primary curriculum you would consider suitable for this approach?

The second part of the lesson is where the main teaching is done. The teacher began by pronouncing the /ay/ sound, placing emphasis on the shape of her mouth and describing her pronunciation as 'stretching' the sound. The children then repeated the sound after her; the teacher put one hand on her chest and said 'My turn' and then put her hand out to the children, saying 'Your turn'. This was repeated several times.

The teacher then explained that the sound /ay/ is made from the two letters 'a' and 'y'; when these two letters meet they do not say /a/ or /y/ but /ay/. Two children came to the front holding a whiteboard each – on one was written 'a' and on the other 'y'. The children moved together and as their whiteboards touched, the class was encouraged to say the phoneme /ay/. The teacher reminded the children several times that there were two letters but only one sound. She asked them what that was called and several children knew the term 'digraph'.

The teacher then introduced the written form of the sound by showing the children a card with the grapheme written on it. This was a resource published by the scheme. The side the children were shown first portrayed a picture and a rhyme which they were told was to help them remember the sound. It is a picture of some children playing and underneath is written the caption 'May I play'.

While holding up the card the teacher repeated the phrase several times using different voices (whispering, shouting, happy, sad, angry). The children copied her using the 'My turn, your turn' routine. The teacher then showed them the other side of the card on which was written just the grapheme. The children said the sound. She then held up the card sometimes showing the grapheme and sometimes showing the picture and the

Figure 3.1 Discrete phonics teaching with 4- and 5-year-olds

children had to say either the rhyme or the sound accordingly. This was presented as a game called 'Can I catch you out?'

Comment

As a teaching sequence this is strong and again follows a behaviourist approach to learning the stimulus is presented with the appropriate response being rewarded by praise from the teacher. So far, apart from the two children who went to the front with their whiteboards, the children have been sitting still. This was an important strategy as it was a physical visual demonstration of how two letters together represent one sound. The children were completely engaged and appeared to be enjoying the lesson, but how far will this learning be transferred to other contexts? Let's look at the rest of the lesson before we try to answer that question. There are two more sections: Practise and Apply.

The teacher showed the group some words containing /ay/ on the IWB; each word had sound buttons underneath marking the individual phonemes. The children were asked to read each word but firstly they had to 'Show me Fred fingers'. Fred is a puppet who talks in phonemes, i.e. he sounds out each phoneme in a word; the children were asked to put up a finger for each phoneme as a way of indicating they were able to break a word down into phonemes. The children 'Fred talked' the word (saying each phoneme separately), then blended the phonemes to read the word. The same procedure was followed for the six words on the IWB.

Comment

This is a very long and explicit way of teaching children how to identify the phonemes in words and then blend them to read the words. There is no doubt it was effective and all the children could read these words. I wonder if there were any children in the group who could already read the words and for whom this process made things more complex than it needed to be. When you next observe or teach a phonics lesson, reflect on that and consider how your lesson takes into account not only individual needs but also individual strengths.

The final part of the lesson was designed to teach the children to apply their newly acquired knowledge of /ay/. They were each given a coin – some had /ay/ words written on them and others had words containing previously learnt phonemes. The teacher said a word; the children had to listen very carefully and consider if it was the same word as that written on their coin. If it was they had to put their coin in the treasure chest – a lavishly decorated box at the front of the class. The teacher chose carefully which word she gave to which child – the more able child was given the word 'crayon'; the struggling children were given a word which had been on the IWB earlier. The game was called 'Locked Treasure' and this ended the lesson.

Comment

As we reflect on this lesson there are several points to be made. Firstly, it must be said that phonics lessons like this are taught every day in hundreds of schools throughout the country. The scheme used is a popular one and I am sure you have already observed several lessons like this. If the purpose of the lesson was to teach a specific GPC then it certainly achieved its purpose. I want to widen out our viewpoint and consider this lesson in the context of teaching children to become readers. Luke and Freebody (1999) identify four identities children need to become effective readers and writers: code breaker, meaning maker, text user and text critic. This phonics lesson was about teaching children how to be code breakers. However, many years ago Clay (1991) found that unless they were told to do so, children tended not to apply synthetic phonics when reading independently but rather identified the initial sound and then used a variety of other clues to read the whole word. And so we are left with the question of the effectiveness of this teaching in the broader context of reading.

Watts and Gardner (2013) argued that we need what they describe as a pluralist approach to the teaching of early reading. This is one whereby teachers identify strategies used by different pupils and build their teaching around that. Their research seemed to indicate that teaching synthetic phonics was not enough, and a look-and-say approach where children were taught to recognise whole words was as effective in teaching early reading.

Davis (2012) described current practice as 'policy driven'; teaching is dominated by organisational routines which do not necessarily relate to children as learners. Wolfe (2015) claimed that following a highly prescriptive scheme such as the one used in the observed lesson restricts and inhibits teachers from making professional judgements about their pupils as learners. An effective lesson becomes one which follows the script closely rather than one which adapts to the perceived needs of the learners. This is the danger of a centrally imposed policy which impacts, through a system of accountability, on the inspection of schools but also on teacher training so that many teachers become less used to making professional decisions during the course of a day as they 'read' what is happening in their classrooms.

Wolfe (2015) expands this point by considering the language used in the lesson by both the teacher and the children. In Chapter 2 the common pattern of interaction between teacher and pupil known as IRF was described. The teacher asks a question, the pupils respond and the teacher gives feedback. There were a lot of such exchanges in this lesson, and it must be said that the manual of the scheme outlines such interactions. The lesson was designed to teach a particular piece of knowledge and a particular skill and it did just that; it did not enable the children to construct their own knowledge about print and how it works. Wolfe says:

> It seems that the debates about early reading miss a fundamental point about the effectiveness of pedagogic interactions, namely the importance of the nature and quality of teacher-learner interactions and suitability of presentational methods or forms of talk for the intended pedagogical purpose. (2015: 511)

This is an important point when we consider how we teach children to become readers. There is a place for the type of teaching in this lesson but it is only a small part of what we do as teachers of reading. The conversations that were held in the first observation have an equal, if not more important, part to play. It is vital that teachers are aware of the need and are able to match 'pedagogical form and intent' (Alexander 2005).

Read

Wolfe, C.S. (2015) 'Talking policy into practice: probing the debates around the effective teaching of early reading', *Education 3-13*, 43(5): 498–513.

Summary: Teaching of early reading

We have looked at two observations and have seen how the different aspects of the reading process are explicitly taught to the children. In the first observation the children were being shown how to behave as readers, they were encouraged to make a personal response to the text and to share these responses with each other. They were encouraged to ask questions and to relate what they were reading to their own understandings. In this lesson they were being taught how to behave as readers.

In the second observation they were learning decoding skills. It was a highly structured lesson with a clear purpose and focus.

It was clear in both observations that talk is a key element in a successful learning activity; children need opportunities to articulate their learning and to explore for themselves with others new ideas and concepts. The skilled teacher supports them in this through scaffolding and sensitive questioning. We will see more examples of this later on – but when observing look at the questions teachers ask and consider how they support and challenge.

The next observation is also a phonics lesson with Year 1 children but it is very different. It does not follow a particular scheme but it also has a clear focus and purpose. As you read about this lesson, compare it to the previous one and ask yourself how what the two groups of children are learning about being a reader differs.

OBSERVATION: Phonics teaching with a group of Year 1 children (ages 5 and 6)

Tables were set out in the classroom in a semicircle with a magnetic board and a box of magnetic letters set out on each table – enough for one between two. As the group of eight children (five boys and three girls) came into the room, they sat on the floor in a semicircle in front of the teacher who sat on a chair.

Comment

The room is prepared for the lesson with the magnetic boards set out and boxes with the appropriate magnetic letters in them next to the boards. This means that valuable teaching time is not wasted by getting resources out.

The teacher quickly showed the children cards with graphemes on and asked them to say the phoneme represented by the grapheme. This is a revision exercise of prior learning and most were clearly recognised.

Comment

This was done very quickly. The children were clearly familiar with most of these phoneme-grapheme correspondences and time is only spent on those which have been introduced recently.

The card shown is /ai/. A child responds with /a/. The teacher replies, 'It would be /a/ but it has a letter "i" next to it and so it is an /ā /'.

Sometimes the teacher prompts by reminding the children of the action that accompanies the sound.

Comment

Here the teacher is relating to all learning styles and making the taught concept very clear. She gives a reason why the answer given was wrong but in her reason shows that it was a reasonable response to have made. She then explains why it was wrong and the symbols that also need to be taken into account. When children have begun by learning graphemes which contain just a single letter, it can be confusing when they progress to graphemes that consist of two or more letters. Including the action will support the kinaesthetic learners. Some children will remember by action, some by looking at the picture and some by the sound and/or the contextualising story. All aspects need to be included in a lesson.

As this part of the lesson comes to an end, the teacher says, 'There are three cards left: /air/, /ear/ and /ure/. Who can come and show me which one says /air/?'

Comment

The children are given the choice so that nobody is put on the spot. The way the question is framed means that most of the children were looking to see if they could rise to the challenge.

A child comes up to the front and points to the card which says /ear/. He then changes his mind and points to /air/. The teacher asks, 'Why did you change your mind?'

Comment

The child clearly felt confident to change his mind. It is important that this is the case in classrooms; we learn by making mistakes and talking about them. The teacher asks the child to talk through his decision-making process. It is being able to explain something to somebody else that indicates real learning. It also allows the teacher to gauge his understanding and use this for further teaching.

The child replies, 'Because it's got an "a" in it'.

Comment

This child is clearly making a visual distinction between the words rather than focusing on the representation of the phoneme. It may be that the letter 'a' acts as a mnemonic for the child. The teacher might want to note this and see if the child can recognise this grapheme on other occasions.

The lesson then moves on to the next phase. The teacher says, 'I wonder if you've been practising your spellings. Let's sound them out'. She holds up a card with the word 'bent' written on it. The children sound out the word phoneme by phoneme and then do the same with 'sent'.

Comment

The children are here practising segmenting with simple phonically regular words. Note the relationship between segmentation (breaking words into sounds) and blending (building sounds into words). Both skills are needed for reading and writing.

The teacher then holds up both cards and asks how the two words are similar. One child replies that they both have 'ent' in them.

Comment

The children have sounded out these words and the teacher is wanting them to recognise them by sight. Ehri (1995) believed that when beginner readers are faced with an unfamiliar word, the ability to phonologically recode the word provides an access route for the visual into the memory. In simple terms, that means that learning the sound–symbol correspondence helps the visual to 'stick' in the memory more effectively than relying on just the visual pattern of the word.

The teacher replies, 'Well done! The "ent" is the same but the first sound is different. We're going to look at the first sounds a bit more. On the tables with the magnetic letters I want you to make "bent". Then we're going to change it to "went" and then we're going to see if we can think of rhyming words'.

Comment

The children are here working on the onset and rime of words. The onset is the sound before the first vowel and the rime is the rest of the word. Monosyllabic words (words with only one syllable) can be changed by putting a new onset on the rime to create new words. If a word has more than one syllable then the same principle applies to each syllable. This exercise is helping children to create new words from words already known. This can be described as using analogy. To complete this task the children are required to both look at the visual pattern and say the sound of the word. Working with these larger chunks of sound can be more supportive for children who struggle with phoneme identification.

The children move to the tables and sit in pairs. They clearly have fixed places in which to sit and working pairs are already established so the transition occurs smoothly. The teacher says, 'First, we're going to make "bent". Tip out the letters to make it easier'. She walks around the tables, checking and commenting to individual children. 'Is that a "b"? No – it's a "d". Can you find me one that is the right way round?'

Comment

Many children of this age confuse 'b' and 'd' and it is not an indication of significant difficulties unless they carry on doing it when they are more experienced readers and writers. Learning the orientation of letters is challenging for some children; when learning to name objects the orientation does not matter but it is highly significant when naming letters. Remember that confusion can also be aural ('k' and 'g') as well as visual.

To another child the teacher says, 'What comes next? Say the word slowly to me. Think about what the next sound is. So – what letter are you looking for?'

Comment

The teacher is encouraging the child to listen to the sounds and segment the word. If this is done orally first, it is easier to identify the grapheme which represents the phoneme. Relate this back to Ehri's theory, which was discussed earlier.

'You've made them. Good! Now look at the "-ent". Take the first letter away. See if you can put another letter in to make a different word. Just try the letters and see if they make real words'.

Comment

The physical manipulation of the magnetic letters helps young children to understand what it is they are doing. It is easier to move and change magnetic letters than to write them down on paper. Note also how the children are encouraged to say the words.

'"Shent" – that's an interesting word. What does it mean? /sh/ is a sound. It's a rhyming word but it's not a real word'.

Comment

The teacher accepts a nonsense word because the child has done exactly what was required – changed the onset while retaining the same rime.

'Brilliant! "Sent" – I sent a letter'.

Comment

By putting the word into a sentence the teacher is clarifying the meaning and establishing comprehension as the prime purpose of both reading and writing.

'That's good. But "gent" is a very silly word. It doesn't start with "j" but "g"'.

Comment

The teacher accepts the word as the child has fulfilled the required task. However, she explains simply that some words do not conform to expectations. Her use of the phrase 'silly word' shows the child that she has not made a mistake, it is just that the conventional spelling is unexpected.

Note what the teacher needed to know in order to teach phonics effectively. Firstly, she had secure knowledge about how the alphabet works. She knew the phonemes and their corresponding graphemes. She does not use the technical terms in her teaching but you will see many teachers who do. It can certainly be less confusing to use the term 'grapheme' when referring to phonemes written down. A grapheme is a letter or group of letters representing one sound.

A teacher needs to be confident in phonic knowledge in order to address the children's misconceptions. This teacher needed to know different graphemic representations of the same phoneme and she needed to know what a child was doing when he identified a grapheme.

She needed to have a language for talking about the sounds, letters and words which is both accurate, clear and able to be understood by the children. She also needed to know about how the sounds are produced (phonetics) and which sounds are so similar that confusion can arise between, for example, voiced and unvoiced sounds (/p/ and /b/, /t/ and /d/, /k/ and /g/).

In this lesson the teacher is using a mixture of synthetic and analytic phonics. **Synthetic phonics** is when children are taught to read by identifying the phonemes represented by particular graphemes. The phonemes are then blended to create a word. The children were doing this when they were reading the words on the flashcards by 'sounding them out'. When they were writing the words by using the magnetic letters, the children were segmenting the words by splitting them up into phonemes and representing them by particular graphemes.

Analytic phonemes is when children analyse patterns in words and identify the graphemes which represent those patterns. The children here were looking at the pattern '-ent' which was common to all the words. This is the rime of the word and by changing the onset they were creating different words by the use of analogy. They used their knowledge of the words 'bent' and 'went' to create new words ending in '-ent'.

It is highly unlikely that you will encounter a teacher of early reading who does not pay close attention to the alphabetic nature of print in English. In the early twenty-first century, teachers are encouraged to rely on systematic synthetic phonics as their main approach. You might like to read some of the debate around this and decide for yourself the best way of helping young children understand the world of print. You might well discover that different ways work best with different children!

Read

Goouch, K. and Lambirth, A. (2008) *Understanding Phonics and the Teaching of Reading: Critical Perspectives*. Maidenhead: McGraw-Hill/Open University Press.

Johnston, R. and Watson, J. (2007) *Teaching Synthetic Phonics*. Exeter: Learning Matters.

Wyse, D. and Styles, M. (2007) 'Synthetic phonics and the teaching of reading: the debate surrounding England's "Rose Report"', *Literacy*, 47(1): 35–42.

The lesson above was clearly part of a systematic programme of phonics teaching. When you are observing in school, ask to see the medium-term or unit plans from which an individual lesson comes. You should be able to trace the development of phonic knowledge and relate what was going on in the observed lesson to the stages of development. Try and look at a copy of *Letters and Sounds* (DfES 2007) which will describe six stages of development in phonics teaching, with lots of practical ideas for games and activities.

This lesson was a discrete daily session and the children were progressing from simple to more complex phonic knowledge and skills, as well as covering one of the major grapheme–phoneme correspondences. The lesson was taught in a small group and the teacher was monitoring understanding continually throughout the lesson. When you observe a lesson, talk with the teacher afterwards about how she or he records the learning achieved and how that prior learning is built upon in subsequent lessons.

The lesson used a variety of teaching and learning strategies. The children were involved in reading and spelling words, in making up new words orally, and in manipulating magnetic letters to spell known words and make up new words, working as a member of a group, in a pair and individually. Effective phonics teaching consists of multi-sensory activities that are 'interesting and engaging but firmly focused on intensifying the learning associated with its phonic goal' (www.gov.uk/government/uploads/system/uploads/attachment_data/file/298420/phonics_core_criteria_and_the_self-assessment_process.pdf).

Task

Draw up a list of multi-sensory strategies that you have observed and include them in your own lesson planning. Remember though that they should be simple and quick and have a very clear focus.

There was a clear sense of progression within this lesson. It began with a recap of previous knowledge, moving quickly through those phoneme–grapheme correspondences which were learned previously and spending more time on those learned recently. The teacher followed up on children's comments and attempts at word creation and used these as teaching points. Note how she took the three graphemes with which the children struggled, and focused on those for a short teaching interaction. She questioned the children, asking them to explain their thinking and so extending their understanding and strengthening the learning.

In a written account of a lesson it is difficult to convey the enthusiasm of both teacher and children and to show how the teacher related to the children. There are some clues in the language she used: '"gent" is a very silly word'; 'just try the letters and see'; 'that is an interesting word'. In her responses to the children the teacher always took them completely seriously. She respected and valued their contributions and took even their mistakes as serious attempts and responded accordingly. She knew the children well enough to know what they would find amusing, interesting or exciting, and she herself was amused, interested and excited with them. In short, she saw the activity through the eyes of 5-year-old children and joined with them in the problem-solving they were engaged in. It is when the teacher works alongside the children as co-learner that an ethos of enquiry is created. Look for examples of this in the lessons you observe.

Shared reading

The first observation in this chapter was of shared reading in a Reception class. Shared reading is a reading lesson with the whole class using either a big book, a visualiser or an e-book on screen. The purpose of shared reading is to teach explicitly reading strategies. In the observed lesson the children were being taught about comprehension – they were learning how to predict and to empathise, to construct images and to question the text, to explore how the author created effects and to respond emotionally to the text. Towards the end of the text they were also taught about the relationship between the written and spoken language. The teacher was using a text which the children would not have been able to read independently and was teaching reading strategies through modelling and questioning.

Guided reading

Guided reading is a reading lesson with a small group of approximately six children, usually of roughly the same reading ability, using a text which the children can read independently with support. In guided reading the children are 'guided' to use independently the reading strategies they have been taught previously and are supported or scaffolded in this by the teacher. The scaffolding may take the form of the nature of the activity or the type of talk; scaffolding is how the teacher supports the independent work of the children.

Read

Pentimonti, J.M. and Justice, L.M. (2010) 'Teachers' use of scaffolding strategies during read alouds in the preschool classroom', *Early Childhood Education Journal*, 37(4): 241–8.

Verenikina, I. (2004) 'From theory to practice: what does the metaphor of scaffolding mean to educators today?', *Outlines: Critical Practice Studies*, no. 2.

OBSERVATION: Guided reading in Year 2 (ages 6 and 7)

Six children are sitting around a table with the class teacher. The rest of the class is engaged in independent reading activities – browsing in the book corner, writing reviews or spotting adjectives in a text.

The teacher starts by informing the children of the learning objective of the lesson, which is 'to be able to recognise adjectives and understand they add detail and interest to stories'. The teacher then asked the children to explain to a partner what they thought an adjective was.

Comment

Understanding grammatical terms is best done in the context of understanding what a word does in a sentence. It might have been better to ask the children what adjectives do and to stress how adjectives tell us more as readers. Adjectives help us to create pictures of characters or settings. For example, 'a tall, thin, grumpy-faced man' tells us more about the character in a story than just 'a man'.

The three pairs then shared their ideas about adjectives and the teacher emphasised the point that adjectives make stories more interesting. The big book *Stellaluna* (Cannon 1993) was then introduced to the children. The children had been read this book before in a read-aloud session and had discussed the power and poignancy of the story. They had responded to the book personally and had talked about the story and the different characters. This guided reading session was to explore how the author created those effects on readers that they had previously experienced.

The teacher read the first three or four pages to the group. Each child had a whiteboard and a pen and they were asked to write down some of the adjectives they heard on their boards. After the reading these words were shared.

Comment

By giving the children a specific task to do while listening to the reading, the teacher was focusing their listening and ensuring that they were engaged in active listening. They were not required to record all the adjectives and the careful instructions meant that the children were not put under pressure. The way in which the adjectives were shared created an atmosphere of collaboration – the children were really working together to identify the adjectives.

When the adjectives had been listed, the teacher re-read the extract, leaving all the adjectives out. The group then discussed their response to this as members readers and the effect the adjectives had on their understanding of the story.

Comment

The whole focus was on reading the text to see how the writer had used words to create particular effects. This is an important strategy called 'reading like a writer' and demonstrates the inextricable links between reading and writing. Children cannot be expected to write brilliant, exciting and imaginative stories if they have not read stories like that, and, perhaps more importantly, also talked about what makes those stories brilliant, exciting and imaginative.

Read

Barrs, M. and Cork, V. (2002) *The Reader in the Writer*. London: CLPE.

The children were then given a copy of a short story called 'Brave Together', written by the teacher, and asked to read it in pairs. Before they began reading they were reminded of the different strategies they could use to help work out words they did not know – use the clues in the picture, use their phonic skills to blend the phonemes to make a word, read ahead for the meaning, leave the word out, go back and start the sentence again, and so on.

Comment

One of the important elements of a guided reading lesson is what is often called a 'strategy check'. This involves reminding the children what they can do to help them work out an unknown word. The main aim of teaching reading is to enable children to read independently, and they will never be able to do that if they do not have strategies to tackle unknown words. It is important that children are given a variety of strategies; there are some words which they will never be able to build up from the sounds and others which they will never be able to work out from the context. Children need a variety of strategies at their disposal. These strategies will be taught explicitly in shared reading and phonic sessions and will be practised and emphasised in guided reading sessions.

The children read the story together, taking it in turns to read aloud in their pairs. This meant that at one time three children were reading aloud at once. The teacher tuned in to each of them, listening to what they were doing and supporting as and when necessary.

Comment

This can be a challenging aspect of guided reading. The children read aloud at their own pace at the same time. You will find that the children are able to do this quite easily and are not distracted by each other. As a teacher, you will have to practise tuning your ear in to each child in turn to listen to their reading and to observe the reading strategies they are using. When listening to children read aloud, we need to make sure that their reading is fluent and flowing. We often use the term 'phrased reading'; this means that the words go together appropriately and the reading is not word by word and does not have pauses in inappropriate places. Listening to how children read texts aloud will often give you an indication of how they are understanding the text.

When the story had been read the teacher led a short discussion on how the adjectives had enriched the story and how the children had responded to them.

Comment

The teacher was continually emphasising that the author had been using language and choosing words in a particular way in order to create a specific response in the readers. Why do you think this is important?

The teacher then brought out a small cuddly dragon toy. After much admiration and discussion, she asked the children to write adjectives on their whiteboard to describe him. They did this very quickly, not worrying about spelling or handwriting. Three children then volunteered to read their words to the group. As they read, the rest of the group were encouraged to look very carefully at the dragon to see how these adjectives related to him and how they would help somebody who was not there to get an idea of what the dragon was like. As each adjective was discussed the teacher wrote them on a large luggage label which was then tied round the dragon's neck. Adjectives chosen included green, smiley, friendly, pointy.

Comment

This time the teacher was using a concrete object as a tool for teaching about adjectives. This meant the children could look at, touch and discuss the dragon, and so think about different words to use. You will see from the list that the children generated that some adjectives relate to the physical observable appearance of the dragon and some are inferential – the children were interpreting what they saw. The whole activity was put in the context of helping somebody who was not there to imagine the dragon – putting into a concrete activity what writers are doing and emphasising the visualisation that many readers do when reading.

The lesson ended by referring back to the learning objective. Each child was given three large coloured and laminated card circles. The red circle would indicate that they did not understand and needed to revisit this topic; the yellow circle indicated that they did understand to a certain degree but needed further work; the green circle indicated that they were confident in what the lesson had covered. The teacher asked the children to hold up a circle – four of them held up green circles and two held up yellow.

Comment

Asking children to evaluate their own learning is a powerful assessment tool and can be used to inform future planning. You must however be sure that they are evaluating against clear and very specific criteria. This means that learning objectives must be precisely phrased and that all activities within a lesson relate to them. Do you think this was the case in this lesson?

OBSERVATION: Guided reading in Year 5 (ages 9 and 10)

We began the chapter with a focus on teaching comprehension in the Foundation Stage and we close with an observation of comprehension in the upper end of Key Stage 2. The observation is part of a unit of work and we will return to another lesson in this unit in the next chapter on writing.

With older children there tends to be less emphasis on practising reading strategies for decoding, and so children will be reading silently or will have read a passage before the lesson, and during the lesson they will be discussing their different types of responses to the text. For the observed lesson the children had read part of Chapter 8 of *Oliver Twist* by Charles Dickens. Although they had read it to themselves before the lesson, the teacher read the extract aloud to them at the start.

Comment

This was a challenging text for these children. In the previous lesson with the whole class the teacher had compared a passage from a book by Roald Dahl with a passage from Dickens. They had discussed the types of language used and the vocabulary. This provided the children with a good starting point. However, they still needed the mediation of the teacher reading aloud to them to help them to fully access the meaning of the text.

The teacher began by asking the question, 'What did Fagin look like?' This was a question which could be answered by direct referral to the text. It is what is known as a 'literal' question. The children did not need to interpret; they just had to read and identify the relevant information from the text. There was some discussion about this and a list of words and phrases were written on the whiteboard describing Fagin.

The next question was, 'What did Oliver find frightening?' This was a slightly different type of question because it required the children to infer from the text. The teacher required the children to quote from the text to say why they said what they did. Every comment was accepted as long as some justification was given. Inferring information from the text is the next level of comprehension. It could be described as 'reading between the lines'.

In this lesson the teacher did not progress to ask an evaluative or application question, which would see if the children could apply the understanding of the text to another context.

Comment

There are different levels of comprehension and in planning conversations around texts teachers need to be aware of and plan for all of these:

- Literal comprehension questions centre on ideas and information that are explicit in a text. They require the recognition or recall of a fact or facts. For example, what was the name of John's dog?
- Inferential comprehension questions require children to 'read between the lines'; for example, how did John's mum feel about the dog?
- Deductive comprehension questions require children to dig deeper into the text. They need to make inferences based on the text and also draw on their own experience and knowledge, thinking about cause and effect. For example, describe how John felt at the end of the story.
- Evaluative comprehension questions ask for an evaluation of arguments or ideas suggested by the text. Readers have to compare the information provided with their own experiences, knowledge or values. For example, was John's dad right in what he said about the dog?

Summary

The teaching of reading takes many forms and cannot be limited either to short lessons or to hearing children read from particular types of books. In 2003 the International Academy of Education published a paper on teaching reading in which it said:

> Both research and classroom practices support the use of a balanced approach in instruction. Because reading depends on efficient word recognition and comprehension, instruction should develop reading skills and strategies, as well as build on learners' knowledge through the use of authentic texts.
>
> Teaching reading and writing is difficult work. Teachers must be aware of the progress that students are making and adjust instruction to the changing abilities of students. It is also important to remember that the goal of reading is to understand the texts and to be able to learn from them. (Pang et al. 2003: 7, 21)

Think carefully about these statements and consider what you will do in your classroom to achieve these aims and help your pupils to become enthusiastic and critical readers.

Further reading

Perkins, M. (2015) *Becoming a Teacher of Reading*. London: SAGE.
Tennent, W. (2014) *Understanding Reading Comprehension: Processes and Practices*. London: SAGE.

4

Teaching writing

Teaching reading and teaching writing are inextricably linked and both are surrounded by talk. This chapter focuses on teaching writing, one of the most challenging tasks for any teacher. The observations look at the process of writing and explore ways in which teachers have made this explicit to children.

Writing is one of the most difficult activities we engage in – I can vouch for that as I sit in front of my computer writing this! You will know how difficult it is when you try to write an assignment or a difficult email or clear instructions for a stranger. It is difficult because it lacks all the elements of spoken language which help us to know that our message is understood – the facial and verbal expressions of the listener, the interruptions and questions, the chance to rephrase and repeat ourselves and the context in which the message is spoken. In writing, the reader is absent, there are no opportunities to have a second go and there are many ways in which a written message can be misinterpreted. These are all reasons why written language needs to be clear and unambiguous – a challenging aim.

When we teach young children it helps to keep five key words in mind.

Composition

This is the process of authoring a text – of sorting out ideas and deciding on the best way of expressing them, of structuring thoughts and making them accessible to others and of expressing what you imagine and dream to others. Composing a text does not have to be done in front of a computer or with a pencil in your hand. As I have been writing this book I have spent a lot of time wandering around the house, making coffee, tidying up and sometimes even doing the ironing! While doing all these things, though, I have been rather distracted and have not wanted to talk to anybody or to read or watch television. That is because I have been composing the text in my head; I have been trying out different ways of expressing what I want to communicate and working out in what order things should be written. When I actually come to the computer I have a fair idea of what I want to say, although many changes are continually made.

It is important that children learning to be writers realise that this is what writing is like. It is about having something to say and working out how best to say it – it is about composing a text. The teaching strategy of shared writing is a way of making this explicit to children and we will consider an example of that later.

Transcription

Once a writer has had an idea and knows how she wants to express it, she then has to pick up a pencil or switch on the keyboard. She needs to know how to form letters or to use a keyboard and how to spell, punctuate and construct grammatically clear sentences. These are important skills and need to be taught and learned. However, I can compose a text and be an author without ever using transcriptional skills – I can dictate my composition to a scribe or use voice-activated software. Very young children can compose texts – they do not have to wait until they have sufficiently competent transcriptional skills. They can dictate their writing to an adult or older child or they can record it using emergent writing.

These two skills, composition and transcription, need to be taught and learned alongside each other. It is no good having brilliant ideas if you are not able to record them for other people to read, and it is no good having neat handwriting, perfect spelling, punctuation and grammar, if you have nothing to say!

Purpose, audience and format

These three work together. Imagine I want to leave a note to my son to ask him to put the wheelie bins at the end of the drive before he goes to school. I am likely to find a scrap of paper and a pen and write, 'Don't forget wheelie bins'. He will know, from prior experience, what that means and will work out that it is from one of his parents. He would be very surprised if I wrote a formal letter on the computer and posted it to him. However, if I wanted to make a complaint to the manager of a shop, it is not likely to have much effect if I stick a note on his door saying, 'TV doesn't work'. He would not know who it was from and would be likely to put the note in the bin, taking no further action.

As a writer, I decide on the purpose of my writing and the audience for my writing and that will determine the format of my writing – the style and layout and use of language. Young children need to be able to make those decisions appropriately.

One of the most influential researchers on the teaching of writing has been Donald Graves (1983). He stressed the importance of seeing writing as a process in which we plan, draft, edit and revise our writing. His thinking has had a great deal of impact on pedagogical practice and recent research confirms his view. Andrews et al. (2009) argued that effective teaching of writing includes a model of the writing process in which planning, drafting, editing and revision are a central part.

Read

Andrews, R., Torgerson, C., Low, G. and McGuinn, N. (2009) 'Teaching argument writing to 7- to 14-year-olds: an international review of the evidence of successful practice', *Cambridge Journal of Education*, 39(3): 291–310.

Graves, D.H. (1983) *Writing: Teachers and Children at Work*. Portsmouth, NH: Heinemann Educational.

OBSERVATION: Composition in Year 4 (ages 8 and 9)

In the following observation of writing with 8- and 9-year-olds, look for evidence of the writing process at work. How are the children being encouraged to plan and draft their writing? You might also want to consider the place of editing and revision. Do you think this needs to happen with everything a pupil writes? How would you justify your answer?

The class were looking at persuasive writing and the work was based on the text, *Click, Clack, Moo: Cows that Type* by Dorothy Cronin. The teacher read the first few pages of the text, finishing up with the large illustration showing Farmer Brown looking very cross, grumpy and rather puzzled.

The children then spent time in groups working out how Farmer Brown was feeling, what he might be thinking and why. They were encouraged to make suggestions, backing them up by reference to the text.

Comment

This activity allowed the children to 'get into the mind' of Farmer Brown. They were putting themselves in his place and by empathising with him were able to consider his emotions and feelings. It also required them to infer things from the text – both the written text and the illustrations. This 'reading between and beyond' the lines is an important skill for readers to develop. Sharing and justifying their ideas in a group also meant that the children were thinking carefully about what they said. They were willing to challenge each other and to debate different viewpoints.

The ideas generated in the groups were fed back as a whole group and recorded on the whiteboard. As each point was made by a child, the teacher required them to justify it and refer back to the text for support.

The children were then set the task of writing a letter from the cows to Farmer Brown. This was done as a shared writing activity in their small groups. The children made suggestions as to what was written, discussed it among themselves and came to a consensus; it was then recorded on a large sheet of paper in felt pen. Throughout this process the children were continually re-reading what had already been written and checking that this was what the group meant to say. Halfway through the lesson the teacher stopped the class and asked each group to read out what they had written so far. She asked for comments from other groups and checked with the writers that they were happy and knew what they wanted to say next. The writing contained many crossings out and arrows moving phrases and words around. Once it was completed the whole text was read to check that the group was happy with it.

Comment

Shared writing is a strategy which makes explicit all the thinking that normally goes on in the head of a writer. It can take one of three forms: demonstration, teacher scribing or supported composition. Demonstration is when the teacher writes in front of the class and makes a running commentary on the whole writing process; she would articulate the decisions she made, try out sentences before she wrote them and change things she was not happy with. Teacher scribing is when the children compose a text and the teacher acts as scribe, writing it down on a flip chart or whiteboard.

This is a useful way for the teacher to model the revising and editing process, showing the children the sort of things they might ask themselves when they are writing.

The example of shared writing in this observation is of supported composition; the children were in Year 5 and it can be assumed that they would have had a lot of experience of the other types of shared writing activity. The children were working together to compose and transcribe and so had to discuss the decisions that writers have to make. The teacher was supporting them in this reflective process and the teaching assistant was acting as scribe for one group.

Task

Observe some shared writing sessions and decide whether it is demonstration, teacher scribing or supported composition. After the observation, think about the respective roles of teacher and children and how they change in the different activities.

This activity allowed the children to empathise with Farmer Brown and understand his reactions and feelings. In the following lesson attention was then turned to the cows! In the book the cows hold a meeting behind the closed doors of the shed to discuss their response to Farmer Brown's initiative. The children became the cows and held their meeting. Before the meeting each child was asked to make notes on what they thought and how they felt the cows should respond to Farmer Brown. Feelings were shared and different viewpoints of an appropriate response were hotly discussed. The children were required to explain and fully justify their views and the group had to come to a consensus after hearing different perspectives. Once this had been reached, each group was required to write a report of their meeting showing how they had reached the consensus. One member of the group was appointed as scribe and the teacher and teaching assistant worked with those children who needed more support. This writing activity followed a very similar pattern to the previous shared writing activity. The more able children were challenged by doing the writing with less scaffolding than previously. Those who needed support were given it and their writing was a guided writing time.

Comment

Guided writing is very similar to guided reading in that it allows a teacher to provide structured and focused support to a group of children who have similar needs at a particular stage of the writing process. In this situation the teacher worked with a group of children who needed help in sorting out their ideas and recording them in a way which was meaningful for the reader. The teacher acted as scribe and the children composed the text, using the strategy of 'oral composition' to try out their ideas. The teaching assistant worked with a group who needed support in working as a group and was there to model and demonstrate collaborative working – ensuring that everybody's voice was heard and that everybody made a contribution to the final product.

Once the meetings had been held and the reports written, the rest of the book was read. The children enjoyed comparing their own response to that of the cows in the book.

In this observation we have seen some quite sophisticated writing practices. Children were writing in role, collaborating with other people and writing in particular formats and styles. You might want to argue that older children should be expected to do this, but it is a skill that is learned and the writing experiences that younger children are given will enable them to write in this way.

OBSERVATION: Writing in a Reception class (ages 4 and 5)

A whole Reception class went on a shopping trip to buy the ingredients to make a Christmas pudding. All 35 children went on a bus to a local supermarket; they were in small groups and each group was led by an adult.

Each group had their own shopping list which they had written themselves. The children were encouraged to read the words on the list and to hunt for the items needed in the shop. In the afternoon the children worked independently to write an account of the morning's trip in their writing journals.

Comment

This piece of writing comes from an exciting, authentic experience. The children were clearly full of what they had done and were eager to record it in their journals. They had something to write about and so could concentrate on how to convey what they wanted to say rather than scratching their heads and trying to think of something. They had a genuine purpose for writing and a personal experience to write about.

All the children have writing journals which are used to write about events in school, to recount home events and to act as a showcase for their writing. From the very beginning of their time in school, journal writing is modelled as something special that can be looked back at and can be a source of personal pride. Teachers frequently use the journals to show children how much progress they have made since their arrival in school. Journals are expected to be illustrated and the illustrations are considered as important as the writing. Most children are keen to do journal work and love to spend significant amounts of time writing and drawing.

Consider

What's in a name? What difference do you think it would make to the children as writers to be writing in a 'journal' rather than on paper or in a 'writing book'?

Comment

The explicit encouragement to the children to reflect on the progress they have made as writers serves at least two purposes. First, they are being shown how to evaluate their own work; they look critically at work done previously in relation to what they have done now and talk about specific ways in which progress has been made. Second, and maybe more importantly, in seeing the improvement in their writing their self-esteem is raised and they feel confident in themselves as writers.

To support the children's early writing, laminated key words are stuck on the wall facing the writing area. An adult usually works with the children doing journal work. Word cards are provided on the table which have key words in alphabetical order on one side of the card and letters with an illustration from the phonic programme on the other, indicating the correct letter formation. All the children are encouraged to write independently and to use strategies to enable them to do this – word cards, thinking of the first sound of the word, using the key words on the wall, and so on. This means the children are always able to read what they have written.

Comment

To support independence the children are given all the resources they need to write. The strategies which the children are encouraged to use need to have been explicitly taught. The class daily play games with the key word cards and they are not a permanent display but used as part of teaching and learning activities in the classroom. Sometimes children will use word cards to create texts rather than transcribing them themselves. Why do you think the teacher would encourage them to do this?

The recount in Figure 4.1 is written by Natasha, a 5-year-old pupil who spent two terms in the nursery attached to the school and wrote this at the end of her first term in the Reception class. She is the third and youngest child in the family, with two brothers who attend the same primary school. Her teacher describes her as a bright, articulate and enthusiastic learner with a mature outlook in the classroom. She speaks English as a second language and her first language is Hebrew. Her parents speak some English but Hebrew is the main language used in the home.

When writing the recount Natasha used the word cards and the key words on the wall and did so without prompting from an adult. She asked for help

Figure 4.1 A recount of a shopping trip written by a 5-year-old

to write the word 'ingredients' but was able to segment it into 'ing – greed – yens', recognising that the first sound was /i/. When 'ingredients' was added as a key word on the wall, she was able to read it and put it into a sentence with the other key words that she already knew.

Comment

This is a lovely example of how the phonics teaching is influencing Natasha's writing. Look carefully at what Natasha is doing. She is not segmenting the word into phonemes but into syllables. Syllables are the most accessible unit of spoken language and can be described as the rhythm of language. Has Natasha identified the syllables correctly?

How would you help her to do this? Clapping, stamping, tapping, jumping while saying the word are just some of the ways to help children feel the rhythm of the words and to identify the separate syllables.

Why is this useful to children? It helps them to hear the phonemes in each syllable. Once a syllable has been identified, they can be helped to segment each syllable into phonemes.

Can you break the word 'ingredients' into syllables and then segment it into phonemes?

When she had finished her writing, Natasha showed it to the teacher and the following conversation was held:

Teacher: Gosh Natasha, what fantastic writing! You did this independently. Wow! I am so impressed that you knew how to write so many words on your own. Look at the beautiful way you've written your letters. And you've remembered lots of finger spaces between the words. Full stops too! Can you read it to me?

Comment

The teacher is effusive in her praise of Natasha, but look carefully at exactly what she is saying. Not only does she praise her but she states very clearly what she is praising her for. What has Natasha done that is worthy of praise?

- She worked independently.
- She was willing to have a go and to use the resources that were made available.
- She formed most of the letters correctly.
- She put finger spaces between the words.

Well done, Natasha! Is there anything else that you might have praised Natasha for?

Natasha: We went to the shop to buy ingredients. We went in a bus. That's me on the bus, look – can you see my head in the window?

Comment

Natasha is here beginning to engage in conversation about the topic of the writing. How might you have responded to this if you were the teacher?

By talking with Natasha about the content of the writing, rather than just transcriptional aspects, you would be responding as a reader rather than just as a teacher.

Teacher: I can. That bus looks full of children going to Sainsbury's. Look how clever you are. Look at the beginning of your journal – beautiful drawing but no words and now, you're writing clever words on your own. I expect in your next piece of writing you'll put nice big finger spaces between each word, won't you?

Natasha: Yes. My finger spaces are a bit skinny in this one, aren't they?

Teacher: They are. But you've remembered we need them. Do you think we need to do something special at the beginning of your sentence too? Can you remember what it is?

Natasha: No. Do we make the letter big? Oh, I know. Captain Capital. I need a capital 'w' for 'we'.

Teacher: Brilliant girl! You're absolutely right. I'm going to write that on a special Post-it for you. You choose which colour and I'll stick it on your journal for next time.

Comment

The teacher is now beginning to challenge Natasha and to give her targets for next time. The targets are ones she identifies along with Natasha and her conversation is modelling to Natasha how she might review her own work and set her own personal targets. Note how she scaffolds Natasha's evaluation of her own finger spaces and leads her towards realising for herself how they can be improved. See also how she encourages Natasha to remember teaching she has had about capital letters and then relate that to her own work. Yet, it is all done within a context of praise for what has been achieved.

Natasha chose a pink heart-shaped Post-it and the teacher wrote, 'Finger spaces and capital letter at the beginning!' She then stuck the Post-it onto the side of her work and wrote a comment on the bottom, reading it aloud to Natasha as she wrote, 'It was a fun trip, wasn't it'.

Comment

In her written comment the teacher is making an affective response to the shared experience and is showing Natasha that she has read what she has written and that what is most important is the content.
   How might the teacher continue this conversation?

We have all been in the position of sitting in front of a blank sheet of paper or a blank computer screen with an equally blank mind, not knowing at all what to write about. In order to help children to become writers, teachers need to understand that experience, drawing on it to know that writers need authentic experiences to write about. When we have to scratch our heads and ponder over what to write next, continually checking the word count button, our writing is not likely to be the best. The best writing comes when we have lots to write about because we are enthusiastic and excited about the content; we may be writing about things that really matter to us or experiences we found exciting, enjoyable or even frightening. Children feel exactly the same about writing. Natasha was writing about an experience she had clearly enjoyed. She was writing about it in a special place and she knew exactly what the purpose of writing in her journal was. Providing these experiences, purposes and tools allows children to develop their compositional skills as authors.

Teachers also need a knowledge of the transcriptional conventions of written English so that they can help children to master them. Do you know what a sentence is? How would you explain it to a child in Key Stage 1 or even in Reception? Could you explain to Natasha where capital letters go? Many children put them at the beginning of each line; that's very understandable but how would you allay that misconception?

What are full stops for? It is helpful to remember that punctuation is generally for the reader rather than the writer. The writer uses punctuation to tell the reader how the text is to be read. Often the best way to explain what punctuation is needed is to read a text aloud.

Teaching writing also needs a strong phonic knowledge. Can you identify syllables in words and can you then segment each syllable into its constituent phonemes? The word 'ingredients' is a challenging one. It has four syllables:

In – gred – i – ents

These are made up of 11 phonemes:

/i//n/ /g//r//ee//d/ /ee/ /e//n//t//s/

A grapheme is the way of writing down a phoneme, so there are always the same number of graphemes in a word as there are phonemes. However, a grapheme can consist of one or more letters, so there are not always the same number of letters as graphemes and phonemes. That is where it can get confusing! 'Ingredients' is difficult because the graphemes used to represent the phonemes are not always the most common; for example, the phoneme /ee/ is represented in two different ways in this word. As a teacher you need to be aware of this but recognise that young children might not be ready to understand complex segmenting. Natasha segmented the word how she said it and so heard it; the most positive response would be not to correct her but to say the word to her and encourage her to repeat it slowly and clearly, making it into a game.

The shopping trip was as much a writing lesson as any shared or guided writing lesson. It served two purposes: it was an integral part of a cross-curricular project (making a Christmas cake) and gave the children a real experience to write about. The children had created a shopping list which they used when they went on the trip and the recount of the trip was for a personal record.

There were many resources within the classroom to support children's independent writing and it is important to note that these were constantly used, referred to and changed. They were not just permanent displays in the classroom. The children were aware of them and accustomed to using them.

In this observation the particular pedagogical strategy which stands out and is worthy of note is the way in which the teacher responded to Natasha's writing and used it to set targets for future development. Key points noticed in the commentary are:

- The teacher responded as a reader – she made comments on the content and expressed her own response to it in writing.
- She praised Natasha for her achievements and was very explicit about what was being praised.
- She helped Natasha to identify her own targets for development. This meant they were attainable in the near future and were clearly understood. She involved Natasha in recording them.

The way in which this activity was set up illustrates how writing is deeply embedded in all classroom activities. The journal had already been established within the classroom as a place to record important experiences and events, and so Natasha was happy with and understood the process. Natasha also knew the resources that were available to her and used them well.

The teacher was clearly aiming to help Natasha become an independent writer and she did this in several ways:

- by using the resources of the classroom
- by treating her as an independent writer
- by evaluating Natasha's current understanding and achievements
- by indicating clear and specific small steps towards improvement
- by modelling to Natasha the process of evaluating her own achievements.

Through the use of praise and by responding to Natasha's writing as a reader, the teacher ensured that the writing experience was positive for all concerned. Notice how positively she supported Natasha in seeing that the spaces between words needed to be larger. How much better than a brusque comment, 'Your word spaces are too small'. Writing is very hard work for adults and children, and any discouragement or setback will be very off-putting.

Talk for writing

Your experiences of writing school and college assignments, letters, emails or even shopping lists will have shown you that a lot of thinking and experimenting goes on before you commit words to paper or screen. Most of us will rehearse ideas in our minds and try out different sentence structures. For young children this is even more important. Talk can help them to structure their ideas and thinking and to investigate the best words to use and the best ways to use them. Before any writing activity children need lots of talk – in large groups, in small groups and individually. They need to hear teachers modelling sentence structures to them and also receive feedback from conversational responses to their own ideas.

One of the most significant influences on classroom practice is the consultant, Pie Corbett. He has published many practical resources to support teachers in their planning and teaching and these can be found in many schools. His work on story is said to be based on the work of the developmental psycholinguist, Traute Taeschner, from Rome. Her work (Taeschner 1991) argued that language acquisition, particularly the acquisition of a second language, is about internalising the patterns of the language.

Corbett based his story-making project on this, transferring the learning of patterns of language to learning patterns of narrative with accompanying actions. Corbett links the ideas of book talk and storytelling with talk for writing, arguing that these strategies give children content, purpose, motivation and skills for writing. He says, 'It is this developmental exploration through talk, of the thinking and creative processes involved in being a writer, that we are calling *Talk for Writing*' (Corbett 2008b: 3).

The point is clearly made, that learning to write is much more than just learning to form letters, to spell and to construct grammatically meaningful sentences. The following observation from a Year 5 class (age 9–10) shows the close relationship between reading and writing. It is part of the same unit of work from which we discussed a reading lesson in the previous chapter.

OBSERVATION: Year 5 class (ages 9 and 10) writing in the style of Dickens

The lesson began with the teacher recapping the two previous lessons. Part of these lessons was described in the previous chapter: a group of children were looking at a section from *Oliver Twist* and were exploring their understanding of it, scaffolded by the teacher's questions. The whole class had also spent time looking at a passage from *Oliver Twist*, identifying the linguistic characteristics. These were recorded in a word cloud which was referred to during this writing lesson and the children were thus reminded of them.

Comment

This reminds us that reading and becoming familiar with the characteristics of the text type the children will be asked to write are really important.

The teacher wrote the following sentence on the board:

Miss Cooke came into school at 8.00 this morning.

The children were asked how that sentence could be changed into the style of Dickens and the teacher demonstrated this through shared writing.

The teacher wrote on the whiteboard, explaining his choice of vocabulary and structure as he wrote. The sentence became:

> *Miss Cooke came into school very early this morning. It was dark, cold, windy and so she was wrapped in a scarf, coat and gloves to keep warm from the chill; then the radiators came on at around 9 o'clock which made her feel warmer.*

There followed some discussion about how close to the style of Dickens it was. The teacher had deliberately not made it 'too good' because he wanted the children to reflect on it critically.

Comment

We all learn from our mistakes and often if we present children with a perfect piece of work it can be off-putting. This teacher gave the children the opportunity to make suggestions for improvement of this writing and this provoked a lively discussion.

The children were then given another sentence and told to rewrite it in the style of Dickens. Some children worked in a group with the teacher in a guided writing session. These were the children who needed more input before they could work effectively independently. Other children worked independently but with the teaching assistant on hand for support if needed.

Comment

Note how the teacher differentiated the activity in relation to the amount of support given. All the children were given the same task but some children were given a lot more help. Relate this back to what you know about the concept of 'scaffolding'. In order to plan this, the teacher needed to know his class very well and to have monitored their learning during the previous lessons.

Halfway through the writing time the children put their work in progress on the tables and all walked round the classroom reading each other's. Sticky notes were placed on each table and the children wrote comments and suggestions.

Comment

This was a procedure used quite frequently by this teacher. He felt that the children were not very skilled at continually reviewing their work and that it would be easier to do this with somebody else's writing. The children then returned to their work to find lots of suggestions. They read and considered them and maybe changed their writing accordingly before carrying on.

This was a challenging lesson for both the children and the teacher. We can identify some points of good practice which can inform our teaching of writing:

- The writing was preceded by reading and by lots of talk about the texts which were read.
- A large amount of talk took place both about the meaning of the text and the linguistic features used.
- The children were given the opportunity to collaborate or work alone in the independent work.
- Those who needed extra support were given it.
- The children were being taught how to review and revise their own writing by commenting on the writing of their peers.

OBSERVATION: Handwriting lesson in Year 1 (ages 5 and 6)

There are times when children, especially young children, need explicit teaching in handwriting and letter formation – the transcriptional skills. It is often difficult to know how to make these lessons motivating for both teacher and children.

The class is sitting on the carpet facing the whiteboard. They are looking at the teacher who is sitting on a low chair facing them to one side of the board. She says, 'Do you remember what we said yesterday – that the next thing we start is very exciting?' There are lots of nods and 'oohs' and 'aahs' from the children. 'We're going to start joined up writing. I love doing joined up writing because it's lovely and flowing and I don't have to lift my pencil up. We're going to look at the letter 'l' and learn how we make it join up.' By this time the children are really excited and eager to begin.

Comment

Many schools begin 'joined up' handwriting from the start and if they do not completely join they teach the children to form the letters with the entrances and exits already present; for example: 'l' instead of 'l'. There are strong arguments for doing this. There is a well-established link between spelling and handwriting. The hand 'remembers' the movements for common letter strings. There are also links between compositional skills and the extent to which handwriting becomes automatic.

Read

Medwell, J., Strand, S. and Wray, D. (2009) 'The links between handwriting and composing for Year 6 children', *Cambridge Journal of Education*, 39(3): 329–44.

The teacher then wrote the word 'tell' on the whiteboard and asked the children to write it with their fingers in the air. As they wrote she talked them through the shape of the letter: 'Instead of starting at the top, start at the bottom. If you get a little loop it doesn't matter'.

Comment

Once again we see the importance of talk. As the teacher talks through the letter shape with the children she not only gives them clear guidance, but also gives them a reminder of what to do and a verbal indication of the shape. A handwriting lesson has been described as a mini physical education lesson. The teacher is talking through the movement, describing what happens at each stage. That is exactly what happens to me at the gym when I am being introduced to a new exercise. Learning to form a letter is no different.

A board with handwriting lines on is then pulled down. The lines are arranged with two dotted lines in between two bold lines. The centre of each letter goes in between the middle two lines and the top and bottom lines show the extent of the ascenders and descenders.

Comment

It is very helpful for young children to have the support of lines; it gives them a clear indication of where to go so they can then focus on the shape. Handwriting lessons are about movement and the emphasis needs to be on the required hand movements.

The teacher modelled how to write several letters on the lined board and each time she talked through the movements she was making: start at the bottom, go right up to the top, go back down on top of the line and then make a flick out at the bottom.

The children were then given sheets on which were printed the handwriting lines. A letter 'l' was written at the start of each line. The teacher gave them clear instructions: 'On your sheet there is one to show you. Do one – if you are unsure put your hand up and somebody will come to show you. First things – put your name – two names – and remember what goes between them – a finger space'.

The children went to their places at the tables and before they began to write they were reminded about correct posture: 'Your bottom should be on the seat, your feet should be flat on the floor and make sure you hold your pencil correctly'.

Comment

Posture is very important for good handwriting. The paper should be held at a slight angle to the left; the opposite applies for left-handed people, and the pencil should be held firmly but not so tightly that knuckles become white! Sometimes special rubber grips put around the pencil can help.

As the lesson progressed, the teacher was continually talking through what was happening to the children. I am going to list the things she said here. Consider how they were supporting the children in developing their skills.

What's the next letter we can see? It's a 't'. It's nearly the same as the 'l' but a little shorter and with a little line across it. Look, start from the bottom, up to the top, down, kick and across.

The next letter is 'i' and it's easier than the other two, so if you can do an 'l' and a 't', it's easy.

It's a little dot. We don't want a football. Who thinks they're going to be able to do joined up writing? I think you all are – because if you do each letter with the join in and the join out then you can put them together.

The next letter is 'h'. I think this is a little more tricky.

Don't hold your pencil too far down or you can't see what you are doing. Make sure your fingers are on the painted bit not the wooden bit.

Does it matter if we make a mistake in our handwriting? No, it doesn't – because we're practising.

One more letter. This is our challenge today because I think it's the trickiest letter – 'b'. It is a 'b' but it looks a little bit different because it's got a joining bit. Some children try and do their 'b' like this … and it looks like a muddle, so we have to remember very carefully the order in which we do it.

By listing all the comments of the teacher I hope you will begin to appreciate that she was providing a running commentary on the handwriting process. By articulating the formation of each letter and highlighting the challenges and purposes, she is providing them with a scaffolding to support their practice.

Task

Look at each of the comments she is making and see in what way it might support the children's learning. What is the role of the teacher during a handwriting lesson?

OBSERVATION: Guided writing with Year 3 (ages 7 and 8)

The teacher was working with a focus group of 11 children; five of these children had English as an additional language. The group had the target of achieving a Level 2 in writing by the end of the academic year. This lesson took place in May. Level 2 is the outcome that is expected for most children at the end of Year 2 and so it could be said that these children were working below expectation.

Target-setting is a central part of life in primary schools. Teachers are required to set targets for their class and for individual children and share these with both the children and their parents. This is part of a policy belief that standards can be raised through a focus on outcomes which are identifiable, measurable and achievable. However, as Einstein once said, 'Not everything that counts can be counted and not everything that can be counted counts', and the too rigorous application of specific targets can be stultifying rather than enhancing.

Task

Talk with a class teacher about how s/he uses target-setting in the classroom, particularly with reference to the development of writing.

Read

Wyse, D. and Torrance, H. (2009) 'The development and consequences of national curriculum assessment for primary education in England', *Educational Research*, 51(2): 213–28.

In a previous lesson the children had listened to stories with dilemmas. They had predicted what was going to happen in the stories and, after sharing their predictions, had written the end of a given story on sticky notes. The learning objective of this lesson was to write the end of a story, focusing on the characters and on making the story interesting for the reader.

The lesson began with the children sitting on the carpet recapping on what they had done in the previous lesson. The word 'dilemma' was revisited and defined as a problem in a story that needs to be fixed. The teacher then introduced the word 'fable' to the group: 'We are going to be looking at more stories with special messages. These stories are called fables. If you listen really carefully and do some really deep thinking you will know the message the story is trying to teach us'.

The teacher showed the children the book *Fables* by Arnold Lobel and read the fable entitled 'The Frogs at the Rainbow's End'. It is a story of three frogs who are sure they will find gold, diamonds and pearls at the end of the rainbow. The teacher read the story to the children up to the place where the first frog met the second frog. She put the children into groups of three and gave each one a number – 1, 2 or 3. The first two had to role-play the conversation between the two frogs, number 3 had to observe and report back to the whole group. The children responded well to this and there were some exciting ideas.

Comment

By engaging in role play as the frogs, the children knew exactly what they were each thinking and feeling. This gave them a solid basis on which to write.

Each group had been given a booklet with images from the text and spaces to write in. Some of these writing spaces were speech bubbles and others were limited text boxes. Each group decided what to write and wrote it together. One child acted as scribe but all were engaged in the act of composition. First, they wrote in a speech bubble what the first frog said. Suggestions ranged from 'Come with me!' to 'You can't be my friend'. Each group reported back, the whole group chose one response and the teacher added this to the slide on the interactive whiteboard.

Comment

The fact that the children had only a limited space to write in meant that they were not inhibited by a blank sheet of A4 paper or an empty page in their exercise book. Alongside the encouragement this gave them was the support of knowing that they had already tried out their ideas in the small group. They were not making themselves vulnerable by writing just their own ideas but in working with a group they were supporting each other.

The teacher then carried on reading and stopped again when the two frogs met the third frog. The activity was repeated and the children talked in pairs about how the two frogs would react to the third frog. When the group was sharing their ideas the teacher used the strategy of lolly sticks to ensure that each child had a turn to speak. Each name was written on the end of a lolly stick and the sticks were put into a pot. The teacher took one out and the child whose name was on the stick spoke.

Comment

This is a useful strategy if some children tend to dominate class discussion or some children never volunteer. It ensures that every child is given an opportunity to speak. Once a child has had a turn, that lolly stick is not put back in the pot. Teachers need to be very sensitive and ensure that questions are modified to suit the child chosen and that differentiation will occur in the responses to the children. In this group there were some children who would call out and dominate and others who were very quiet and liked to hide in the background. This strategy meant that all children had a chance. Milly, who is normally very quiet, expressed creative ideas eloquently, for example 'The treasure would only be gold dust and so the frogs would have to leave it behind as it was too small to share'.

The teacher then read to near the end of the story when the three frogs arrive in the cave. Again, the children discussed what would happen in pairs and shared their thoughts on what would happen. As groups they completed the story in their booklets. The teacher then read the whole story to the children right up to the end. The frogs went into the cave and ... you will have to read the story for yourself if you want to find out the shock ending!

Comment

This last observation is similar to the first one in this chapter. Can you identify the similarities and differences? What key aspects of teaching writing can you see demonstrated in this lesson?

OBSERVATION: Authentic writing

I want to close this chapter on writing by emphasising the variety of texts we write in our day-to-day lives. At the start of the last chapter I asked you to list all the things you had read during the previous 24 hours. If I were to ask you to do the same thing but in relation to writing, I wonder what would be on your list. I would imagine that for most of you, the texts you wrote would have been very brief, very functional and often not for publication. Very few would have written a story and, unless you are reading this during assessment season, not many would have written much continuous prose. Consider why there is such a discrepancy between the writing we ask children to do in school and what happens at home.

One way in which to redress the balance is to assert the need for ensuring that children have authentic writing experiences. These may be embedded in topic or other work across the curriculum or may be part of normal classroom life. For example, why not ask the children to write the labels for wall displays, to write letters home to parents inviting them to class assemblies or such like, or to write instructions for how to use a computer, visualiser or other piece of classroom equipment. Look at the two pieces of writing written by 8-year-old Nathan (Figures 4.2 and 4.3).

The first piece was prompted by a trip Nathan had made with his parents to see a performance of *A Midsummer Night's Dream*. He had been learning about Shakespeare at school and knew the story well but had not read the original text in any form. The performance he saw was a completely unabridged version performed in the open air by an amateur company. His parents were slightly worried as to how Nathan would cope but he loved it! He was particularly excited when the actor playing Sentinel came to talk to them after the performance.

Figure 4.2   Nathan's account of seeing a Shakespeare play

At school Nathan had been given an exercise book in which to record what he did over the summer holiday. Any of you who have had to do such a thing will know how tedious it can be. Nathan adopted his own strategies to make his writing convey his enthusiasm without giving him too much work! Look carefully at how he did this in Figure 4.2.

Comment

This is a wonderful multimodal text – it uses a variety of media to convey the key message. Notice how Nathan cut out the title of the play from the programme and stuck it in as the heading of the writing. He then used an arrow to point to the title rather than write it all out again. Nathan was taking control of his writing as the author and making decisions about how he created his text. Similarly, the strip of stars at the bottom of the writing conveys how much he enjoyed the experience; he is using visual imagery rather than print. The writing he has done shows that Nathan is actually an accomplished writer with sophisticated vocabulary choice. The whole thing shows that he is also an accomplished creator of texts using a variety of different ways to create his message. It might be too much of an assumption, but I like to think that he described the play as 'unspeakably brilliant' to avoid having to write any more! It reminds me of the lines from Gareth Owen's poem 'Miss Creedle teaches creative writing':

If there are indescribable monsters

Tell me what they look like...

As you look at this piece of writing, consider how you might have responded to it if you were Nathan's teacher and he had written it in school.

Now look at another piece of writing by Nathan.

It was a week before the annual family camping holiday and Nathan was getting worried that his parents did not seem to be preparing for this holiday. He decided to take matters into his own hands and wrote a series of lists. Again, Nathan organised his writing in his own way in order to serve his own purpose. Think about how he has done this and relate it to what you know about how lists are written.

Figure 4.3   Nathan's list

Comment

Nathan has physically divided the paper into two parts – inside and outside – and then for each part he has different sub-headings. His writing represents the way in which he is imagining the holiday – the different sections within the tent and the area surrounding it. He created smaller texts and then stuck them on a large sheet of paper to create the larger text. Which do you think came first – the organisation of the whole or the individual lists?

It is interesting how in both these pieces of writing Nathan has manipulated the positioning of the text and used different ways of constructing the final piece of writing. He has done this by hand but, in my mind, the process is very similar to creating a digital text, for example a web page.

Both these pieces of writing are examples of authentic texts and as the author Nathan is very much in control of them. Look through the writing done by children in a class where you might be placed or be working and ask yourself how authentic it is and how much control they had over it.

Being a writer is all about making decisions, and in learning to be writers children need to be given the opportunity to make those decisions.

Summary

The writing process is very complex and, like the reading process, contains many elements which all need to be taught and yet need to be seen as an integrated whole. As you observe writing lessons, consider the relative place each element plays in the lesson and how a teacher demonstrates to children the integrity of the process.

We have seen in the observations in this chapter how the elements of composition and transcription work together and yet need not coexist. We have also seen that writing is much more than putting marks on a piece of paper or tapping the keys on a keyboard.

Above all, we have seen the importance of talk for writing. Children need to have experiences to write about and they need to have talked about those experiences so they can rehearse the vocabulary and the grammatical structures they will use in their writing.

It can all be summed up in the fact that writing is a process and needs time to develop and come to fruition. We want children to join with James Michener (n.d.), the American author, when he said: 'I love writing. I love the swirl and swing of words as they tangle with human emotions'.

Further reading

Chamberlain, L. (2015) *Inspiring Writing in Primary Schools*. London: SAGE.
Cremin, T. and Myhill, D. (2011) *Thinking Critically About Writing: Writers' Voices in the Classroom*. London: Routledge.

5

Teaching grammar, punctuation and spelling

This chapter explores the teaching of spelling, grammar and punctuation – something which has gained in prominence and significance since the first edition of this book. There are several reasons for this – the specificity of what is to be taught within the English National Curriculum and the introduction of concepts which previously had been taught much later; the influence of the testing regime where spelling, punctuation and grammar (SPaG) are assessed out of any meaningful context; and the strong accountability agenda where the results of these tests impact on teachers and schools.

Grammar

Watson (2012) talked to a group of secondary English teachers about their perceptions of teaching grammar and found there were two contrasting views. Most of the teachers described having to teach grammar as threatening, reactionary and dull but there were some who found it inspiring, fascinating and empowering. I wonder into which category you would fall? The teaching of grammar has gained prominence since the introduction of the current National Curriculum; there must have been very few primary teachers who did not look at the programmes of study and the glossary of terms with a sinking heart. The huge increase in the specificity and quantity of grammatical terminology put pressure on teachers' subject knowledge. Many of them had never been taught grammar and for them it was unknown territory, while for older teachers like myself, it seemed as though the names and definitions had changed since I last 'did' grammar at school.

The way in which grammar is taught is hugely influenced by the way in which it is tested. We will see in Chapter 7 how assessment and pedagogy are inextricably intertwined and this is particularly evident in the teaching of grammar. The way in which the SPaG test is designed asks pupils to label words and parts of sentences, and there is little requirement to consider the impact vocabulary choice and sentence structure have on the meaning of a text and the impact on the reader. Look at these examples from the 2016 test (Figure 5.1):

Tick one box in the row to indicate if the sentence is in the present progressive or the past progressive.

Sentence	Present progressive	Past progressive
Joey was playing football in the park after school.		
Joey's football skills are improving all the time.		
Joey is hoping to be a professional footballer.		

Which sentence uses capital letters correctly? Tick one.

The athlete won four gold medals at the olympic games in london.

The athlete won four Gold Medals at the Olympic Games in London.

The athlete won four Gold medals at the Olympic Games in London.

The athlete won four gold medals at the Olympic Games in London.

Write a sentence using the word <u>point</u> as a **verb**. Do not change the word. Remember to punctate your sentence correctly.

Write a sentence using the word <u>point</u> as a **noun**. Do not change the word. Remember to punctuate your sentence correctly.

(2016 Key Stage 2 English grammar, punctuation and spelling Paper 1: questions. © Crown copyright and Crown information 2016)

Figure 5.1 Questions from the 2016 SPaG test

Task

Try and answer the questions yourself and then reflect on why you found them easy or challenging.

For me in the first question the challenge was the words that were used. I studied languages for A' level many years ago and learned to describe verbs in the past tense as the 'perfect', 'imperfect' or 'pluperfect'. I then learned to call them the 'continuous past' or the 'simple past'. I did not know the term 'past progressive' or 'present progressive'. I understand the concept completely but needed to think twice about the words used.

In the second question I could understand why somebody would indicate the second sentence as using capital letters correctly. 'Gold Medals' are extremely significant and I would certainly want to highlight them if I were an athlete. However, that is incorrect; the final sentence is the only correct one.

For the third question, look at Michael Rosen's blog entry (www.michael rosenblog.blogspot.co.uk) on Monday 23 May 2016 under the heading *How SPaG wastes space and wastes the mind* for his analysis of this question. It makes interesting reading!

The point of this is that the way in which SPaG is set out in the National Curriculum and the way in which it is tested implies a notion of correctness. In one way, that makes it easy to teach and to assess; you tell children what they need to know, give them lots of practice in the sort of questions they will meet in the test and hopefully they will be successful. Safford (2016) quotes a teacher from her research who said, 'It's very easy to train children to do well'. The trouble is that when you start looking at literature or real-life language you immediately come across all sorts of ambiguities. When I am teaching grammar subject knowledge to trainee teachers, my heart always sinks when one of them says, 'but what about this?' You can guarantee it is a sentence where it is not always easy to apply 'the rules'. A view of grammar which believes in rules and prescription is very different from one which sees it in terms of conventions and description.

Myhill (2000) argues that our discussions about grammar are shaped by political and ideological views and this is certainly true. The way in which grammar teaching is constructed in schools today is determined by a particular view of what grammar is and what it does. Safford (2016) found that the time spent teaching grammar has increased enormously since the introduction of the 2014 National Curriculum and it is now taught explicitly and formally as a regular part of classroom routines. This is a direct consequence of the format of the assessment.

So, is there any value in teaching grammar? I would want to answer a definite 'Yes' to that question but only in the context of real texts of all types in which the impact of the author's linguistic choices are discussed. Let's look at some lessons to see how this can happen.

OBSERVATION: The subjunctive with Year 6

A series of lessons was based around the book *The Boy in the Dress* by David Walliams (2013). This book addresses some challenging issues and at least two children in the class would have been affected by similar events in their home lives. In the first lesson the teacher read the first chapter to the class. Together, looking at the text under a visualiser, the class identified sentences in the chapter which told us about the characters John, Dennis and Dad. This activity required the children to think carefully about what the text was saying and to use their inferential skills. The sentences they identified included the following:

> Dad banned John and Dennis from ever mentioning Mum again.
>
> John was full of silent rage with his mum for leaving.
>
> After Mum left, Dad didn't say much, but when he did, he would often shout.

The children then worked in pairs to list what they knew about each character and the questions they still had. They made notes and then compared notes with another pair.

Comment

You may be wondering why this lesson is included in a chapter on teaching grammar. Be patient because the grammar will appear in the third lesson! Remember that the previous chapter finished with a reminder of the importance of authentic writing. There is evidence from research (Andrews et al. 2006; Hillocks 1986) that teaching grammar out of a context has little if any impact on children's reading or writing. However, Myhill et al. (2012) found there was a positive effect when teaching was done using real texts to explore how the language features of a text enhance the writing. In this first lesson of a series the teacher was demonstrating to the pupils how to 'read between the lines' and how an author can convey information both directly and indirectly.

The class then came back together and held a discussion about the Dad – the question the teacher gave them was 'Is Dad neglecting the two boys?' The class was used to dialogic work like this and the discussion was lively, with different views being expressed. The teacher took little part in the discussion but recorded the main points on the whiteboard.

Comment

This is a good example of the importance of talk for writing. The children were using the text to generate ideas and opinions; they were challenging each other's views. They did not yet know, but what they were talking about was relating directly to what they would soon be writing about. They were rehearsing vocabulary, ideas and justification and hearing new ideas. They were also seeing their ideas written down and these remained on the working wall as a resource for independent writing the following day.

The second lesson took place on the next day and continued the focus on Dad. The teacher read the second chapter to the class and after the reading posed the questions 'How does Dad feel? What do we know about him?' This was a sensitive question for this class but the teacher had deliberately put the focus on the Dad in order to encourage empathy and to help those children in the class who were sharing the experiences of John and Dennis to look at their situation through other eyes. In groups the children did a role on the wall exercise. They had a large gingerbread man figure on a sheet of A3 paper – outside the shape they wrote descriptions of what Dad was looking like and inside the shape they wrote what he was feeling. They were required to support everything they wrote by reference to the text they had read so far. At the end of the session the teacher gave the children homework: they were to think about how Dad was coping on his own and ask themselves if he needed help.

Comment

Once again the children were building up ideas and thoughts for their writing. They were being challenged to take their thinking even deeper through conversation and thought. In doing so the teacher

(Continued)

(Continued)

was recognising that composition does not begin when you put pen to paper but starts much, much earlier. By the time they come to do their writing, these children should know what they want to say and so be able to focus their attention on how to say it.

The learning objective of the third lesson was that the children should recognise vocabulary and structures that are appropriate for formal writing, including subjunctive forms, and build on their ideas from their homework. The children were asked to imagine they were a social worker assigned to the family; most of the children in the class were familiar with the role of social workers. They were asked to think back over all they had learned about the family situation and to consider what would help. After a few minutes discussion the class was brought together and told that, as social workers, they were required to write a report on the family. They were reminded that this would be a formal piece of writing and some of the characteristics of formal writing were introduced, for example no abbreviations, no slang words, no question tags.

The teacher then introduced the subjunctive form of verbs. He gave the class lots of examples drawn from traditional tales and nursery rhymes. For example: *If the mice were to stay up the clock, the farmer's wife would not cut off their tails; If Jack were not to fall down when going up the hill, Jill would not tumble over him.* The subjunctive was described as a wishful verb when the action was thought unlikely to happen. It is only found in formal writing and usually in subordinate clauses. The children then worked in pairs writing sentences based on Dennis's family using the subjunctive. For example, *If Dad were to eat more healthily, he would have more energy.* Each pair read their sentence to the class and the subjunctive was highlighted.

Comment

Now the grammar teaching starts! Note however that while there is some discrete teaching about the subjunctive, it is always done in the sense of how the use of the subjunctive impacts on the meaning. Because the examples given were based on 'stories' which the children knew well, the meaning is more accessible to them and so they can consider the language use. They know that the mice did run down the clock and so can understand that the clause, 'If the mice were to stay up the clock' is highly unlikely and rather like wishful thinking. Understanding this enables them to try out the language structure using what they have discovered about Dennis's family. They know what life is like for the family and so know what is likely and/or unlikely to happen.

The teacher then showed the class an example of a social worker's report on the IWB. This was one the teacher had written about Jack and his mother based on the story of Jack and the Beanstalk. The report contained two subjunctive verbs and these were identified by the class along with other characteristics of formal writing. The children were then set off on the task of writing a social worker's report on Dennis's family. This took the remainder of this lesson and the whole of the next.

Comment

The teacher modelled to the children the report they were going to write before they began to write independently. They had been given an insight into the emotions experienced by different members of the family, they had talked about the events and what might happen, they had used the vocabulary and linguistic features of the genre and they had been shown a framework for their writing. They eagerly began to write.

The observation above showed how grammar teaching can be incorporated into a unit of work which is based on a quality text and demonstrates the interdependence of talk, reading and writing. Some of the findings of the work of Barrs and Cork (2002) can be seen in these lessons. While observing Year 5 pupils and carrying out detailed case studies of six of them, they found that indirect planning prepared children more effectively for writing than planning with a writing frame or a planning model. This is what was happening in these lessons.

OBSERVATION: The passive voice with Year 6

The children had been looking at newspapers; they had looked at a range of newspapers, reading reports of the same events in the different papers. In the previous lesson they had re-written a report using the range of linguistic features they had identified – headline, introduction with 5ws (Who? When? Where? What? Why?), photo and caption, embedded clause, chronological order, direct and reported speech. At the start of the observed lesson they were told they were going to work for different newspaper companies and each write a report using all the linguistic features they had discussed. The teacher showed them a report under the visualiser and the children identified all the features they had been taught about. The teacher then read out the examples of the passive voice within the report and asked the children to tell her what effect this had on the report. This was discussed in pairs and then shared with the whole class. In the discussion the teacher introduced words like 'agent' and asked why newspapers might not want to indicate who had carried out the action. They also identified the subject and object and together worked out a definition of active and passive verbs.

Comment

Again, the starting point is the text; the teacher was looking at the passive voice and, rather than just giving dry facts, was considering why it was used and the effect it had on meaning for the readers. Secondly, the children were investigating for themselves – they were working out the conventions rather than just trying to apply rules to random sentences. Reedy and Bearne (2013) came up with the REDM sequence for teaching grammar in context. It is:

1   Reading and investigation
2   Explicit teaching
3   Discussion and experimentation
4   Making controlled writing choices

So far in this sequence of lessons we have seen the first two elements of this sequence.

The teacher then put the class into mixed-ability groups of about six and informed them of the name of the newspaper for which they would be working. She told the class that the editors of each newspaper group wanted to be sure they could write reports appropriately before giving them a 'big' story to cover, and so they were given a report which had been written by a junior reporter with which the editor was not happy. The children were asked to see if they could improve it. The report had been written entirely in the active voice and the children soon appreciated they needed to change it into the passive voice.

Comment

The explicit teaching in this lesson had given the children a vocabulary to talk about the reports. This is often known as a 'metalanguage' - a language about language. This illustrates one of the key reasons for teaching about language or teaching grammar. If we want children to behave as writers they will need opportunities to revise and edit their writing, and if this is to be done effectively they will need common terminology and an understanding of the conventions of usage.

The children then watched a news clip from BBC's *Newsround* programme and were told to work in their groups to plan the structure of the newspaper report and to write the first sentence of each paragraph together. One child in each group was appointed as scribe, another was given the role of ensuring that everybody in the group was given the chance to contribute and a third was asked to keep reading what was being written to ensure it made sense! There was much lively discussion as the groups began work and some heated debate about what were the essential elements of the story that needed to be conveyed to the newspaper's readers.

Comment

Remember that these were mixed-ability groups and the teacher wanted to be sure that nobody dominated and everybody had an opportunity to contribute; she allocated the roles very carefully based on her knowledge of the children. The use of the TV extract made the story very accessible to all the children and gave everybody access to the information. The groups took different approaches to planning their report: two groups drew the story in what was practically a story board; one group wrote numbered notes; two groups did a mixture of drawings and writing; and the other group created a comic strip along with speech bubbles. They all used the terminology they had learned earlier and some members of the last group were very fervent in their desire to make sure their sentences were in the passive voice, even though all their other writing was in the active voice.

At the end of this lesson each group had a clear structure for the report and the first sentence of each paragraph. The teacher gathered them together and they rehearsed the linguistic features of a newspaper report with special emphasis on the passive voice. Later, the teacher made copies of the plan for each member of the group so that on the next day they could write their individual reports.

Comment

All the children were now in a strong position to move to the final stage of the sequence and make controlled and informed writing choices. The framework for their writing had not been imposed on them but they had constructed it for themselves based on the teaching they had received. The grammar teaching had a purpose, which was to enable them to write in a particular genre, and they had been given an explanation as to why it was important.

OBSERVATION: Slow writing in Year 6

The next observation is of something called 'slow writing'. This is a technique which, as its name implies, makes children think really carefully about their technique and to focus in on particular forms of language structure. It seems to have first appeared in a blog named *The Learning Spy*, which is written by a secondary teacher called David Didau. There are some interesting ideas and thoughts there. The lesson below was taught by a trainee teacher and he was exploring this technique to enable children to create a piece of writing which is mysterious and full of tension. It is with a Year 6 class.

The lesson began with the children in pairs reminding each other of the story of *Little Red Riding Hood*. They had looked at different versions of the story during guided reading in the previous week and so should have been familiar with it. While they were talking the teacher played some creepy music to enhance the feeling of fear and anticipation.

Comment

At the very start of the lesson the children were engaged in re-telling the story. They would not all have looked at the same versions and so during this talk partners were comparing notes, identifying similarities and differences. The music was not mentioned by the teacher but it added to the mood and, almost unconsciously, it helped to focus the children's thinking on how to create a sense of mystery and tension.

The children then watched the opening section of the film *Chaperon Rouge* (www.youtube.com/watch?v=XyTDRzV9IcM). The first 1 minute 44 seconds introduce the character and the setting. The children watched the section twice – firstly they just watched and on the second viewing they were asked to make notes – jotting down words which they thought referred to Little Red and her feelings.

Comment

Here the film is being treated just as a written text. The first response is purely that of a 'reader' – what impact did it have on you and how did it make you feel? What connections do you make between previous versions of the story and this one? What questions do you have about what you have seen? Secondly, read as a writer. How can I convey this experience I have had with a visual text through written language? Again, as in all the examples we have seen, the private response is enhanced by the subsequent talk. Always, the children were required to justify their views by reference back to the text.

The children then began a piece of 'slow writing' based on the Little Red Riding Hood. The teacher gave them instructions for each sentence; they wrote individually but were writing just one sentence at a time in response to the instructions from the teacher. These were:

1   Begin with a verb
2   Start with an emotion
3   Include at least three adjectives
4   Include 'very' and then an adverb
5   Include a simile
6   Include a very short sentence
7   Include an ellipsis
8   End in the word 'sleep'

The process of writing was slow and the children were encouraged to think carefully about each sentence. The instructions forced them to consider word choice and sentence structure. They knew there would be eight sentences but they did not know what they would be like to start with.

Comment

At first, the children found this very disconcerting and were looking around at each other and the teacher for reassurance. Some wanted to rush on and found the slowness inhibiting. Others found it frightening because, as they told me afterwards, they did not know what was coming next. Some enjoyed it because at each stage they knew exactly what they had to do and they found that supportive.

At the end of the time, the children were given the opportunity to read over their eight sentences. They were advised to read their writing aloud to a neighbour to make sure it made sense. They were allowed to make changes but not any changes that would fundamentally alter the structure they had been given. They then read their writing to another person and were asked to respond as readers – did you get a sense of mystery and tension?

Comment

It was important that after the detailed focus the children were allowed to step back and look at their writing as a whole. Many of them were surprised at how good their writing was. One child, who usually writes a lot, had initially expressed frustration at the slowness and being held back, as she perceived it, but at this stage she recognised that her writing was of a higher quality. The teacher talked to her and then to the whole group about how, as a writer, you have to make every word count, and this exercise helped the children to appreciate this for themselves.

Note also how the response of the reader remained a key factor. This is essential for any writer; writing (except for personal journal writing) is not an indulgence but is primarily for the reader. As I am writing this I am continually going back to ensure that it makes sense, that it flows and that the sense of what I want to say is coming across. If I have failed in any way, please let me know!

The children then watched the next stage of the film up to the part when the girl wakes up (1 minute 26 seconds). Again, they watched it twice and the second time the children were asked to write down words and phrases which came into their mind while watching. The instruction was as unspecific as that because the teacher wanted them to be able to record the feelings and emotions generated by the extract of the film.

After the film the class discussed what had happened – had they realised it was a dream while they were watching or was that only clear to them when they saw Little Red waking up? Or had it been real and the wolves just went away when she woke up? As you can imagine, that discussion was quite lively, with different views being expressed.

The children then worked independently to write a second short paragraph about the 'dream'. The teacher told them their aim as a writer was to convey the emotions they had had while watching the film. She used the expression 'show not tell' to describe to the children what they were to write. They were to convey emotion and not events. She reminded them of some of the language structures they had used in the first paragraph and suggested they might like to consider if they would add to their writing in this paragraph.

Comment

The control was lessened now but there were still quite tight constraints about what the children were to write. This forced them to focus both on what they were saying and how they would say it. The teacher reminded them of the techniques they had at their disposal and gave them the choice of how or if to use them.

Finally, the children watched the rest of the film and for homework were given the task of planning the final paragraph of their writing. The next day the writing was completed.

Comment

This is another lesson where the grammar teaching is embedded in a consideration of real-life texts and of the impact on readers and writers. In my opinion, that is the best and probably the only effective way

(Continued)

(Continued)

to teach children about grammar and how they can have control of language and use it, as writers, to convey the intended meaning.

However, teachers are placed in the dilemma of needing to prepare children to take the SPaG test which, as we saw at the beginning of this chapter, requires children to label words and phrases in decontextualized sentences and their answers are then marked as right or wrong with no scope for variation. Some commentators have written powerfully about this (e.g. Michael Rosen at http://michaelrosenblog.blogspot.co.uk) and others who believe grammar should be taught in its own right have responded (e.g. Bas Aarts at https://grammarianism.wordpress.com/2016/01/25/is-the-grammar-punctuation-and-spelling-test-for-key-stage-2-too-hard/), and the debate continues on Twitter and other media.

However, I would say that it is important to distinguish between how you teach something and what you are teaching. I do believe that even though I do not think it is the best way, it is possible to teach decontextualised grammar in an exciting and relevant way so it is not boring for the children.

We have looked at grammar teaching at the top end of the primary school; let's now observe some lessons in Year 1. The programmes of study include the requirement that pupils should know how words combine to make sentences. To be able to separate out individual words is not as easy as one may think and it is a knowledge we often take for granted when we work with young children. In Reception most children who have had experience of print will be aware of this but there will be others who are not. I remember Andy who arrived in his Reception class very excitedly one morning clutching an empty cereal box. He thrust it in front of his teacher, pointing to the name of the cereal, saying 'Look! I've found a word!' His teacher responded sensitively and shared his excitement, putting Andy's cereal box on display with the word labelled. Over the next week or two other members of the class brought in words and soon a whole display board was covered with a miscellany of words. This activity could be extended in Year 1 by asking the children to bring in words related to a theme – family members, cars, names of animals, etc. The focus on words helps increase awareness of what a word is but also demonstrates that more words are needed for anything meaningful to be communicated – and that is where consideration of what a sentence is comes in.

Kress (1982) argued that the sentence is the most important concept for beginner writers to understand, but often it is something with which they struggle. It is a common experience that when children first discover the use of the full stop they put it on the end of every line of their writing, confusing a line with a sentence.

OBSERVATION: Sentences with Year 1

The teacher was aware that many of the children in her Year 1 class did not really understand what a sentence was and so were struggling to demarcate sentences with capital letters and full stops. She decided to use a book which was well-known and well-loved to explore this idea. The book was *We're Going on a Bear Hunt* by Michael Rosen. The sentences are simple and short and suited to the planned activity. The teacher read the book to the children in the classroom and they all joined in with her. The class then went out into the playground to go on their own hunt – they were hunting for sentences. Firstly, the class marched around the playground reciting the story and taking one stride for each word they said. This took several attempts as some children were confused by the two syllables in 'going'. No reference was made to the sentences – the children marched to the words, saying *'We're going on a bear hunt. We're going to catch a big one. I'm not scared. What a beautiful day!'* taking one step for each word.

Comment

By using a really well-known story the children were confident and every child was able to join in. Walking in time to the story allowed children to identify the separate words; they had to concentrate because the two syllables could be confusing but they soon came to see that each step matched a word. This was a step on from previous experiences when they had marched in time to syllables. Listening for the words gave them more of a cognitive challenge – it could not just be 'felt'. In their own way, the children were investigating how the text was constructed. It might be much simpler than the investigation about the passive voice in the previous observation, but it was still exploring how texts were constructed.

Once all the children were confident doing that, the teacher gathered them around her and asked them, 'What are we doing?' In one voice, the children replied, 'We're going on a bear hunt'. The teacher praised them and congratulated them on replying in a sentence. She asked them how she knew they had said a sentence. One child started to say there was a capital letter but stopped halfway through his sentence and laughed. You could see him thinking hard! The teacher talked to them about the fact that the words they had used together told her what she wanted to know and that they made sense and did not need anything else. She then showed them a large laminated black circle which represented a full stop; they repeated the first sentence several times and each time she held up the full stop to show they had got to the end. Several children had a go doing this for themselves, and when the teacher was happy they said all four sentences clapping their hands when they paused, with the teacher holding the full stop in the air.

Comment

Lots of repetition and physical action meant that the children were hearing, feeling and understanding where a sentence ended.

The teacher then gathered the children together and asked them to stand next to their learning partner. Each week the children had a different learning partner with whom they worked together during lessons. The teacher gave each pair a large piece of card on which was written one word from the first page of the text. Four pairs were given a large full stop. The children were told to find the other words in their sentence and to stand in the correct order with the full stop at the end. Once this was done, the whole class read the sentences together.

Comment

In this final part of the lesson the children were problem-solving. They had to find the correct words – matching with the text if necessary – stand in the correct order and make sure they had a sentence at the end. This was the end of the lesson but you could have carried on inside, asking the children to stick words in the correct order in their books and write a full stop at the end. This lesson lasted no longer than half an hour. The children were completely engaged and most had made progress in their understanding.

There are lots of different ways in which technology can support learning in school but one which is excellent for teaching direct and indirect speech involves a mock-up of text messages on a phone. Look at Figure 5.2 below.

Figure 5.2   Using texts to teach direct and indirect speech

I have created this on the site www.fakephonetext.com. The speech bubbles show clearly the turn-taking effect of conversation and can be used to discuss direct speech and then the conversation can be written down as indirect speech, exploring how it would be punctuated. Let us now move on to consider punctuation.

Punctuation

The important thing to remember about punctuation is that it is there for the reader; it is the punctuation which tells a reader how a text is to be read. Consider the following sentences:

1   We're not scared.
2   We're not scared?
3   We're not scared!

Read each of them aloud and you are likely to find that you will naturally find yourself reading each one in a different way and with different expression. It is the punctuation that informed that decision. If there is no punctuation it is much harder for a reader to access the meaning of the text. Taking all the punctuation out of an extract from the class novel and asking somebody to read it aloud is a simple but effective way to make that point.

There are also many jokes which illustrate how significant punctuation is when creating texts. The one in Figure 5.3 is well known and will probably elicit a groan from you!

Let's eat Grandpa.

Let's eat, Grandpa.

Correct punctuation can save a person's life.

Figure 5.3   Punctuation matters!

This just emphasises how important punctuation is. Various strategies have been introduced to teach punctuation and one very popular one is *Kung Fu Punctuation*. Have a look at this video to see it in practice: www.youtube.com/watch?v=VZHUt0MY0Xw. I do not know the amazing Mrs Briggs but just watch the children's faces and see how they are involved and listening carefully to see what punctuation is needed in each of the sentences.

Within the programmes of study there is always an explanation of the reason for the use of particular punctuation and that is useful. For example, in Years 5 and 6 pupils should be taught to use hyphens to avoid ambiguity. Examining a text to see how authors use hyphens in this way is the best starting point. Remember that the texts you use to do this do not have to be restricted to those published for the purpose of teaching grammar and punctuation. Clark (2013) argues that children are surrounded by a huge variety of ways of using written language and see and experience many different ways of structuring language and of using punctuation. However, it is often the case that the way we teach grammar and punctuation in school 'perpetuates the myth that there is one correct way of language use which is fixed and invariant'. This is a challenge but an exciting issue to explore with older children at the top of Key Stage 2. Does it matter how we write? I would argue that is does in certain contexts; many job applications are rejected because of poor spelling, grammar or punctuation. But knowing the conventions gives you the freedom to break them!

I was not able to find a teacher who taught punctuation on its own and I found that encouraging. Learning how to use punctuation is an integral part of learning how to be a writer.

Read

Truss, L. (2009) *Eats, Shoots and Leaves: The Zero Tolerance Approach to Punctuation*. London: Fourth Estate.

In this edition there is even a 'Punctuation Repair Kit' so you can put stickers over signs in shops which frustrate you because the punctuation use changes the meaning! There is also a children's version which is very funny.

Spelling

Rutherford (2016) argues that there is a point at which teaching discrete phonics becomes superfluous and he claims that this comes when a child realises a word can be spelled in different ways. Rutherford uses the example of a bird's beak – which could be spelt 'beak', 'beek' or 'beke'. He says,

> The child does not require further teaching on phonics but needs to learn which one of these spellings (all of which are potentially phonetically correct) is appropriate in the context in which it is being used ... The only way for the child to realise that a bird has a 'beak' and not a 'beek' is to root their understanding in the context of written text. (2016: 190)

In my opinion there is no more to be said about the teaching of spelling, but again it is the pressure of the SPaG test and the strong accountability agenda which drives many schools to teach spelling in discrete lessons. Resources and schemes have been published and the temptation is for teachers to follow these so they can be sure everything is covered and that records of the discrete phonic patterns and spelling rules that have been taught can be kept. I have the details of one scheme in front of me now which argues that a daily 15-minute spelling lesson from Year 2 through to Year 6 will 'embed impressive spelling skills'. If there were no other consideration, the impact on a child's day of a 15-minute phonics lesson and a 15-minute spelling lesson, never mind any quick mathematics lessons, is considerable and reflects an interesting perspective on the nature of learning and how we learn.

It is all so much more tidy and systematic than an investigative approach which delights in exploring how words are written down, where they come from and how spelling has changed over time. I love playing with words and investigating them. Here are some thoughts for you to ponder:

- Many people now spell the past tense of learn as 'learnt' but people like me still like to spell it as 'learned'. Why has the change happened? Do the different spellings mean different things? Does it matter?
- Do you think that the increased influence of technology and the power of American software manufacturers will eventually mean that we will all spell 'colour' as 'color' and car 'tyres' as 'tires'?
- Will the use of text speak and abbreviations affect our spelling? Will words like 'soz' and 'lol' eventually find their way acceptably into more formal written communications?

These are the sort of questions I love to think about and they can be set as challenges for older children. Why not suggest they take such a question home for homework and survey the views of family, friends and neighbours.

It is of course true that spelling matters because written language is all about communication, with no author available to mediate. Words are important and need to be a focus of classroom discussion. Just as Andy's teacher used his enthusiasm to create a class focus on the nature of words, so in Key Stage 2 a 'word of the week' can stimulate all sorts of investigations. There are lots of books available which will give ideas for creative ways to teach spelling and this is not the purpose of this book.

I want to focus on just one aspect and that is the notion of 'emergent spelling'. This was a key part of teaching during the 1980s in the era of the National Writing Project and was encouraged as a way of supporting children to engage in composition without being hindered by transcriptional difficulties. These would be addressed later in the editing phase. Children were encouraged to write down whatever sounds they could hear in the word even if it was only the initial sound. Sometimes children could not even manage this and so drew a line where the word was supposed to be and this became known as the 'magic line'.

This has not entirely disappeared, but some phonic schemes place a strong emphasis on children only reading or writing those GPCs which they have learned. Not only does this limit children to rather boring texts, but it also denies them the creative opportunity of listening to and recording the sounds with words. The word 'sorser' is perfectly readable if not conventionally spelled and yet it could be correct if the conventions were different. I believe that encouraging children to write in this way means that they are actively thinking about how sounds could be written down and so seeing spelling as something that is worked out rather than just learned. This can also be done in lessons, as the observation below demonstrates.

OBSERVATION: Using the Year 3 classroom environment as a resource for spelling

The focus for the week was words containing the prefix 'sub'. The children had been introduced to this on the previous Friday and had been asked to keep an eye out for words starting with 'sub'. On the Monday they had brought in words mainly from the environment but some from books and magazines they had read. The teacher had prepared a display where all these words were put on the wall.

First thing every day the class looked at the words that had been collected. On Monday several children had brought in the word 'Subway' from the sandwich shop and this prompted a discussion about why a sandwich shop should be called Subway and where the word comes from. Some of the children had gone shopping and knew about subway rolls but this still did not answer the question of where the word came from. About half the class had heard the word subway being used on television programmes or had been on holiday to the States and had heard the word used there. The class decided that the word came from the 'subway' – the American term for the underground – and after looking up pictures of subway rolls on the Internet they thought the shape was similar to the tunnels through which the trains travelled and this had led to the name.

Comment

This is a discrete spelling lesson but one which takes an investigative approach and starts with words as they are used in the children's familiar world. The teacher did not give the children the answers but required them to work these out for themselves; they drew on their own knowledge and other sources to create a hypothesis which they would test as the week progressed.

During the week the children brought in many words starting with 'sub'. The teacher wrote them on cards and laminated them, creating several sets of the same words. On Friday the children were put into groups and asked to sort them, putting them together as they thought best. This prompted some interesting discussion. After some time each group was asked to choose one word from each of their sets and explain why they thought the words in that set went together.

Comment

During the group activities the children were having lively and fascinating discussions about the words. They were looking at the spelling of the words and working out what the root word was when the prefix was removed; they were talking about the meaning of the words and putting them into sentences when they were unsure to try out ideas. Choosing one word to represent each set was challenging for them – the process took quite a while and caused some to rethink their reasoning. The process here was much more important than the final product; the conversations the children were having were powerful and focused on the written form of the words.

The final part of the lesson consisted of discussion about the words to try and work out what the meaning of the prefix 'sub' is and how it changes the meaning of words. It was fairly straightforward when discussing words like 'submarine, 'subterranean' and 'submerge' but the children were more confused by the word 'subterfuge'. They were trying to find out if there was such a word as 'terfuge'! Some children extended the activity by taking a word and adding the prefix 'sub' to see if they could make another meaningful word – 'subtalk' was one they invented for talking quietly while the teacher was talking! I rather like that.

Again, it was the process of the conversation that was important and the investigations by looking up dictionaries and thesauri.

At the end of the lesson the teacher recapped on what a prefix is and what it can do to words and gave the children three different prefixes with the challenge to see how many words they could find for each one.

Comment

An alternative approach to this lesson would have been to give the children a list of words starting with 'sub' and ask them to put each one into a sentence. They could then have taken the words home to learn and be tested on them the following week. How boring – and yet this is what many children have to do each week.

OBSERVATION: Word investigation in Year 6

This investigation was not in a lesson as such but was an ongoing activity in the classroom over a week. The children worked on it when they had a few spare minutes and every day, either at lunch time or at the end of the day, the teacher drew their attention to what was happening. There was a word investigation board in the classroom and each week there was a different focus. The children built up the display on the board and changed it as they found more out.

The investigation began with the children being asked to find as many words as they could containing 'sign'. Each word was written on a Post-it note and stuck onto the display board. After a few days a very large sheet of paper was put up with the word 'sign' in the middle. The children were asked to re-arrange the Post-it notes so that similar words were together and a spider diagram was created. On the final day a question was put on the board which asked what all the words had in common. The final class discussion looked at this question.

Comment

The children came to realise quite early on that in some words the pronunciation remains the same but in others it changes, for example 'signature'. They began to collect words according to those different criteria.

(Continued)

(Continued)

The discussion then forced them to reflect on what was similar. After a long time, with considerable 'interthinking' and co-construction of knowledge, the children identified that there was something due to the meaning which united the words. The teacher introduced the concept of 'morpheme' and the investigation turned to thinking of definitions of each word to test their conclusion.

It is true that the spelling of some words has a morphemic origin rather than a phonemic basis. Other words are spelled the way they are because of their origins or because of historical coincidence. There is no point in pretending to children that spelling in English is anything but very complicated and very challenging; if you do not tell them they will soon find out! However, it can be fun looking for patterns and explanations.

Read

O'Sullivan, O. and Thomas, A. (2007) *Understanding Spelling*. London: Routledge.

Summary

This chapter has looked at the teaching of grammar, punctuation and spelling, which, since the introduction of the English National Curriculum in 2014, has received much more attention. The separate SPaG test has caused much controversy and is challenging for pupils and teachers alike. In this chapter I have tried to plead the case for text-based teaching which has an investigative problem-solving element. In my opinion this will foster an excitement about language and how it works in children which will only enhance their development as readers and writers. As David Almond (2016: 1) wrote:

> Words enter our mind to stimulate, inform, entertain us. They flood our minds with images. We continue to become more sophisticated, more experimental, more controlled. The process is miraculous, astonishing and very very ordinary.

Further reading

Waugh, D., Warner, C. and Waugh, R. (2016) *Teaching Grammar, Punctuation and Spelling in Primary Schools*, 2nd edn. London: SAGE.

Literacy across the curriculum

6

The purpose of this chapter is to help you think about the nature of the curriculum you provide in your classroom and in your school and the role literacy plays in that. The National Curriculum changes with different governments, but classrooms and schools continue to be places where teaching and learning happens. What sort of learners do we help the children to be and how do we help them to become effective literacy users for the twenty-first century?

In considering literacy across the curriculum it is important to clarify what is meant, first, by the curriculum and, secondly, by literacy. People have different ideas of what the curriculum is. The Latin root of the word (currere = to run) has the implication of a course or track; we start at the beginning and follow the prescribed route to the end. Often the word 'curriculum' is used synonymously with the word 'syllabus' and this also has connotations of something that is externally defined and can be tested.

The Rose *Independent Review of the Primary Curriculum* in 2009 was intended to inform the introduction of a new primary curriculum in September 2011. This review recommended that the curriculum be formed around six broad areas of learning in which subject teaching would be complemented by cross-curricular work. This would give an increased focus on literacy and numeracy, including a major emphasis on speaking and listening.

As plans for a new curriculum were made it was argued that this approach was supported by international evidence, because eight out of 10 countries that have recently reviewed their primary curriculum have moved to a design based on areas of learning. Ofsted (2002), in its report on the curriculum in 31 successful primary schools, found that although teachers planned and taught largely through separate subject areas, they were adept at making clear links across subjects. Alexander, in his response to Ofsted, argued that a broad curriculum is essential:

> One reason why I get impatient with those who think that the way to raise standards in the basics is by cutting back the rest of the curriculum – my main reason of course is that it sells children short – is that this essential symbiosis between the basics and the rest has been common knowledge for a quarter of a century. (2002: 4)

This was echoed by views expressed by parents in a survey carried out by the DCSF in 2009; over 80 per cent agreed that children should learn life skills such as effective communication, teamwork and creative thinking at primary school, over 90 per cent thought young children should learn through play and 92 per cent thought that integrated learning would help children develop their reading and writing skills.

The new curriculum was planned for introduction in September 2011 with an emphasis on key skills, a real-world context to learning, and clear connections between and within areas of learning. The coalition government was elected in May 2010. The planned theme-based curriculum was abandoned and a review looking to establish a 'proper knowledge-based curriculum' was set up. The Education Minister argued that:

> People know that the place of knowledge at the heart of our curriculum is not what it was and not what it should be. More and more children should be given access to that kind of education. A proper knowledge-based curriculum should be available to all rather than just a few. (Gove 2009)

While the introduction to the English National Curriculum is clear that the curriculum should 'prepare pupils at the school for the opportunities, responsibilities and experiences of later life', the programmes of study give a lot of detail for the content which is to be covered, fulfilling Mr Gove's desire for a knowledge-based curriculum. In English there are word lists and grammatical terminology broken down into year groups.

In Scotland the Curriculum for Excellence is less precise in its content. It aims to enable pupils to become successful learners, confident individuals, responsible citizens and effective contributors. It has been criticised for being incoherent, atheoretical and potentially individualistic (Gillies 2006; Priestley and Hughes 2010) and Watson argues that it 'is concerned with setting out not what children are expected to *know* but how they should *be*' (2010: 99, original emphasis).

There is immediately a big tension between both the aims and the content of a curriculum and so the question of what counts as the curriculum remains unanswered. The National Curriculum (DfE 2013: 5) stated in its introductory section that 'The school curriculum comprises all learning and other experiences that each school plans for its pupils. The National Curriculum forms one part of the school curriculum'. For some schools this is an important distinction and leads to a consideration of the learning experiences offered to children. The National Curriculum is a minimum requirement and is placed within a broader framework which considers what children in the twenty-first century need to know.

> **Read**
>
> The document about the curriculum at the Wyche Church of England Primary School: www.wyche.worcs.sch.uk
>
> Consider how the elements of the school curriculum relate to the requirements of the National Curriculum. How does this work in schools in which you have been?

The focus of this chapter is on literacy in the whole curriculum. It is usual to have daily literacy lessons in most schools, but it is also clear that no other lesson can take place without the children using literacy skills. I often tell my students that literacy is the most important subject in the curriculum – and I am only half joking! Without effective literacy skills no other curriculum subject can be fully addressed. It is very important, therefore, that children are given opportunities to use literacy in ways which are powerful in all sorts of areas and subjects. In this chapter, we begin to explore some ways of doing that.

OBSERVATION: Writing in a nursery class (ages 3 and 4)

In this classroom every morning the teacher puts up a flip chart with a message or a question on it. As the children arrive with their parents or carers they respond in writing to that message. On the day I was there the message was that shown in Figure 6.1. As each child arrived they went to the board, read it with their parents and responded in writing.

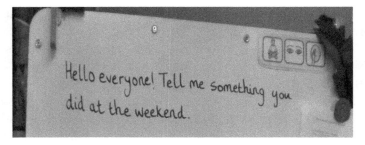

Figure 6.1   A nursery teacher invites children to respond to her question in writing

Comment

We know that the children who are the most successful literacy learners are those who understand the purposes of literacy. What were these children learning by taking part in this activity?

The little girl in Figure 6.2 is clearly concentrating very hard as she writes her message. What does she need to know and be able to do in order to complete this activity?

Figure 6.2   A 4-year-old responds to the invitation

Comment

There are several positive things that can be said about this child as a writer:

- She is holding the pen correctly.
- She appears to be forming the letters correctly, although we cannot be precise about that unless we are watching her actually write.
- She is writing from left to right.
- She appears to have something to say; she is writing purposefully.
- She is aware that there is a 'correct' way of writing things; she is thinking about what letter comes next.

It is difficult to make such judgements from a photograph, but I observed her and was able to see her confidence and attitude. When you observe literacy activities it is important to look also at the attitude of the children participating. Ask yourself questions such as:

- Are they carrying out the activity confidently or are they doing it slowly and having to think very hard about what comes next?
- Do they appear to be enjoying the activity?

Consider what sort of behaviours you might expect to see in a child who is confident and enjoying an activity.

Read

Chris Pascal and Tony Bertram did a lot of work looking at the engagement of young children in activities (Effective Early Learning Project). They used the Leuven Involvement Scale for Young Children (Laevers 1994).

Pascal, C. and Bertram, A.D. (eds) (1997) *Effective Early Learning: Case Studies of Improvement*. London: Hodder and Stoughton.

If we look at the finished board (Figure 6.3) there are several things we can note about it as a literacy learning activity and some of these might take you by surprise.

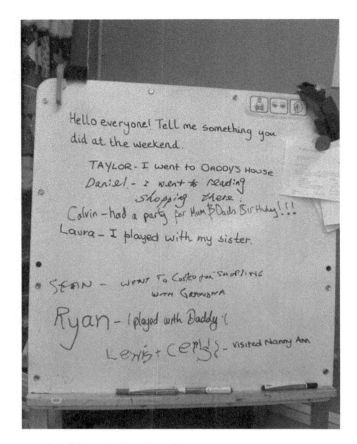

Figure 6.3 Several children in the class also responded

Task

Look at this board and list all the things you think are worthy of note concerning the writing on it.

It is clear that there are lots of different styles of print on that board – upper case, printing, joined writing, children's writing and abbreviations. Notice the ampersand in the middle of the board. There was a time when teachers were very anxious about the types of print to which young children were exposed. Think, however, about all the print that children will see around them – in the home, in the local shopping centre, in places like a doctor's surgery. All print will be different and children need to learn what differences are significant and what are not. This can be challenging.

When I learn about objects and what they are called I soon know that objects can be different but still be called the same thing. A chair might be an upright wooden dining chair or it might be an office chair on wheels, a sagging old armchair or an ultra-modern barstool.

Letters do not always work in the same way. This is an 'a' but so is this 'ɑ' and 'a' and 'a' and 'a' and A. It can be very confusing. It is through the experience of print in many different contexts and in many different ways that children learn to understand significant differences.

Secondly, look at the use of the exclamation mark in the third line down. Calvin 'had a party for Mum & Dads birthday!!!'

Consider

What do the exclamation marks tell us as a reader? How do we read and respond to this piece of text?

Punctuation is generally there for the reader. It tells us how to read a text – the expected expression and response. It can set the tone. I later observed the teacher read through the comments on the board. She remarked on the punctuation marks by saying, 'Calvin's Mum and Dad must have had a really good time at their birthday party'.

Consider

What did that remark tell the children about the use of punctuation? What impact would their own life experiences have on their understanding?

Read

Dyson, A.H. (1993) *Social Worlds of Children: Learning to Write in an Urban Primary School.* New York: Teachers College Press.

The boards in that nursery class were just part of the literacy environment providing opportunities for children to behave as readers and writers. The next observation allows us to think about that in a little more depth.

OBSERVATION: Literacy in role play in a Reception class (ages 4 and 5)

This classroom was set up to be full of literacy resources and opportunities for the children and I want to describe just three that I observed.

The role-play area was set up as a home and contained many of the tools for literacy that you might expect to see in many homes. By the armchair was a pile of newspapers and magazines; next to the phone was a telephone directory, notepad and pencil and a calendar was hanging above on the wall; next to the cooker was a pile of recipe books and by the entrance a pile of junk mail. Four-year-old Andy was sitting in the armchair, his legs crossed, reading a newspaper. He looked away from the paper, appeared to be listening, got up and answered the phone. He spoke, listened and wrote a note on the pad. He then opened the telephone directory, ran his finger down the list of names, stopped at one and then made a phone call before returning to his newspaper.

Talk

Find a friend and share your impressions about this observation. What was Andy showing about his understanding of literacy in this short incident?

I expect you will have come up with quite a long list of positive comments about the value of creating a print-rich classroom environment. We can now think about this a little more and see what is missing and how it can be encouraged.

Read

Marsh, J. (2003) 'Connections between literacy practices at home and in the nursery', *British Education Research Journal*, 29(3): 369–82.

In this article Marsh argues that there tends to be a dissonance or mismatch between the literacy practices of school and those of home. Go back to the observation of Andy in the Reception class and think about the resources that were provided there. What was missing?

You might observe that there was no computer, no iPod, no television or game console, no mobile phone. Now consider all the uses of literacy you have engaged in over the last 24 hours and list them. When I did that, my list included the following:

- sent several text messages
- read messages on a social networking site and wrote a few responses
- sent several emails
- looked for articles on a search engine
- checked the schedule for this book and made notes of the observations I want to include in pencil
- wrote several hundred words of this book on my laptop.

That is not an exclusive list. What do you notice about the sort of literacy activities I engaged in? How similar was your list? Most of the reading and writing I have done today have been on screen. In the article cited above, Marsh claims that the literacy behaviours of young children in the home tend to be centred on popular and cultural texts and that these behaviours do not influence the literacy opportunities offered in school.

Task

Plan to make a classroom for young children as print rich as possible by including the types of texts and opportunities they would encounter in the home.

In one part of the classroom was a display bench on which was a collection of several musical instruments. Alongside this was a music book showing both the words and the music of a song the children had been learning. Often the children would stand at this bench playing the instruments and singing as they 'read' the music. Jason had drawn a picture of a large colourful rainbow and below it he had drawn several musical notes: ♪♫♪♫♪. The teacher asked what it was he had drawn. He looked rather perplexed at this question as though the answer was obvious and replied, 'I've written the rainbow song'.

Comment

Jason was aware of different types of symbolic representation. He wanted to write a song and knew that the symbols used for this were different from the letters he would use to record words. He had learned this because of the provision the teacher had made in the classroom. The music area had taught the children that music was written in a particular way. He had not learned this just because the resources were there. The teacher referred to it explicitly. Each week a different song was put there; the class sang it together and the teacher showed them the music and showed them that she was putting it in the music area so that they could play and sing it for themselves. She did a shared reading lesson with the words and musical notation.

On another occasion I was in the classroom observing some of the literacy behaviours of the children. I sat at tables watching the children in their play and independent activities. I had a notebook and a pencil and was continually writing, recording all that I heard and saw. I noticed that Tracey was sitting at the next table, writing in a handmade book she had found in the writing area. I went and sat next to her, asking what she was doing. She answered, 'I'm doing what you do – I'm writing down what the children are doing'.

Comment

Nobody had told Tracey what I was doing. She had watched me and worked out what I was writing. She wanted to do the same and her notebook was full of play writing which looked very like my untidy notes. What had she learned from this? She was learning one purpose of writing and was experimenting by using it for herself. This was a powerful learning experience for Tracey. She came from a home where she would not often see adults writing continuous prose and the fact that she took what I was doing and made it her own demonstrated a growing understanding of what writing could do for her.

The next observation is another example of how children represent their understandings through the use of symbols. This is older children recording their learning in science.

OBSERVATION: Science in Year 4 (ages 8 and 9)

The class had been studying the germination and growth of seeds. They had planted seeds and watched them grow and the teacher wanted them to record this in a way which would demonstrate their understanding. They did this by creating an animation of a plant growing. Each pair of children created an animation on screen showing the growth of a plant from planting the seed to the full-grown healthy plant. In creating these animations the children were thinking hard about how the 'reader' would understand their text. Each animation was slightly different and the children were able to discuss different approaches at various stages in the process.

Comment

The children were creating a text but it did not contain any words. What were the similarities and differences between this act of composition and how it would have been if they had recorded the growth process more traditionally by drawing and writing? Langer said, 'The distinction I wish to make is between literacy as the act of reading and writing and literacy as a way of thinking and speaking' (1986: 6). How does that distinction relate to the observations we have just been considering?

The observation above shows how literacy is more than written words. In the activity they were finding ways of expressing ideas and in doing so they had to consider how those ideas needed to be structured and related to each other in order to best communicate the essential concepts to the reader. In choosing the best images and movements the thinking process was very similar to that of choosing the best words and linguistic structures. The following observation shows another group of children making the same sort of decisions as they authored a text.

OBSERVATION: History in Year 4 (ages 8 and 9)

The class had been studying the Vikings and had researched a lot of information about them. They had begun by sharing all the information they knew and recording it in a large mind map. They then looked at that information and, in groups, identified the questions they still had about Vikings. These questions became the focus of their research and they collected a huge amount of additional information. They then had to decide what to do with all this accumulated knowledge.

The class had used a variety of sources for information gathering and was excited at what had been found out. The children wanted to convey this excitement as they reported their research and were reluctant to 'just write it down'. They decided to create an animated interactive encyclopedia using PowerPoint.

Think

How does the chosen media affect the process of presenting information? What skills and knowledge were required by the children to do this?

The children began by sorting out their information into chapters or slides. The original questions gave them a starting point for doing this but the final version did not exactly follow the themes of the questions. They eventually came up with a list of headings:

- Fast facts
- Fast facts 2
- Viking work
- Vikings at sea
- The longboat
- Viking death.

Each group took a heading and went away to work on their slide. The slide on 'Vikings at Sea' is shown in Figure 6.4.

Each of the pictures was animated; the waves became storm like and the Viking boat was tossed as it moved through the choppy sea. Clicking on the symbols at the bottom right of the slide activated sound files: one was of the sea, the second of the farm animals and the third one of a Viking 'song'.

The centre 'home button' took the reader back to the contents page.

A superficial look at this slide might lead you to think that this was an unchallenging writing task for these children, but look again and

Vikings at sea

- The longboats could travel at about 10 mph.
- A ship carried everything needed at sea – drinking water, dried meat and fish to eat, tools and weapons, and furs to keep warm.
- The Vikings could sail down rivers and streams and they beached it on the side of the river they got out and slaughtered everyone.
- Cargo ships carried families and farm animals too.

Figure 6.4 One slide from an interactive encyclopedia created by a group of 8-year-old boys

consider what needed to be known, to be understood and to be able to be done:

- In writing the text the children had to be aware of the limited space provided by one slide. It took a lot of discussion before they were happy with the words. The first text had to be drastically pruned and it proved challenging to convey all the information in not many words. There was a lot of oral composition and editing during the process.
- Secondly, the pictures had to be chosen. Those children who had been given the responsibility of doing this looked carefully for a picture of a Viking boat. They rejected many, drawing upon their knowledge of Viking boats. They then placed it on the sea and introduced the animation.
- Thirdly, the group doing the sound files had to think carefully about what to choose. The sounds of the sea and the farm animals were fairly simple, but choosing a sound of a Viking song was difficult. The group found the following quotation from a tenth-century Arab merchant on the Internet: 'Never before have I heard uglier songs than those of the Vikings in Slesvig (in Denmark). The growling sound coming from their throats reminds me of dogs howling, only more untamed'. They then had great fun trying to replicate and record this sound. They experimented many times before deciding on the final version.

Comment

This is a good illustration of the fact that the final product does not always do justice to the work that went into its production. This single slide involved talk of many different kinds, research and creating texts.

Once each group had produced their individual slides, the whole encyclopedia had to be put together. The children decided on the order and then created the contents 'page'. One group decided it would be good to add a slide with links to useful sources of information and so went off to research and create this. Another group made a slide with a Viking-based game on it and a third group wrote the index and the 'blurb'.

Consider

What literacy skills were used for these activities?

Read

Merchant, G. (2007) 'Writing the future in the digital age', *Literacy*, 41(3): 118–28.

Putting together a text such as this gave the children opportunities to experience the different structures of a text. The text they created was not linear and some children found it challenging to consider that there was no prescribed order and readers would create their own pathway through the text. They followed many different routes through the text because they wanted to know what it would be like for each reader. In this way, the children were coming to an understanding of how readers bring their own meanings to a text and use a text for their own purposes. For some children the experience of creating this text made them more efficient users of information books.

In the following observation we revert to presenting information through the written word. The children were, in focusing on persuasive language, also developing their skills as critical readers. This is a crucial aspect of what it means to be a good citizen, taking one's place in a democratic society. If one is aware of how authors use all aspects of a text, written or otherwise, to get across their message, one is more able to resist persuasion and manipulation. The children in the following observation were considering how vocabulary choice, design, colour and images are used on packaging. If they had also been considering television advertisements they might have included a consideration of sound and camera angle.

OBSERVATION: Year 6 creating promotional texts for biscuits (ages 10 and 11)

The focus of work in this class had been 'Change' and this had covered the subject areas of Science and Design and Technology. In Science they had been exploring the idea that some changes are reversible and some are irreversible and had been using cooking to do so. In Design and Technology the cookery theme continued and the children designed and named a Christmas biscuit.

Comment

This is an example of when different subject areas are linked by a common content. Another way of linking is by identifying common skills or concepts rather than units of knowledge. For example, the link between Science and Design and Technology is rather tenuous in this example and may well not have been apparent to the children. The skills and concepts required in each area were not similar at all, and so one could question the link.

The learning objective of the Design and Technology lesson was to write an effective promotional description of a biscuit and to be able to write concisely and revise work to constraints.

Comment

This was a literacy-focused learning objective. Although the content used was design and technology based, the children were, in fact, experiencing a literacy lesson.

In previous lessons the children had made and tasted biscuits from a given recipe and had designed their own decoration for a biscuit. The lesson began with the teacher showing the children pictures of different types of biscuit on the interactive whiteboard. He asked the children to look at the biscuits and then list words that could be used to describe them. These words were recorded on the flip chart. The teacher then showed them photographs of the packets of these biscuits, focusing on the text which described them. An example of these texts was, 'They're not just any biscuits'.

In groups, the children focused on the language used and its effectiveness. They came up with some criteria for effective promotional writing about a biscuit. It should:

- say what the biscuit looked, smelt and tasted like
- compare the biscuit to something the reader would know
- tell you what was in the biscuit.

They realised that this was a tall order as none of the texts they were analysing fulfilled all these criteria.

Comment

Note how the lesson began by reading and analysing texts of the same kind as the children were being asked to write. This is known as familiarisation with the genre and should be the starting point of all your units in literacy. Before they can write, children need to have read and discussed lots of texts. Discussions will focus on how the writer of the texts achieved the purpose of the text and will identify the linguistic features of that type of text.

The children then worked independently to create their own texts. They were allowed to choose how they wrote – some used laptops, some used whiteboards and some used paper and pencil. They were given a strict time limit for their writing and told that they had only between 50 and 60 words with which to promote their biscuit.

At the end of the 20 minutes they were given, some examples which the teacher had identified during the independent time were shown to the class on the visualiser and analysed according to the extent to which they fulfilled the criteria, in the same way as the original texts had been analysed.

Comment

What literacy skills were used in this activity? The children first analysed the linguistic features of the text type they were about to write; they discussed it and shared ideas; they composed orally with a partner and then chose how they would transcribe their work.

So far in this chapter, observations have focused on how both planned lessons and the planned opportunities within the classroom environment can provide occasions for literacy learning across a variety of contexts. The remaining part of this chapter focuses on the school library.

Consider

Why do you think I have included a focus on school libraries in a chapter on literacy across the curriculum?

Figure 6.5   A school library

The school library

I had first intended to write about school libraries in Chapter 8 where the focus is on the centrality of narrative in literacy learning. I visited a school to talk with a class teacher who is also the school librarian. As I talked with her, it became more and more apparent to me that the library was central to promoting literacy within the whole curriculum. After our conversation, the teacher was kind enough to write for me her thoughts on the use of the library, and I reproduce that next with my comments interspersed.

OBSERVATION: Conversation with a teacher/school librarian

I think that it is important to make the presence and reading of books common-place and evident to learners as soon as they enter school. Making the library a regularly visited space sends a message about the importance of books to the children and makes a statement about a school's values. Display boards use bright warm colours so that the library does not seem a bland or uninviting place. Three times a week some mums come into school on a rota basis to listen to children read in the library. Every year, six Year 6 pupils are chosen by me to help run the library. They are responsible for keeping the books shelved and tidy, advising pupils who need a reading book and logging books in and out of the library computer system. It is a popular role, mostly I think because they get to sit at my desk in the librarian's chair and be in charge! However, this does help to give the library a positive image – the children feel that it is theirs. Often children who are not official librarians will help out in the library simply because they enjoy it.

Comment

Notice the emphasis the teacher/librarian is putting on the physical environment of the library. Just as in the classroom, the library environment can give positive or negative messages about the value and importance accorded to literacy. The involvement of both parents and children in caring for the environment makes it a busy and used place. It is good that pupils want to be there and to be involved.

I encourage the librarians, and others, to pass on their ideas of what works in the library and what they think needs changing. There is a 'post-box' in the library in which children can write down the titles of books that they would like to read and think should be in the library. In previous years I have asked pupils to help me create library quizzes for the rest of the school to investigate and complete in conjunction with school Focus Week or World Book Day. There is a school council who can put forward what they would like to see change in school in general.

Recently the librarians and other Year 6 children took it upon themselves to give the library a bit of a 'face-lift'. Unknown to me, they closed the library to others and during break times that day they tidied books away, straightened and reorganised shelves and found posters to put on display boards. I think that children of all ages find 'playing at being in charge' and making their own mark thrilling, and making the library a desirable place is certainly an important part of promoting reading. The pupils sent me an email together and couldn't wait for me to come and see what they had done. Others were aware that something was going on and liked the idea of taking something into their own hands – it created quite a buzz and drew people in.

Figure 6.6 The school library designed by pupils

Comment

Pupil voice is an important element in the development and working of this library. These children were seeing the library as their own and felt comfortable and empowered to take control and improve the environment. If you were the teacher, what would you do if the children had rearranged the library in a way you did not like? Would that matter? Try and ask some children about books in their school. Is there a library? What do they think about it? How would they change it if they were in charge?

In general, if I were not also a full-time teacher, I would like to 'interfere' and interact more with all the teachers at school in order to maximise use of the library's resources and make room for a greater proportion of routine independent learning. I would also like to organise more events within school in conjunction with the library using books (popular tales, themes, authors, creative writing, experiencing an event to inspire creative writing) as the inspiration and starting point. Ideally, the librarian should be able to monitor the reading habits of children through the library computer system and liaise with class teachers to keep them informed and so that the teacher can advise the librarian of any books that she or he thinks the child should be reading or vice versa. This better ensures that learners are reading books that: (a) are of a genre likely to be enjoyed; (b) contain enough familiar vocabulary and a complexity of language that is manageable and will boost confidence and enjoyment, allowing the story and its meaning to flow in a complete narrative; and (c) contain enough unseen vocabulary and some more complex language in order to challenge the reader and ensure that the reading process is also a literacy teaching tool – a learning experience.

Comment

Do you think librarians should 'interfere'? There is a significant amount of evidence which suggests that school librarians have an impact on pupils' academic achievement. Barrett (2010) says that librarians need to be highly qualified professionals and learning specialists, work collaboratively with teachers, be information mediators, teach the skills of information literacy within the context of the curriculum, be reading experts, inspire, encourage, create and model high-quality learning experiences and be leaders in schools, regarded on a par with teaching colleagues. That is a tall order for anybody! Barrett argues strongly that librarians need to know about teaching and learning as well as about books if they are to be truly effective in a school.

Read

Barrett, L. (2010) 'Effective school libraries: evidence of impact on student achievement', *The School Librarian*, 58(3): 136–9.

So many classrooms have their own collection of books that it can render the library rather redundant, which I think can be a common problem. I have pondered over a solution, but I think it is a must to have books in the classroom and so don't exactly want to discourage this! Having members of Year 6 helping in the daily running of the library is a necessary arrangement; however, I cannot be on hand if there is a technical fault with the scanner or system, or someone has a question that they cannot answer. Ideally, a full-time librarian is needed to get the most out of the library and out of the opportunities for the children to learn therein. I would like to see whole classes using the library for research, but this does become difficult when teachers see how much they have to cover on the curriculum and are reluctant to give up time within that to visit the library; it is much quicker to tell the children about something than to facilitate them discovering it (or not) for themselves.

Encouraging teachers to make more routine use of the library with their classes could also go some way to balancing the use of Internet search engines in order to find information and learn. Though there is a wealth of fantastic information from many different, diverse voices on the Internet, when similar key words are used for a topic in a search engine, it is probable that the same few websites, including Wikipedia, will be visited, and therefore the same, not always entirely accurate, information is taken on board. Books still contain more reliable sources of information and, in a well-stocked library, many different standpoints and variations. The ability to use a library gives independence to the user, whereas Internet search engines in some way dictate which sources are accessed and used. It would be a shame if children were not taught the skills, and benefits, of taking the time to use a library at school.

I would like to see official library book-changing times for each year group so that regular contact with the library is timetabled rather than left to personal choice. Many children get books from home, which is no bad thing, but it would be better to be able to keep track through the library computer system of what each child is reading and for me to then have the time to liaise with teachers in order to keep them abreast of this, so that both I and they could make sure that readers were reading books with enough familiar material to keep their confidence boosted and the story line flowing, but also enough new vocabulary and higher-order language that they are also being challenged and are learning from the reading experience.

Comment

The teacher/librarian is here exploring the nature of knowledge and arguing that the library can help children to be more critical readers and evaluators of sources of knowledge. Critical literacy is an important concept and is part of the empowering and liberating effect of becoming literate. A critical reader will be able to read a text and see how the author has used particular effects and linguistic structures to locate the reader in a certain way and to manipulate the understanding of the text. A critical reader will also notice how the author's choice of language can either include or exclude.

The teacher/librarian argues that access to books can help children to see different ways of knowing and so become more critical and independent. Do you agree?

Read

Vasquez, V. (2010) 'Critical literacy isn't just for books anymore', *The Reading Teacher*, 63(7): 614–16.

Schools are essentially places of learning – both knowledge and skills. I think that how a school's library is maintained and promoted can send a statement to the pupils about what the school values and says something of its ethos. A library that is central to a school can be an inviting, interesting hub that is overtly valued by teachers and sends an essential, positive message of constructive, proactive learning values connected to books, to learners from backgrounds where reading and/or learning are not on the scene/part of the scenery/on the radar/part of life. Learning to access the non-fiction section of a library is important if you believe that teaching children how to teach themselves is an important aspect of school experience. Indeed, for those aspiring to higher education, the ability to read texts in the form of books and articles is still central; as the sometimes vast libraries of such institutions testify. In terms of fiction, a library has the responsibility to not only house the necessary variety of books to accommodate, challenge and interest readers in order to build on their comprehension, but also to cater for and attract those who are more reluctant (as well as maintaining the confidence and interest of those who can already decode, comprehend and hopefully enjoy reading). Certainly, having the correct reading material and incentive to read is still vital in the sense that growing children and young adults are forever learning to decode unseen vocabulary and need the opportunity to expand and progress by having a variety of books that will challenge and engage them at the right level and that will enthuse them to continue their efforts. Also, being able to decode texts accurately doesn't of course mean that the individual words or text as a whole are understood; continued reading and discussion of what has been read continues to build on comprehension of language and use of this language in communication, and essential life skills.

There is interesting discussion surrounding the impact of our continually advancing information technology on what a library – school or otherwise – should be/provide for its users. The word 'library' derives from a Latin word meaning 'book' and I think it is fair to say that libraries are still thought of as being places where, predominantly, collections of books are kept. When the word 'library' was first widely used, books (in the form of parchments, records, scrolls, and so on) could be said to be synonymous with 'information' – other than the spoken word, few other means of sharing information existed – and so the word library was a suitable one for a place where information could be gained. In this postmodern era, however, we are all accustomed to the fact that the Internet and other computer technologies have become perhaps the primary means of sharing information. Thus the word 'information' is now not only synonymous with 'book' but also with the various information technologies that we have. Should school libraries seek to uphold their identities as places where books are collected and promoted against the rising tide of technology, or should they further and/or fully re-adjust their identity so that all sources of information provision become synonymous with the word 'library'?

In my mind, in order to distinguish it from an ICT [information and communication technology] suite and remain in part true to its name, a library should certainly remain a place where books are promoted as a valuable and desirable means of discovering information, or furthering/enjoying understanding of the written word. However, it is essential to reflect on the fact that children born particularly within the last decade have no recollection of a world without computer technology and the prevalence of the Internet as a means of understanding the world and communicating. To not include any elements of this in school libraries runs the risk of condemning libraries as increasingly antiquarian places that bear no relevance to their experience of the systems in which they exist. In part, I think, the children need the experience of researching in books and the pleasure of holding a book in their hands, but the Internet utilised well opens up a superb wealth and variety of information and learning opportunities. This constructive use of computer technology needs to be incorporated into the library experience and used in conjunction with and to enhance books (and perhaps vice versa).

Comment

Reflect on your own viewpoint. The teacher/librarian has argued eloquently about the important role libraries play in schools in supporting children's literacy development. This is so much more than learning to decode or even to understand the words within a text. To become literate means a very different thing for children who are in primary schools in the twenty-first century than it was for me when I was in primary school in the mid-twentieth century. How do our pedagogical practices reflect that difference?

Read

Mullen, R. and Wedwick, L. (2008) 'Avoiding the digital abyss: getting started in the classroom with YouTube, digital stories and blogs', *The Clearing House*, 82(2): 66–9.

Cross-curricular learning

As you talk with teachers you will hear the terms cross-curricular, creativity, theme-based, creative curriculum and many other variations on a theme used.

Do they mean the same thing? The observations in this chapter have been very varied. In the early years settings we have seen how teachers provide resources and allow the children to respond and make use of them as they wanted to. Is that creative? In the observations from Key Stage 2 we saw teachers focusing on literacy skills but using content from other subjects of the curriculum to do so. Is that cross-curricular teaching?

As you consider these questions you might also want to reflect on the term 'creative learning'. Is that what we want children to encounter? Is that what will serve children well in the twenty-first century and enable them to become educated and informed citizens? We know that uses of technology and knowledge in Science are growing faster than we can imagine. Joubert (2001) claims that 75 per cent of the scientific knowledge we will need in the middle of this century has not been invented yet. Jeffrey (2006) proposes that creative learning includes elements of creativity like experimentation, innovation and invention and that the element of intellectual enquiry underpins the learning.

The National Curriculum for England (DfE 2013) claims to promote creativity and the word appears several times within the introduction. However, some might see a tension between a desire to constantly raise standards in 'the basics' and creativity. Wyse and Ferrari (2015) argue that the claim of creativity in the National Curriculum is not carried through into the different programmes of study.

Berry Billingsley is the principal investigator of the LASAR (Learning about Science and Religion) project which aims to explore areas which might be thought to be incompatible. Working with trainee teachers, she looks at the ways in which different disciplines would answer questions. For example, how would you answer the question 'Why did the Titanic sink?' Billingsley (2016) argues that a scientist would model the ship and the iceberg and investigate the forces that created such a large hole, while a historian might want to discover the circumstances which led the ship to be in that particular area. It is interesting to reflect on how other disciplines would address the question. Billingsley says that in this way teachers 'build students' appreciation of the way that disciplines can work together to paint a rich picture of what being human means' (2016: 288).

Push this approach into your teaching; by framing the starting point as a question, opportunities for cross-curricular work naturally emerge.

Observation: Year 1 cross-curricular planning

A Year 1 teacher began a term's theme by asking the question 'What makes a good story?' Her planning was text based and so the explorations were grounded in quality texts. The first text was *I am Henry Finch* by Alexis Deacon and Viviane Schwarz. This delightful book is about a bird who wants to do great things. It was a starting point for two weeks' work in which the children discovered what they could do and listed what they wanted to do and how they could achieve it. This addressed many different areas of the curriculum, as the children, like Henry Finch, strove to achieve their dreams and recorded their aspirations and attempts in many different ways. The next text was the classic *The Jolly Postman* by Allan and Janet Ahlberg. This was used as a way of looking at lots of traditional tales and rhymes and talking about what makes a good story – plot, setting or character? Finally, the class looked at the Christmas story and reflected on the impact of values and beliefs on how we understand and respond to stories. In looking at different versions of the Christmas story, including the Biblical account, the children began to consider the nature of story within religious belief.

Comment

Many of these ideas might seem challenging for 5- and 6-year-olds but it is amazing what can be achieved within a meaningful and relevant context. The curriculum informs the learning but is not necessarily the vehicle for the learning.

Reflect

How does literacy learning fit into that? Think back to the observations in this chapter and match them against the criteria for creative learning proposed above by Jeffrey (2006). Do they match?

If we consider the observation of Jason writing his song using musical notation, we can see if it works. He was certainly experimenting in using musical notation to represent a song; he was being innovative, as nobody else had, as far as we know, done the same thing. He was not actually inventing but he was using a symbolic system, which was new to him, for his own particular purpose. He was certainly engaged in intellectual challenge as he was working out how to represent his song. Do you think we can argue that this observation is an example of creative learning? How does that relate to Jason's developing literacy skills?

Literacy is more than reading and writing and it is not constrained to the written word. I once saw a cartoon in which a child was unwrapping a Christmas gift of a book. His parent looked on sympathetically and comforted him with the words, 'Don't worry, we can swap it for the DVD!' The joke relies on the assumption that it is 'easier' to read a film than it is a book. I would question that assumption and argue that 'reading' a film can be challenging. For me, watching the film *Inception* (Warner Bros. Pictures 2010) was as challenging as reading *Ulysses* (James Joyce 1922) and I still do not fully understand either of them! Booth argues that the literacy of school is falling behind the literacy of society and the home:

> children are dealing with a greater network of meanings and our literacy curriculum needs to match that to set them up for the future ... there is a pronounced difference between the literacies children are developing at home and the literacy of school. It is a divide that needs to be understood and explored. (2006: 59)

As you consider the observations of this chapter in the light of that comment, consider also the literacy that you see in classrooms but also in the world around you. Talk with your friends, with children and with teenagers about their experiences of literacy and consider how the curriculum in school reflects this.

Read

Meek, M. (1991) *On Being Literate*. London: Bodley Head.

Has our understanding of what it means to be literate changed in the years since Meek wrote this?

Summary

In this chapter we have begun to explore the edges of some big ideas. As the curriculum develops and changes, these ideas will need to become more formulated and yet remain plastic enough to accommodate the rapidly changing world of communication and knowledge. There is much to think about and it is probably best to summarise this chapter with a list of questions:

- Is literacy more than reading and writing?
- What are literacy skills?
- What does it mean to be fully literate?

- What is critical literacy?
- How can the classroom environment help or hinder literacy learning?
- Is there a place for the book and the library in twenty-first century schools?

Further reading

Barnes, J. (2015) *Cross-curricular Learning 3–14*, 3rd edn. London: SAGE.
Craft, A. (1999) *Creativity across the Primary Curriculum: Framing and Developing Practice*. London: Routledge.
Goodwin, P. (ed.) (2005) *Literacy Through Creativity*. London: David Fulton.

Assessment and planning

In this chapter we look at the way in which teachers decide what they are going to do in their classrooms. The children's learning lies at the heart of this decision-making; teachers are continually monitoring learning and adapting and changing their plans accordingly. This chapter looks at detailed lesson plans by some teachers and more open unit plans by others.

The link between planning and assessment

Planning can be described as the process of thinking and developing ideas, putting those ideas into an order and creating plans which act as a guide for a lesson. It is certainly true that planning is an important part of being an effective teacher and yet it is possible to become too focused on ideas and things to do within a lesson and forget that the whole purpose is to ensure that the children learn. Children's learning is the key responsibility of teachers, and all that you do must be clearly planned with that in mind.

So which comes first – assessment or planning? That is a bit like a chicken and egg question because they are each completely dependent on the other. Since the introduction of the English National Curriculum in 2014 assessment has been in a state of flux, as, with the removal of levels, schools and teachers are trying to find new ways of describing learning and progress.

The first question to ask yourself as a teacher must be, 'What do I want the children to learn?' Once you have decided that, everything else will begin to fall into place because you can then begin to think about the different sorts of activities and experiences that will help children to learn. It is also important to tell the children what the purpose of the lesson is and what they are supposed to learn from it. Knowing this will give children something to work for and a basis on which to judge their own learning and achievement. In order to do this however, children have to, firstly, know what the expected learning looks like and, secondly, believe that they can achieve it.

It is not the intention of this chapter to describe how to set about planning for learning but rather to explore the relationship between planning and what happens in the classroom. Most trainee teachers are required to create detailed lesson plans for everything they teach and the following is one of those plans.

OBSERVATION: Year 3 lesson plan on connectives (ages 7 and 8)

There are times, especially at the beginning of a teaching career, when it is important to plan in detail. Figure 7.1 is an extract from a very detailed lesson plan. This is the plan for just 15 minutes of a lesson lasting an hour and a quarter.

There are several good points which can be made about this plan:

- There is clear differentiation between the ability groups.
- The teaching assistant knows exactly what she has to do during this part of the lesson.
- Teaching points (TP) are made explicit so that the teacher knows the purpose of an activity or a discussion.
- Management and organisational points are included.

However, if I were this trainee's tutor I would want to make several points to the student, particularly in relation to the detail in which things are planned.

Task

Look carefully at the plan (Figure 7.1) and consider if the trainee understands what is meant by 'engagement' and 'ownership' of learning. What evidence from the plan can you use to support your opinion?

Development/Main Activity	Building on prior learning	Mrs A to work with
WALT: explore different connectives to extend sentences. WILF: connectives written on Post-it notes. **ASSESSMENT: Do pupils know the difference between a time and joining connective?** Introduce the nursery rhyme 'Incy Wincy Spider' and read it aloud to the children. Encourage them to stand up on their feet and join in. Q: What is the purpose of a connective? TP: A connective links clauses or sentences together. Q: What connective is used in the nursery rhyme? TP: Explain that pupils often overuse 'and' in their own writing. Q: Can you think of a more exciting connective than 'and'? Q: How else could you link the ideas together? TALK PARTNERS: give time to discuss connectives on the spider's legs. USE LOLLIPOP STICKS (fair selection). Explain that children are going to work in small groups to improve sentences from the nursery rhyme by experimenting and changing the connective. Split pupils into mixed-ability groups to provide peer support. Provide LAPS with connective cards so they can contribute ideas and access the learning task. Set the time expectations for the learning task. Ask pupils to write down their best connective on a Post-it note and add to the working wall.	The questions will enable pupils to draw on what they understand about connectives and suggest examples. **Ensuring engagement in learning** To ensure engagement I will give them ownership by choosing what sentence they will improve and experimenting with connectives. **Learning task** Pupils work in small mixed-ability groups. They select a sentence from the nursery rhyme. They discuss alternative connectives to improve the sentence. They have to read the sentence aloud to ensure it makes sense. They may have to add pronouns, e.g. 'it', to make sense. Then later in the lesson pupils will go on to write their own sentences about the spider using their own connective to add another clause/information. **Differentiation** HAPs: Write own sentences about the spider independently. **WILF: use time and joining connective.** MAPs: Write own sentences about the spider in pairs. **WILF: use joining connectives**. LAPs: Work as a group to cut and stick connectives into sentences **WILF: connectives make sense.**	child LG and his group. Support child LG's contribution to the learning task and ensure positive behaviour for learning is reinforced. Mrs A to pass child LG the connective cards and support his contribution to the group learning task. Then Mrs A to work with Yellow table during the writing activity to help pupils cut and stick connectives into sentences.

Figure 7.1   Lesson plan for a literacy lesson written by a trainee teacher in the early stages of her training programme

It is not sustainable to continue planning in such detail for your whole teaching career; often it can take longer to plan a lesson than the lesson itself actually takes! However, the reason why it is important to do this in the initial stages is to ensure that you have planned for progression, for individual needs and for organisation and management. It is easy when sitting at home in the evening to think that it looks very straightforward. However, every teacher has been in the situation of having 30-plus faces looking at them on the carpet and a completely blank mind! The lesson plan provides no help at all because all it says for this time is, 'Discuss'. It is for times like this, especially when there are no reserves of experience to draw on, that detailed planning is essential.

Comment

My analysis of this lesson plan extract might seem a little harsh but remember that it is written in the first few weeks of a teacher training course and also was written in a context which did not accommodate many of the points I want to make. I do not want to be critical but I want to use this as a vehicle for raising some key issues about planning and assessment.

Learning objectives

The WALT (We are learning to...) says the focus of learning is exploring different connectives to extend sentences. The WILF (What I'm looking for) is 'connectives written on Post-it notes'. Consider what this actually means.

The focus of the lesson is not learning about connectives but learning to explore connectives. What does that mean the children will be doing? It could mean they are identifying lots of connectives within a text, it could mean they are using different connectives in writing or it could mean they are joining sentences together with different connectives. Does the WILF help? Are the children going to write one connective on each Post-it or several on one? Do they have to sort the connectives in some way? What is going to be done with the Post-it notes? Do you see that the learning objectives and intended outcomes here are not clear? If you were to share them with a class, would they know what they are supposed to be learning?

Clarke (2008) asks what makes for effective learning objectives and describes them as a means which allow pupils to be in control of their learning.

This is a very important point and the implication is that within any lesson the identification and explanation of the learning objective needs to be done in collaboration with the pupils. Clarke identifies learning objectives as being either open or closed; the latter are either right or wrong with no indication of quality, and the former are skills where there will be a difference in quality between one pupil and another. One child might have written down two connectives on Post-its and one might have written down 15 and sorted them into different types, but they will both have achieved the learning objective. It is therefore important to have some indication or means of identifying what quality learning will look like.

Clarke (2008) also stresses the importance of identifying the context of the learning. In this lesson plan, if you read on, the context is the nursery rhyme 'Incy Wincy Spider'. In case you have forgotten it, here is the rhyme:

Incy Wincy spider climbed up the water spout.

Down came the raindrops and washed poor Incy out.

Out came the sunshine and dried up all the rain

And Incy wincy Spider climbed up the spout again.

It is clear that the connective 'and' is used three times in this rhyme. Note that after the children have stood up and recited the rhyme they are asked the purpose of a connective. This will tell the teacher a lot about what the children know about connectives and their grammatical function, and so the teacher might want to adapt the subsequent plans – but let us look at what the plan says. In mixed-ability groups children are asked to improve the nursery rhyme by experimenting with and changing the connectives. The 'low ability' children will be given examples of connectives on cards. What impact do you think this will have on the way the group functions? How would you feel if you were the only one in the group who had been given the words to use? Try the activity for yourself – take the first sentence and see what other connectives could be used; more changes need to be made to the sentence to accommodate a change in connective but this could generate a lot of discussion. Consider how that would relate to the learning objective.

Differentiation

In this lesson plan the trainee teacher has identified four 'levels' of difficulty for the task. Look carefully at these and see what the difference in challenge is. Personally, I would find it much more challenging to write sentences with somebody else than on my own. The challenge would be to my social and collaborative skills rather than my cognitive ability! The difference in these differentiated tasks is in how they are carried out not in what they are.

It is also important to ensure that the difference in the tasks is also one of cognitive challenge. I once saw a teacher give three groups three different activities – they were writing acrostic poems about a seaside visit. The low-ability group had to write a poem based on the word 'sea'; the middle-ability group on the word 'beach' and the high-ability on the word 'seaside'. Can you see that there is no difference at all in the cognitive challenge of these three activities?

Peacock (2016) discusses the idea of giving children 'choice and challenge'. She argues that often, as in our example lesson, differentiated tasks are given according to assumptions about children's capacity to learn. As teaching assistants often work with the 'low ability' group, this can lead to a 'learned helplessness' in the children. Children who are motivated and enthusiastic about learning will choose an activity which gives challenge because they are excited by learning.

Peacock advocates offering children the choice of activities, which she claims encourages 'children to build intrinsic motivation to challenge themselves in their learning, rather than passively waiting for others to judge their performance' (2016: 52). This approach takes time to introduce and is closely related to the work of Dweck (2006). Dweck identified two different kinds of mindset – the fixed and the growth. A fixed mindset sees intelligence as a limited resource – each person only has a certain amount at their disposal and this leads to a tendency to withdraw from things which are too challenging. Let me give you an example. I am about to go on holiday to Scotland, and at the gym this morning I asked my personal trainer, Jenny, if she thought I was capable of climbing the Cairn Gorm mountain. She replied that physically I am capable of doing it but she is not sure my mind is capable of letting me. In terms of physical activity I have a fixed mindset and that is something I have learned throughout my life. In contrast, a growth mindset sees intelligence as something that can be increased by effort and loves the challenge of mastering something new.

Let's go back to the lesson plan. In predetermining the group to which each child belongs and the activity which each group does, children are being limited in what they might achieve. It is possible to teach and model a growth mindset in the classroom. We can emphasise the importance of process and make children aware when they need to work extra hard to achieve something; we can praise children for effort rather than achievement; and we can reward perseverance and determination. Making the success criteria really clear, as we have already discussed, also tells children exactly what they need to do to succeed. In other words, we make learning explicit to children and talk to them about what and how they are learning.

Most teachers tend to work from their unit or weekly plans and only write detailed lesson plans when they are being observed. These plans tend to be much less detailed, but can be so because the information about organisation and management is embedded in practice.

Read

Black, P. and Wiliam, D. (1998) 'Inside the black box: raising standards through classroom assessment', *Phi Delta Kappan*, 80(2): 139–48.

Black, P., McCormick, R., James, M. and Pedder, D. (2006) 'Learning how to learn and assessment for learning: a theoretical inquiry', *Research Papers in Education*, 21(2): 119–32.

Continuous monitoring of learning is a key element of the teacher's role and effective learning cannot take place without it. Responding to the children's needs and adapting teaching accordingly is what good teaching is about. This is perhaps the most important element of effective teaching – decide what you want the children to learn, make sure you are clear how you will know if they have learned it, and continually observe them and what they do and say to monitor their learning. In the light of this monitoring, adapt and change your teaching and the learning opportunities you provide to ensure learning. Remember that when you are planning, you are planning for learning – decide what that learning is and then use whatever content is most appropriate and relevant to the class to teach it.

The National Curriculum in England (DfE 2013) sets out very clearly and precisely what children are expected to achieve in each year group of primary school. Expectations for the end of each Key Stage are specified. Schools are expected to have an assessment system which enables them to know if each pupil is on track to meet expectations and to inform parents of their child's progress. A key factor for schools was the removal of levels, which were seen as an 'easy' way of tracking progress and achievement. Teachers and schools have since been looking for ways of assessing progress which are meaningful and useful, and we shall explore some of these ways later in this chapter. As an overall comment, a statement by Michael

Armstrong cannot be bettered: 'In our concern of the predetermined standard we miss the value of the individual work' (in Peacock 2016: 65).

However, teachers and schools are accountable to parents, headteachers and the government, and need to ensure that children are making progress according to specified criteria. These criteria define what progression looks like and can sometimes make a very complex idea appear too simple. To illustrate this, let us consider what, in my opinion, is one of the most difficult things to teach – writing. The programmes of study for writing are dry, with the emphasis on the technical, and need a strong injection of inspired creativity to make them come alive.

How do I know if a piece of writing is effective? I know that my writing is effective if it fulfils its purpose and is appropriate for the audience. I know that by the response I get to my writing. If I am reading a novel, that writing is effective if I enjoy the book and want to carry on reading – if I sympathise with the characters, can imagine the setting or feel scared, amused or charmed. Good writing serves its purpose well. There are times when good writing is very simple, as illustrated by the opening of Jill Murphy's *Peace at Last*:

> The hour was late.
>
> Mr Bear was tired.
>
> Mrs Bear was tired.
>
> Baby Bear was tired.

Here the writing consists of four simple sentences. The same pattern is repeated and there are no 'wow' words. Yet, it is an extremely effective piece of writing. As the opening of a story it sets the scene well. It establishes the unity of the Bear family and their shared feeling of tiredness. This emphasises the isolation of Mr Bear later when he is the only one who cannot get to sleep. Sometimes simple writing is very powerful.

However, if Jill Murphy had been 11 when she wrote this she would not have demonstrated many of the statutory requirements for Years 5 and 6. She might have been encouraged by her teacher to edit her writing so it offered more evidence of her ability. For example:

> Sitting on the sofa late one night, Father Bear, a large gentle-appearing bear, was feeling very weary. Dressed in her nightclothes next to him, Mother Bear drowsed while an extremely sleepy Baby Bear snuggled on her warm expansive lap. As it was past their usual bedtime, the bear family decided to go to bed. The stairs seemed steep as they followed each other, slowly climbing from one step to the next. Baby Bear clung to his father's neck as he was

carried and the lamp was held high by a loudly yawning Mother Bear. If they were more tired, they would not be able to reach their bedroom at the top of the long flight of stairs.

Did you notice the expanded noun phrases, fronted adverbials, passive voice and subjunctive in this piece of writing? Yet – which piece of writing do you think is the most powerful? We have to be careful how we are assessing children's writing, that we notice what is most important for the author and how the reader is affected. Armstrong says that when assessing writing, rather than checking against a set list, teachers should be 'questioning the authors, sharing perceptions, exchanging interpretations, speculating together about the story's plot or its language, its characters and their circumstances, its twists and turns, its significance as a story' (2006: 180). Of course, it is important to measure children's achievements at specific points in time to ensure that those achievements have reached the nationally required standards and this is the role of summative assessment.

RAISEonline is a data analysis system which enables individual schools to analyse their performance data against national standards. This allows schools to compare the achievements of their pupils against those in other schools and so plan in order to raise achievements. This data is used by a variety of people to make judgements about the school.

Task

Ask a school to show you their RAISEonline profile and to talk it through with you. Talk with teachers about how this impacts on their planning and teaching.

Each school will have targets relating to achievement which they need to address; these will inform targets set for each class or year group and similarly each child will have targets to address. All this is in order to raise standards and levels of achievement. It is easy to forget that progress in literacy is not always quantifiable and is usually determined by context and purpose.

Progress in reading and writing

In order to be able to effectively support children in their journeys towards becoming readers and writers, teachers need to have a strong understanding of what progress looks like. This is a complicated process and it is all too easy to oversimplify and to break the processes of reading and writing down into a checklist of observable and measurable characteristics. Most teachers need guidance in avoiding this. The Centre for Literacy in Primary Education has provided such a support for teachers.

The Reading and Writing scales are available as a free download from www.clpe.org. They were created by CLPE in close collaboration with the main subject association concerned with the teaching of literacy. They are a development of the scales which were a part of the *Primary Language Record* (CLPE 1985). The aim was to provide a 'rich framework for teachers to help them identify each pupil's current stage, analyse progress and consider the next steps'. They are grounded in research and there are many references which give strong theoretical underpinning and establish a clear framework for the scales.

The scales are said to describe the journeys children make as they become literate and it is noticeable that they describe behaviours. They look at progression and are definitely not designed to be used as checklists for summative assessments. Do not read them in a linear way. You will notice that they are not age-related either – in some of the descriptions it says, 'older children at this stage ...' I would have liked to see more on how the nature and demands of the text affect the reading and writing behaviours, but that is something that can easily be taken into account when referring to the scales.

Both the scales for reading and for writing indicate the development from dependence to independence. The first stage in the Reading Scale is described as the beginning reader: 'The main feature of this stage is that readers are not yet able to access print independently and may not yet have the awareness that print carries meaning. They are likely to need a great deal of support with the reading demands of the classroom'. The scale goes on to describe further characteristics, but the most important bit comes below the description and that is the next steps – how to support the beginning reader in developing independence as a reader. This shows how teachers can create environments, opportunities, resources, conversations, demonstrations and models, etc. to support children's journey as readers. This is the power of these scales – not only do they provide rich descriptions of progression in reading development but also strategies for ensuring that progression takes place.

Assessment of writing development

In spite of all that has been said above, it is important that teachers are able to look at children's writing and to respond to it, showing them how they can improve as writers. The CLPE Writing Scale gives good support for doing this but it must be remembered that it is not designed to provide checklists for an individual piece of writing, but rather to support a holistic picture of the child as a writer. One piece of writing can only give a snap-shot of a moment in time and is not always a true reflection of the whole. The Writing Scale also provides a strong support for the teacher's subject knowledge and acts as a model for feedback.

How does all this relate to the whole question of assessment without levels? In 2014 the government produced a document looking at alternative approaches to assessment being tried by a range of teaching schools across the country. There seemed to be two key commonalities which emerged:

1   Pupils must be at the centre of the assessment process; this meant that formative assessment would often take place during the work and pupils were very clear about what would make their work better.
2   The tracking models created were very close to the detail of learning and progress within a subject, rather than the 'best-fit' approach used with levels.

It can be seen how the Reading and Writing Scales match these two prin-ciples but let's look at some actual examples of children's writing:

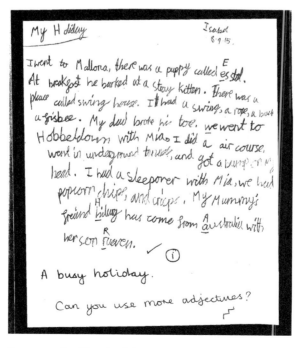

Figure 7.2   Isabel's account of her holiday

Isabel was writing a recount of her holiday. Look carefully at her writing and imagine how you would respond as a teacher.

Comment

There are many positive things that can be said about this writing:

- There are clearly demarcated sentences; they are all mainly simple or compound sentences.
- There is a good use of commas in the list.
- Good use of the possessive apostrophe is evident.

However, the writing is not particularly exciting to read and does not engage the reader. As a reader there are lots of questions I want to ask and more detail I want to know. Look at the comments made by the teacher. Would they help to make the writing more interesting? Does the comment 'a busy holiday' suggest that the teacher has engaged with the writing as a reader? Why does the teacher give the target of including more adjectives? Would that make the writing more interesting?

There is no indication of any involvement of the pupil in the assessment of her writing. It is likely, although I do not know for sure, that she would have maybe looked at the teacher's comments when she opened her book to do the next piece of writing. Is she supposed to edit this recount and insert more adjectives or is she just supposed to remember to use more adjectives in every subsequent piece of writing?

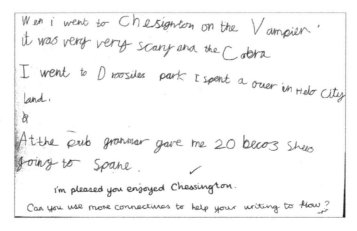

Figure 7.3 Another holiday recount

Look at this next piece of writing (Figure 7.3) by another child, again writing a recount of his holiday. Read the writing carefully and then identify the strong points about it. How does it make you feel as a writer? What emotions does it evoke?

Now look at the teacher's comments. How do you think the pupil felt when he received these comments? Why would using different connectives make it a better piece of writing?

Comment

You will see marking like this in many classrooms around the country; teachers will have carried home bags full of books and spent most of their evening marking. The good points may well have been written in pink and the 'targets' in green so that pupils were clear about what was to be done. There are, in my mind, two unspoken questions. The first is 'Why?' and the second is 'What now?' Ask yourself these questions and see if you can come up with any answers!

We now turn to two very different pieces of writing and very different responses to them by teachers. Before we look at them it needs to be said that they both come from a text-based teaching programme where reading is the starting point for writing. You will see that the children have been reading *The Iron Man* by Ted Hughes. They had responded to it as readers and then had read it like writers, looking at how Ted Hughes created the effects he did through his language choices.

This is quite difficult to read so I will transcribe it with the comments:

The Iron Man **(1)** saw the cliff. "What was it" he thought, what treasures lie beyond. **(2)** He started climbing. Climbing **(3)** higher higher and faster faster. He could just hear the sea, until he finally saw it. The colour was fantastic he ran, then stopped, there was a sound, the sound beckoned **(4)** him to come closer and closer, till he tumbled **(5)** off the cliff...

(6) His legs went faster, all the rusty nails that held him together, fell off leaving his body a wreck. He tumbuled into the water and ... then washed up on the beach. **(7)** Days, nights, weeks, months, years went by until a boy came along, he saw all the metal scraps he decided to make something he didn't know what he was making he let his mind take him away. **(8)**

Several days later he finished his art. **(9)** He had created the Iron Man again. Hadn't known anything.

I read lots and lots of books and I choose favourite sentences.

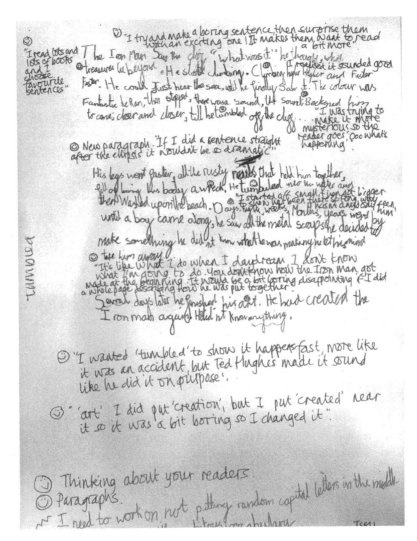

Figure 7.4   Responding to The Iron Man

I try and make a boring sentence, then surprise them with an exciting one! It makes them want to read a bit more.

I realised it sounded good

I was trying to make it more mysterious so the reader goes 'Ooo, what's happening'?

New paragraph. If I did a new sentence straight after the ellipsis it wouldn't be so dramatic.

I started off small then got bigger to show he's been there so long and hasn't anybody found him

It's like what I do when I daydream, I don't know what I'm going to do. You don't know how the Iron Man got made at the beginning. It would be a bit boring, disappointing if I did a whole page describing how he was put together.

I wanted 'tumbled' to show it happens fast, more like it was an accident, but Ted Hughes made it sound like he did it on purpose.

'art' I did put 'creation' but I put 'created' near it so it was a bit boring so I changed it.

☺ Thinking about your readers

☺ Paragraphs

I need to work on not putting random capital letters in the middle of sentences.

Comment

What a difference! There is so much that can be said about this piece of writing and the teacher's comments about it.

1 It is evident that what is written on the text is the product of a conversation between the teacher and the pupil and the teacher has recorded the child's comments. The comments are detailed and the whole piece of writing has evidently been discussed. The teacher had committed quite a bit of time to this child.

2 It is clear that the class had carefully read and discussed *The Iron Man* and had read it as writers. This meant they had talked about the sentence structures and vocabulary choices that Ted Hughes made; they had responded as readers and then analysed how the writer had generated that response in them.

3 The child is aware that somebody is going to read his writing and has the audience in mind as he composes. This influences his vocabulary choices, his sentence structures and the layout of the writing. He has thought carefully about what he is writing before he writes.

4 He knows that writing is a continuous process of decision-making and that sometimes you change your mind or try out different ideas. He is not afraid to do this and is able to explain his choices and the reasons for them.

(Continued)

(Continued)

5   He has a metalanguage for talking about his writing; he knows the correct terminology and is able to use it fluently and confidently.
6   He knows what would make his writing better and is able to identify what he can do to improve as a writer. He is also able to identify what is good about his writing.

What is also evident from this piece of writing and the comments the teacher has made is the strong subject knowledge of the teacher. She firstly knows the book on which the writing is based and has been able to discuss its linguistic and authorial style in depth. She also has a firm understanding of development in writing and of what progress looks like.

Task

Read the descriptors from the CLPE Writing Scale and notice the language that is used; consider how it can support you as a teacher when you respond to children's writing (www.clpe.org).

Let's look at one more piece of writing on the same theme:

The iron man came charging **(1)** through the trees. As he came to the very **(2)** brink of the cliff. The iron man stopped he heard the glistening **(3)** shiny stars, he looked again. He **(4)** shone like a star in the wild **(5)** staring moonlight. When the iron man turned and turned he tripped on a rock. With no warning **(6)** the iron man fell then no more iron man.

Before you read the comments of both the pupil and the teacher think what you might say about this piece of writing. Look generally and then look at each number and see what you would pick up at this point. What would you suggest this writer needs to do to improve?

I put 'charging through the trees' to make it sound like he was in a hurry, so he might accidentally run in to the sea, but he didn't, he tripped. I didn't want it to sound like on purpose like Ted Hughes, I wanted to make it more of an accident.

'glistening shiny stars' – he's got big ears so he can hear them. It gives you a full explanation of how shiny they are.

The light is bouncing off the metal, you can't actually see what it looks like so it's more scary.

wild, staring moonlight 'It's more dramatic'

He didn't see the stone, no-one could tell hi

It sounds like he's not alive anymore, I wanted to do something different. Ted Hughes makes you think it's not over.

☺ Much better full stops

☺ Choosing dramatic words

☺ Thinking about the reader

→ Keep checking spellings

→ Work on paragraphs

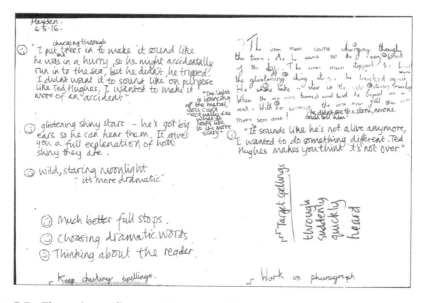

Figure 7.5 The writer reflects on his own writing

Comment

This writing is not as rich as the previous one and there are more transcriptional issues and yet the writer has still been very thoughtful and intentional about what he is saying and the effect it will have on

(Continued)

(Continued)

his readers. It is a strong piece of work. I love the way that the child knows what Ted Hughes did and very deliberately decided he wanted to do something different. He has real confidence in himself as a writer and that can only have come from the teaching and experiences he has had.

This teacher knew about the relationship between reading and writing and had learned how to read like a writer and teach children how to do this too. She took part in the CLPE *Power of Reading* project which started by developing teachers' knowledge of children's books. We know that this can be a problem through the work of Cremin et al. (2008). As a result of their increased knowledge, teachers were encouraged to introduce three strategies into their classrooms: create an attractive book area; read aloud to the class regularly; and involve children in open-ended discussions about reading. They were then supported in planning cross-curricular sequences of work which were text based. Five years of data showed that these relatively simple practices resulted in children who:

- choose to read more often at home and school
- talk about their reading to their teachers
- read at greater length or with greater focus
- are more confident to browse and choose books
- are more willing to seek out deeper meanings in texts
- show greater confidence in talking about books
- are more motivated to write. (Cremin and Myhill 2011: 186)

This approach impacted not only on children's motivation to write but also on their skill as writers, as can be seen in the two examples above. The comments demonstrate the high degree of ownership and intentionality the children had over their writing. They were the authors and they made the decisions about their texts, even though they were very different from the decisions Ted Hughes had made!

This strengthened teacher subject knowledge demonstrates the intimate relationship between planning and assessment and perhaps goes some way towards explaining why I found it difficult to decide which comes first at the start of this chapter. It is the pedagogical priorities of teachers which support progress, and the knowledge of what learning and progress look like which enables teachers to support children's development.

Assessment of reading development

When looking at progress in reading the simple view of reading is a useful reminder of the key elements. An effective reader will be good in both word identification and language comprehension. However, it is not always as simple as that and reading is a much more complex process than that statement might suggest. In assessing reading development, teachers need the skills of looking and listening to all that children say and do not say, and of making judgements, based on their understanding of what reading is.

Read

The Reading Scale from CLPE, which you can download free of charge from www.clpe.org.uk

Perkins, M. (2015) *Becoming a Teacher of Reading.* London: SAGE.

These two texts will give you an introduction to all the different research perspectives which are used to understand the reading process and what they have to offer us as teachers.

One very useful strategy for assessing reading is 'miscue analysis' or 'running record'. This was first devised by Ken Goodman in the 1970s and involves listening carefully to a child reading an unknown text and noting what is said when 'errors' or 'miscues' are made. This can indicate to you what knowledge the child is drawing on when reading and so indicate the future teaching that needs to be done. What follows is an example of such an assessment of an individual child's reading.

OBSERVATION: Reading of a Year 1 child (age 6)

The teacher listened to the child read aloud and recorded everything the child said. The child was given as little help as possible so that the teacher could identify their degree of independence as a reader and the strategies the child used to work out an unknown word.

Comment

Children need to be independent and have a variety of problem-solving strategies at their disposal when they come across an unknown word. This is the basis of independent reading. The knowledge of strategies used by a child will inform the teacher of the teaching and scaffolding the child needs in subsequent shared and guided reading sessions.

The first 'error' the child made was when attempting to read the word 'said' in the sentence, 'Mum said, come in the car, Nick'. The child attempted to sound out the word using single phoneme–grapheme correspondences. This lead to /s//a//i/; at this point the child realised that it was a vowel digraph and read the word as 'say'. It appeared as though the effort of working out the phonemic structure of the word was such that once a recognisable word was reached the child was content! She then started reading again from the beginning of the page, realised that 'Mum say …' did not make sense, saw the/d/ and self-corrected to read 'Mum said …'.

Comment

The first strategy used for decoding the word was phonics. The child was confident in simple phoneme–grapheme correspondences but less so when it came to vowel digraphs. It was re-reading and using the meaning of the sentence that enabled the child to realise the decoded word did not make sense, to self-correct and eventually to get to the correct word. This example emphasises the importance of phonics in tackling unknown words but also that it is not enough on its own. If this child's ear was not tuned in to the sense of what she was reading she would not have realised that what she said did not make sense. She would have learned this from her experiences of read-aloud sessions, shared reading and guided reading.

The next 'error' made followed a similar pattern. The text on the page was, '"Here I come," said Nick'. The child read 'Her I come'. This shows that again it was the vowel phoneme which was causing this child difficulties. She recognised the capital 'h' and decoded using the simple phoneme–grapheme correspondences /h//er/, failing to notice that the word actually contains a split digraph.

Comment

A pattern is beginning to emerge in this child's reading. She again self-corrected when she realised that her first decoding attempt did not make sense. She used the meaning of the text to inform her. Do you think this is a positive reading strategy adopted by this child?

As the child read on she began to relate more to the sense of the text, making comments on it as she read. These comments often referred to the illustrations: 'He looks scared'. The text was a very basic text and did not offer much in terms of subtlety of meaning. The child was making more meaning by referring to the illustrations and also by relating the text to her own experiences. After reading the sentence 'Here is Teddy', she commented, 'I've got a teddy bear too'.

Comment

It is clear that while using phonics as a key strategy for decoding, the child is also drawing on her experiences of life and her knowledge that texts usually make sense to read this book. How does this relate to what you already know about the reading process?

The final 'error' the child makes is on the very last page. The book has a large illustration of a little boy hugging a very large teddy bear. The words are 'Teddy is in the car too'. The child spent a long time looking at the illustration and then read 'Bear is in the car too'. She then stopped and said, 'No, not a bear. His name is Teddy'.

Comment

Here we have evidence of the meaning of the text having priority in the mind of the child. She was drawing on her knowledge of the text so far and relating it very closely to her own experiences of life. It seems that it was her prior knowledge of the text that caused her to self-correct here and not her phonic knowledge, although it is clear that she would have been able to decode that word. What does this tell you about the process of learning to read?

An overall analysis of this child's reading would indicate that she has a growing confidence in reading and is able both to recognise high-frequency words and relate what she reads to her own personal experiences. She has a sound grasp of simple phoneme to grapheme correspondences but is not so confident with more complex vowel phonemes. She tends to look only at the first part of a word when blending the phonemes and does not blend throughout the whole word. She recognises when she has misread and will usually self-correct. She made a personal response to the text, relating it to her own experiences.

Comment

What would you say were the priorities for teaching with this child? Consider discrete phonic teaching and also the teaching of reading in its broadest sense. Identify some of the things you would do if you were this child's teacher.

The analysis of a child's reading in this way gives teachers many pointers to future teaching. Of course, it cannot (and should not) be done on a daily basis, but done regularly and systematically will inform teachers' planning to enable their approach to be more focused and appropriate to individual needs.

With older children it is helpful as a strategy to identify the needs of struggling readers in particular.

One of the most significant ways of assessing older children's under-standing and response to a text is to hold a conversation with them. This can be done at an individual level, and for that the best framework is Chambers's *Tell Me* (2011):

- Tell me about your enthusiasms for the text – the things you like and the things you don't like.
- Tell me about the questions you have which you want to put to characters in the text or to the author.
- Tell me about the patterns you see – in relation to language, recurring themes etc. within the text; in relation to characters, settings, plots and themes of other texts or in relation to memories of places, people or experiences in real life.

This simple framework can generate a lot of information about children as readers and how they are engaging with a text. It can also be used in group discussions about a text. If older children read a text or part of a text beforehand, a discussion helps them develop a shared understanding. Just as when I go to my book group, the comments of other people start me thinking in different ways. Often, after the group meeting, I want to go home and read the book again! Group talk can have the same motivating and challenging effect on children.

Look at the double-page spread from Shaun Tan's book *The Red Tree*, shown in Figure 7.6. It is a perfect example of a picture book suitable for older readers.

Figure 7.6   Without sense or reason from *The Red Tree* by Shaun Tan. (Reprinted with permission from Hachette Australia)

Task

Spend some time looking at this image yourself and responding to it as a reader. You might find it helpful to use Chambers's framework.

Now read the transcript of the children talking about the image:

1	Dolce	Ummm, this is from…. The paper… the man with the paperhat or the paper man hat [I forget]
2	Ellie	Oh yeah, I'd forgotten about that… it looks like it's all cardboard and paper, isn't it?
3	Dolce	Yeah so it's like… [indistinct]
4	Ellie	And then it's got…
5	Dolce	I made one of those little things where you had the square and it had…
6	Ellie	Yeah… But look, did you notice that at the top?

(Continued)

Figure 7.7   (Continued)

7	Dolce	Oh yes… so we know it's from that because the top was…
8	Ellie	Yeah… it was all, um, writing wasn't it?
9	Dolce	Yeah and decoration….
10	Ellie	But what sort of things does it say on here?
11	Dolce	It says turn(?)
12	Ellie	Ummmm Yeah it does but look it says falling, falling, falling, falling…
13	Dolce	"Falling"
14	Ellie	And then we've got algebra over here, haven't we? Look… um
15	Dolce	[Reading] Without size or rest…
16	Ellie	Without sense or reason… Look can you see the little robots… they're all little robots… that's like a mailbox.
17	Dolce	It is.
18	Ellie	What does it even say?
19	Dolce	It's an Egyptian mailbox.
20	Ellie	That's not Egyptian.
21	Dolce	But it has Egyptian writing on it.
22	Ellie	That isn't Egyptian writing, that's Chinese.
23	Dolce	Oh, it's a Chinese mailbox then… pa pa pa pa…
24	Ellie	Umm that's got 6 on it.
25	Dolce	There's airplanes… that's fascinating.
26	Ellie	That's an airplane… look there's one right in the middle there. Look at this… can you see that right there?
27	Dolce	Um hm.
28	Ellie	That's all algebra on… so we've got it there, there…
29	Dolce	Oh, a little girl.
30	Ellie	Look it says hello.
31		Both laughing
32	Dolce	I'm a little girl.
33	Ellie	Look, there's all robots down here.
34	Dolce	Why robots? Oh, because robots are fascinating…
35	Ellie	Let's try and see what this says. It says biology… look there's all stamps…
36	Dolce	Wow… 199.
37	Ellie	Is that your age?
38	Dolce	But, that says 199
39	Ellie	Is that your age?

40	Dolce	No
41	Ellie	How old are you?
42	Dolce	8
43	Ellie	Oh, ok… What does… I'm trying to look at what this is from…
44		PAUSE
45	Ellie	Hmmm… Look can you see it, in every single picture you've got the shadow behind it… look.
46	Dolce	shadow… fascinating
47	Ellie	Let's try and see what this says at the top
48	Ellie	[Moves] Ok… it says
49	Ellie	Dolce, look…
50	Dolce	What?
51		Both giggling
52	Dolce	It says a story… No
53	Ellie	No it looks like a story, but it's not a story. Wait what does it say? 'Scan-den-sa Planner 199' This looks Egyptian…
54	Dolce	Yeah
55	Ellie	….but it's not, it's Chinese.
56	Dolce	That looks like Egyptian but it's Chinese.
57	Ellie	Umm hmm
58	Dolce	Oh, another house, another house… a house
59	Ellie	Look, that is from the paper thing because there was all little houses weren't there?
60	Dolce	Oh yeah! The Paper M… no
61	Ellie	The Paper Man Hat? No
62	Dolce	I'm looking at you sir, what is it?
63	Ellie	[Laughs] What was it called?
64	Teacher	Do you think it's from The Paperbag Prince?
65	Ellie	Yes
66	Teacher	Ok, why do you think it's from The Paperbag Prince?
67	Dolce	Because it has writing all over it and it always has…
68	Ellie	And all those little houses that was in The Paperbag Prince thing
69	Dolce	And there's writing at the top
70	Ellie	And that's what it was like… I think
71	Teacher	It's not

(Continued)

Figure 7.7   (Continued)

72	Ellie	Oh my god
73	Dolce	[Laughing] Oh my lord… all I was thinking about it was now not…
74	Ellie	How / What is it then?
75	Teacher	So if it's not from that, talk about what you think is going on in it.
76	Ellie	I have not got a clue.
77	Dolce	Oh, a village… a village, it's from our country, village! Village…
78		Both laugh
79	Dolce	I think it's from Micr-actually, I don't know / Oh, look, some stairs… aaahh, I've fallen down the stairs /
80	Ellie	Oh, there's millions of stairs Look and then, look, look, there's all little house here
81	Dolce	Oh look some little /
82	Ellie	No that's a road
83	Dolce	Yeah
84	Ellie	This is a building, this is a building, this is a building
85	Dolce	That's a girl… how can she fit through there?
86	Ellie	I don't know… I won't be able to fit through there. Look my head, don't even fit through
87		Both laugh
88	Dolce	Sir's thumb will… not
89	Ellie	No it won't… my finger won't even, my hand won't even fit through there
90	Dolce	My finger will.
91	Ellie	Yeah, my finger will… [both giggle]… What about our ears? No, they won't fit.
92	Dolce	No, no… We need to find a bigger [indistinct]

Figure 7.7   Dolce and Ellie discussing an illustration from *The Red Tree* by Shaun Tan

What does this transcript tell us about Dolce and Ella as readers? How are they engaging in the reading process as meaning makers and text critics (Luke and Freebody 1999)?

Comment

This is a complex text and these two Year 4 girls were attempting to make meaning from it. In order to do so, they were engaging in several different strategies; they were asking questions of the text – *'writing wasn't it?'* – and hypothesising on what it was all about. Maine (2013) calls this process the 'co-construction of meaning' and identified the 'dialogic space' where meaning is constructed. She identified two main strategies used by children for making meaning of texts together.

The first involves them embedding the text in a different context, often one which makes more sense to them. Is this happening in our example? Look through the transcript and identify places where they are using a familiar context to make sense of an unfamiliar text. One strong example of this is when Dolce and Ellie both think the illustration comes from *The Paperbag Prince*. Dolce makes the connection immediately (Line 1) and the idea is returned to between lines 60 and 70. The children find lots of reasons between them to justify this hypothesis and when the teacher tells them it is not from this book in line 71, they temporarily do not know what to say. Can you find any other examples?

Secondly, Maine claims that there is a 'hypothetical modality'; the children are attempting to propose what the text means through the suggestions they make. This is stronger than prediction where it could be argued they are trying to guess what the author wanted to say, but rather they are generating their own hypotheses. Is this happening in our example? Between lines 53 and 57 they are suggesting what nationality the text is – firstly they propose Egyptian and then Chinese – hypotheses are proposed and then adapted when closer examination of the text indicates they are not correct. Between lines 84 and 89 they are together constructing a village which they see as the setting of the story. How do they develop this idea as an attempt to understand the text?

How do conversations such as this help a teacher to assess children's understanding? It is only by listening carefully that teachers can identify how pupils are reading the text and relating it to their own experiences. Teachers can also observe how children identify key words and points in a text and are able to use the skills of inference and deduction in order to read between the lines. Reading conversations or conferences are a useful regular occurrence within classes in order for children to discuss their attitudes to reading and demonstrate the strategies they adopt to make sense of texts.

Phonic screening check

It would not be possible to write a chapter on assessing literacy without some mention of the phonic screening check. The first time this was administered was in June 2012 and it is administered every June to Year 1 pupils. The check is carried out individually by the teacher and the child has to decode 40 words and non-words; some have three or four letters and the rest have five or six. The check is designed to ensure that every child is able to decode; it is important to remember that this is designed to assess the ability to decode and not the child's ability as a reader. It is only since the introduction of the check that teachers have begun to teach children how to read non-words. One might ask what purpose being able to read non-words serves, apart from being able to read non-words in a check. Just imagine if that time was spent reading quality texts aloud to children! However, in 2010 the government was concerned that the increase in phonic ability had stalled at 80 per cent of primary-aged children leaving primary school with the expected level of phonic knowledge, and so the check was introduced to make sure all children were achieving appropriately and to identify those who needed extra help. Duff et al. (2015) looked at the check to see if it is valid (i.e. it measures what it claims to), if it is sensitive (i.e. identifies those children at risk) and lastly if it is useful (i.e. tells teachers something they did not know). They found that it was valid and it was sensitive but it did not assess phonic knowledge any more successfully than teachers did and so it was not useful. There are probably many Year 1 teachers who could have told them that!

What have we learned about assessment of reading?

- Assessing reading needs to take account of the text that is being read and how suitable it is for the reader.
- Assessing reading needs to focus on the growing independence of the reader.
- Assessing reading should focus on the strategies that are used to read unknown words.
- Quality of reading depends on quality of text.
- Assessing reading should consider word reading skills and also levels of comprehension as well as the pleasure gained from reading.
- Assessing reading needs to support effective planning for teaching.

OBSERVATION: Reading journals

In one Year 5 class lots of volunteer helpers come in and spend time reading with individual children (age 9–10).

The teacher reads aloud to the children, talks with them about texts, does shared reading with the whole class and guided reading with groups but does not often hear individual children read aloud to him. He does, however, encourage children to read to volunteer helpers as often as possible.

Think

Why does the teacher himself not hear individual children read?

Why does he encourage them to read to volunteer helpers?

You may have come up with several thoughts on these questions. It is helpful to consider what the teacher is in the classroom to do. It might sound really obvious but the main role of the teacher is to teach! This is done through all those activities listed above. The purpose of reading aloud is either to assess individual achievements or to give children the opportunity to practise the skills they have learned.

In this classroom the teacher keeps a large book in which everyone who hears a child read records what they have heard. Here are a few examples.

There are four different handwriting styles in Maisy's reading journal – her mother, her father, the teaching assistant and a volunteer parent:

21/9 – Work on expression and spotting punctuation. Read very well. 'creatures, people, rocket, climbed, spacesuit'

27/9 – self-correcting, needs to try to blend eg cl br but she read well

28/9 – finished book. She corrected herself but got stuck on the word 'thought'. She kept saying 'thinking'

24/10 – 'Underground Adventure' – finished book making very few mistakes, self-correcting if necessary. However got very stuck on 'visit' – could not blend it.

Comment

It seems evident from these comments that Maisy reads with understanding. She reads with expression, using the punctuation. Remember that punctuation is there for the reader; it can sometimes be fun with Key Stage 2 children to change the punctuation in a passage and see how it would change the way in which they read it.

Maisy also self-corrects. This implies that she is listening to what she reads and notices if it does not make sense.

She is having some difficulty blending some words. Why do you think she struggled with 'visit' but coped well with 'people'?

Benjamin:

> *28/4 – tried very hard but kept on getting the word 'origin' wrong and made some silly errors*
>
> *18/10 – good reading/decoding. Crumpled/staggered/pathetically. Should see some of this great language in Ben's writing*
>
> *24/11 – good reading – must make sure he stays on a coloured banded book – really check if only decoding or comprehending. Keep an eye on punctuation.*

Look at the comment made about Benjamin's reading on 24/11. He seems to be reading well but the person listening is not sure whether he is really comprehending the text or just has good decoding skills. There is a hint that he is not using the punctuation in his reading and so it lacks fluency.

Comment

How would you respond to this if you were Benjamin's teacher? Relate these comments to the simple view of reading which stresses the importance of the relationship between word recognition and language comprehension. The aim is that children are in the quartile where both are good. What sort of questions would you want to ask Benjamin about a text to ensure that he is really comprehending what he is reading? Remember you do not want to monitor his recall but to evaluate his understanding of the essential meaning of the text.

In addition to this ongoing assessment, the class used a sentence-based reading test as a way of tracking progression over the year. This can be a useful way of measuring progress but be careful that you always bear in mind the holistic nature of the reading process and do not think you are assessing reading when you are only assessing one aspect of it.

Principles of assessment in literacy

One of the key influences on thinking and practice in assessment has been the work of Shirley Clarke, and much of her thinking can be seen implemented in primary classrooms. She has listed seven key strategies involved in formative assessment (Clarke 2008: 11) and, in concluding this chapter, it is worth considering them with specific reference to literacy:

1 *Creating a classroom culture in which all involved see ability as incremental rather than fixed.* This means that there is no standard way in which all children will develop and achieve. What it means to improve as a reader and a writer will be different for each child and will depend on the text, the social and cultural context of the literacy learning, and the purpose and relevance of the learning event.

2 *Involving pupils in planning both appropriately pitched content and meaningful contexts.* Literacy is highly dependent on the social and cultural context, and children need to understand the function and relevance of literacy if they are to succeed in becoming literate. For many children, what being literate means in school will be very different from what being literate means at home. Children will be more successful if they feel comfortable with the literacy experiences offered to them and are also able to make decisions about the literacies they use.

3 *Clarifying learning objectives and establishing pupil-generated and therefore pupil-owned success criteria.* We saw this in practice when we looked at the examples of children's writing and the success criteria which had been generated by the reading and analysis of texts. This meant that the criteria were fully understood by the children because they could relate them specifically to texts they had read and so knew what success looked like in concrete terms. They used language they understood to create them and understood why these ideas would make their writing better.

4 *Enabling and planning effective classroom dialogic talk and worthwhile questioning.* Throughout this book the centrality of talk to the learning process has been emphasised. We know true learning has occurred when we can explain what we have learned to somebody else. Talk is a real indicator of learning. Teacher questions are important as a way of probing learning; questions which invite explanation and discussion provide evidence of deep learning rather than closed questions which invite repetition rather than recreation.

5 *Involving pupils in analysis and discussion about what excellence consists of – not just the meeting of success criteria, but how to best meet them.* The development of a unit of work in literacy gives many opportunities for children both to analyse and discuss what makes for a good text or piece of writing. By reflecting on how an author creates a particular effect, children are shown how to create that effect themselves.

6   *Enabling pupils to be effective self- and peer-evaluators.* The use of talk and/or response partners and the generation of success ladders are just some of the strategies which enable children to evaluate their own work. As a learner, you will be very aware that your work only really improves when you understand why it went wrong and how it can be changed to be made better. Children are no different.

7   *Establishing continual opportunities for timely review and feedback from teachers and pupils, focusing on recognition of success and improvement needs and provision of time to act on that feedback.* The process of becoming a reader and writer is a complex one and requires time and practice. An effective literacy teacher will have the subject knowledge to be able to see what children are doing, to know what needs to come next and to create opportunities to extend and challenge learning. Monitoring learning is a continuous element of teaching, and planning must be flexible and open to allow the children's needs to be addressed.

Read

Clarke, S. (2008) *Active Learning Through Formative Assessment.* London: Hodder Education.

Summary

The worst thing you can think about both planning and assessment is that they are both fixed practices which are done and dusted so that teachers can then move on to the real business of teaching. That is not the case at all. Both assessment and planning are ongoing and permeate the whole of that strange and complex business called teaching. They feed from each other and need to be both precise and yet open-ended at the same time. Planning cannot happen without assessment and, in a way, assessment depends on planning so that teachers know what to look for. However, both are concerned with children's learning. We plan to make a difference to children's knowledge, skills or understanding, and we assess to see how that difference manifests itself.

Further reading

Peacock, A. (2016) *Assessment for Learning without Limits.* London: Open University Press.

Teaching with story

8

This chapter explores the role of story within the curriculum and its impact on learning. The observations, across the primary age range, look at story through role play and oral storytelling as well as analysing stories in preparation for writing. It argues that story is an essential part of being human, and working with story can enhance our understanding of both ourselves and the world in which we live.

What does 'story' mean? Spend some time thinking about what comes into your mind when you hear that word. The term 'story' can cover a whole range of texts – oral, visual and written. Traditional stories tend to be those which we consider to have originated in the oral tradition. They include myth, fable, legend, folk tale and others. Even in the twenty-first century, however, stories come in all forms. They can be written, drawn, told, acted and filmed. Stories are told, read or remembered fictional or factual accounts. There is a huge range of story types – sagas, anecdotes, dramas, to name but a few. If I were to ask for your favourite story, I am sure you would be able to name several. I am also sure that if I asked several people their favourite stories there would be many common ones identified. Telling stories is an essential element of what it means to be a human being, and we all read, listen to and tell stories each day of our lives. Why is story so important in our lives?

- Story helps us to make sense of our experiences: by creating a story I am able to come to terms with events in my life. For example, several months ago I drove into the back of the car in front of me, and when telling the story about this to other people I emphasised the rain, the fading light, the busyness of the road with cars and pedestrians crossing in between cars and my tiredness at the end of a long day. It was this storytelling that made me feel better about what was clearly a mistake on my part and also generated sympathy in my listeners and made me feel better. I constructed a story to make sense of that rather unpleasant experience.
- Reading and hearing stories helps us to enter into experiences which might otherwise be outside our normal lives. This explains the popularity of romantic fiction, of spy thrillers and of crime detective novels. Story gives me vicarious experiences.
- It is these vicarious experiences that allow me to extend my understanding, my vocabulary and to explore my own values and beliefs. Story expands the database of experiences within which my cognitive development takes place.
- There is also a huge social and cultural aspect to story. I recently read *Toast* by Nigel Slater and his descriptions of the food of his childhood immediately took me straight back to my childhood and I could see and taste the food he was describing. Some stories reinforce social and cultural understandings and others broaden experiences and help readers and listeners understand the social norms of others.
- Story introduces readers and listeners to the rhythm and power of literary language. The first page of *Peace at Last* by Jill Murphy reads 'The hour was late'. That is not the language that is used at bedtime in my house and I suspect not in yours, but it is literary language. It prepares the reader that something is going to happen and creates an atmosphere of wonder and anticipation.
- Stories introduce listeners and readers to huge concepts about the world – good and bad, honesty and deceit, poverty and wealth, kings and woodcutters. At the same time they consider the most intimate aspects of our lives – both personal and universal.

For these reasons, and others, stories have been the most powerful method of teaching since the beginning of history. Hardy (1977) famously described narrative as 'a primary act of mind', arguing that it is the way in which we make sense of our experiences. She wrote that we use story in our head ('inner storytelling') and told to other people ('outer storytelling') to make sense of our lives and the events in them. Story is central to understanding and learning and so should be central to our teaching.

In this chapter many of the observations focus on the written form of story, but this is not to undervalue the importance of storying and storytelling. These two should have a place in the curriculum in their own right because of their impact on children's learning. Do not think that children move seamlessly from listening to, telling or reading stories into writing. The place of story within the curriculum is more holistic than that.

Read

Grainger, T. (1997) *Traditional Storytelling.* Leamington Spa: Scholastic.

Grugeon, E. and Gardner, P. (2000) *The Art of Storytelling for Teachers and Pupils: Using Story to Develop Literacy in the Primary Classroom.* London: David Fulton.

OBSERVATION: Storytelling in a Year 1 class (ages 5 and 6)

One of the most important features of working with story is storytelling. It is difficult to capture this in an observation because often it is spontaneous and it is difficult to record everything that is said and the responses that are made. I watched a teacher tell a story to her Year 1 class after a very windy playtime. The story she told was very roughly based on Aesop's fable about the wind and the sun, where they try to find out who is the most powerful by attempting to make a traveller remove his coat. The children came into the classroom loudly; their hair was blown and their faces red. It had been very windy outside and they were talking loudly about how they had been blown about and had to chase scarves and so on across the playground. The teacher sent them to hang up their coats and come and sit down quickly because she knew a story which was exactly about what had happened during their playtime.

Comment

Instead of ignoring the children's excitement about the wind, the teacher harnessed this and used it to focus their attention. They immediately wanted to listen and become involved. She had used the 'hook' of their own experiences to draw them in.

When the children were settled, the teacher began telling them the story – but with a difference. She told a story about a class of children outside in the wind. The wind was trying hard to make them take off their coats and scarves and throw them away and wanted to make the children naughty. In telling the story, the teacher named every child in the class, picking up on what they had told her about their adventures outside.

Comment

The children quickly realised that this story was about them and once the first name was mentioned were carefully listening for their own name. They were hanging on her every word.

The story lasted for only about five minutes but at the end the children were quietly settled and ready to begin the next lesson. The teacher told them that there was a story very similar to 'theirs' and during the lunch hour she found a copy of the Aesop's fable, read it to them and put it on display in the book corner.

Comment

This was not a planned lesson and lasted for a very short time but it served three very powerful purposes. It calmed the children down and focused them back on the teacher and into a listening frame of mind. It introduced them to a traditional fable and motivated them to read that for themselves and go on to read other fables later. Lastly, it demonstrated to them the power and universality of story – linking an ancient story with their own very recent experience, helping them to make sense of both.

It is important to remember that much learning that happens in the classroom is unplanned. This was an experienced teacher and she had the confidence to take five minutes from the planned lesson. She also had the subject knowledge of Aesop's fable to be able to draw on that and use it to make the link with the children's immediate experiences.

OBSERVATION: Guided reading with an EAL group in Year R (ages 4 and 5)

The next observation is of a teacher reading with a Reception class. It was a guided reading lesson and she wanted to support them in making meaning from the text. The group of children had not been in school for long and the majority of them did not share the social and cultural background of the story. The teacher, therefore, wanted them to experience this in order to enhance their understanding. She did this through role play.

This lesson was with a group of six children who were at the start of their second term in school. They did not have much English. They were working with a teacher, looking at a story called *Getting Up* by Roderick Hunt.

The lesson took the form of role play. The teacher took on all the roles and the children joined in with her, using the props and echoing her language. Props used included toothbrushes and toothpaste, coats and scarves, wellington boots, etc. The teacher turned to each page in the book and showed it to the group. She gave them some time to look at the picture before asking for comment.

Comment

Thinking time is important, as we have already seen in preceding chapters. In this instance, it allowed the children to look carefully at the details of the pictures and to relate them to their own experiences. The frequent emphasis on pace and 'correct' answers can sometimes contradict what we know about how learning takes place through the co-construction of knowledge and understanding. The article cited below considers how the use of the interactive whiteboard (IWB) can support children's understanding and encourage the use of dialogic teaching. It is mainly about work with older children, but as you read it, consider the similarities and differences between how the IWB was used with 12–13-year-old pupils and how the Reception teacher in our observation used role play for the same purpose.

Read

Mercer, N., Hennessy, S. and Warwick, P. (2010) 'Using interactive whiteboards to orchestrate classroom dialogue', *Technology, Pedagogy and Education*, 19(2): 195–209.

These children became part of the story in order to understand what was happening. They were able to use language in authentic situations, and because they had experienced the scenario were able to tell the story. The lesson was recorded and the children returned to it many times, looking at the book and the video and retelling the story to each other.

OBSERVATION: Year 1 children (ages 5 and 6) retelling the story of *We're Going on a Bear Hunt*

The next observation is of a group of children in a Year 1 class during independent activity time. The class had been working on the text *We're Going on a Bear Hunt* by Michael Rosen and there were multiple copies of this in the book corner. Alongside this was a story sack related to this text.

Story sacks were originated by Neil Griffiths. A story sack is a cloth bag full of resources to encourage children and adults to enjoy reading together. The sack is based around a well-known picture story book and usually also includes a non-fiction book on a similar theme. There are also a variety of artefacts: soft toy characters, props and scenery and also a game, a CD of the story, an activity guide and a guide for parents.

This sack was rather unusual in that it contained a copy of the book and nothing else but some lengths of different types of material. There was a length of textured green linen, a length of patterned material in different shades of blue, a length of brown satin, a length of rough dark brown hessian, a length of white netting and, finally, a piece of heavy black cotton.

A group of children was sent to explore this resource during the independent time of a literacy lesson and told to prepare a storytelling for the rest of the class. A teaching assistant was supporting them. They began by opening the sack, taking out the material and waving it about.

Some of the material was more fluid than others and the children soon noticed this and commented to each other: 'This is like a flag', 'This won't wave about – it's really heavy', 'I can see through this', 'I don't like the feel of this – it's scratchy'. They took about five minutes doing this, passing different materials from one to the other and comparing them.

Comment

At the beginning of this activity the children had not even thought about the story which was the focus of their task. Do you think this was a waste of time? If not, what was the purpose of this part of the activity?

After several minutes of exploring and discussing the contents of the bag, the children had a good understanding of what each length of material was like and had developed a bank of strong descriptive words for talking about the materials. The teaching assistant then picked up the text and suggested they look at it. The children were very familiar with the text and so immediately began considering how to match the materials with the different settings in the story. They turned immediately to the coloured 'grass page' and did not bother to look at or read the pages before. One child immediately picked up the green material and waved it in the air while the whole group chanted 'Swishy, swashy! Swishy, swashy! Swishy, swashy!'

The group worked through the book, looking just at the coloured pages and matching the lengths of materials to the pages. There was almost complete agreement except for the two brown lengths of material – the satin and the hessian. This was the only occasion when the decision was not based on colour alone. There was a heated discussion between the children:

Child 1:   I think this [the satin] is the forest because you can't see through it.

Child 2:   But it's shiny!

Child 1:   So are the trees [pointing to the trunks of the trees].

Child 3:   Well I think this [hessian] is better for the trees because it's prickly like all the twigs and branches

Child 2:   Hey look – don't you think this shiny stuff looks wet like the mud.

Child 3:   Oh yes, I never thought of that.

Child 1:   But you can't see through it.

Child 3:   I think the shiny stuff is best for the mud and the prickly stuff for the forest.

Child 2:   I'm happy with that. Let's go for it!

Child 1:   OK then.

Comment

There were at least two influences on this conversation. First, the children knew the story really well. They had had it read to them many many times and it had been in the book corner for them to read independently. They had also talked about the book in class

(Continued)

(Continued)

and had discussed what it would be like to squelch through the mud and stumble through the forest; they had role-played the story and experienced those actions. Secondly, they had experienced and talked about the different materials. The relatively long time that they had spent 'playing' with the materials at the start of the activity was now bearing fruit because the children knew what each piece felt like and had a vocabulary to describe it. The judgements they were making to match the materials with the text were therefore informed decisions.

The teaching assistant then asked the children how they could use the material to tell the story to the rest of the class, as instructed. They first said that they could just wave the materials in the air at the right time while somebody read the book but, when asked by the teaching assistant if they could make it even better, they began to think more closely about the text. They focused on the first page and identified the words 'over', 'under' and 'through'. Two children held an end of the blue material and another child stepped over it, then they moved it over that child and then one child let go of his end while the child walked through it. They got excited about this idea and looked through the book to check that each page was the same. When they found it was, they decided that two children would hold all the materials in turn while the other children would be the walkers and would 'tell' the story. This they did and the resulting 'performance' to the whole class was impressive.

Comment

Notice how the children's knowledge of the text modified what they did. They needed to be focused initially, but once this had happened they took control and planned the whole thing themselves. They could do this because they possessed the required knowledge. This text had become part of the children's thinking because they had heard it and talked about it a lot. They knew the story and so were able to make it their own.

An approach to storytelling devised by Pie Corbett to support children's writing of stories is described as 'Talk for Writing'. It involves the children memorising a story through repeating the lines and linking them to actions, and also works well as a family literacy activity. Corbett identifies three stages in the development of storytelling and argues that each stage must be fully internalised before moving on to the next. The three stages are:

- *Imitation*. This is where children listen and join in with stories, becoming very familiar with just a few so they can internalise the structures and linguistic patterns of the story. Corbett suggests that during Reception and Year 1 (ages 4–6) teachers focus on just two to three stories a term, although the children will hear a range of quality stories in addition. The stories which become the focus of attention are repeated and learned.
- *Innovation*. When a story is well known then one or more aspects can be changed. These changes may range from the very simple, such as the name of a character, to the setting or to the resolution of the dilemma within the plot.
- *Invention*. Having spent time getting to know stories and playing with their structure, Corbett argues that children are ready then to create their own stories.

Read

More information about this can be found in the DCSF publication of 2008 called *Talk for Writing*.

Comment

Relate Pie Corbett's model to the *We're Going on a Bear Hunt* activity described above. The children were clearly engaged in an 'imitation' activity. However, the teacher and the children had not consciously learned the story, nor had they learned appropriate actions to go with the words. One could almost say that the book itself had enabled them to remember and repeat. The rhythm, rhyme and unforced repetition of the text lent itself to natural action. Can you think of any more stories for which this is the case? Look back to Chapter 1 and think again about what Margaret Meek and Vivienne Smith say about what texts teach readers.

It is interesting to put this strategy into a theoretical framework. In Chapter 4 we saw how Corbett's work is based on that of the developmental psycholinguist, Traute Taeschner, from Rome. Her work (Taeschner 1991) argued that language acquisition, particularly the acquisition of a second language, is about internalising the patterns of the language. Myhill and Jones (2010) have explored the theoretical underpinning further in relation, particularly, to the idea of 'oral rehearsal'. They found that there was much confusion in policy, in strategy writing and in teachers' thinking about what oral rehearsal actually is.

Myhill and Jones's research looked at how oral rehearsal is used in early years classrooms. They found that there is no clear theoretical conceptualisation of what it is and, indeed, the guidance in policy documents is often contradictory. However, they did find that it seemed to have a positive impact on children's writing. The next observation shows how children built on their knowledge of a text to create a text of their own.

The next observation shows how young children used work on a text to develop their emerging identity as writers, using oral composition to engage in the authoring process.

Observation: Year 1 children (ages 5–6) responding as writers to *I am Henry Finch*

A class of 28 children began the first year of Key Stage 1 needing a lot of support and work on self-belief, learning skills and behaviours and group cohesion. They had had a troubled year in Reception and their teacher felt

Figure 8.1 The children made their own pictures of Henry Finch

it was necessary to almost start again. There were six 'special' children in the class and many of the children did not have a positive view of themselves as learners. The teacher chose *I am Henry Finch* as a text which might address those needs. On first reading she was not sure how this class would respond – but they absolutely loved it and it led to two weeks of exciting literacy lessons.

Comment

What was it which attracted the children to this story and prompted such a focus of thinking and writing? What does it mean to say that the children were responding as writers to the book? The book is simple and complex at the same time. The main character, Henry Finch, is simply portrayed and his enthusiasm for life and willingness to think and challenge the status quo are inspiring. Many of the children warmed to him and identified strongly with him; one of the special children made a picture of Henry Finch which was put on display in the classroom – it was the first time she had ever volunteered a response to anything which had happened in school.

Over the next two weeks the class carried out many activities related to the book:

- they thought about thinking and what they would think if they were Henry Finch
- they shared what they were good at and what they would like to get better at
- they made a flock of finches with their thumb prints and discovered how they could create different characters with just a few pencil lines
- they were scared of the beast and drew their own beasts, describing them with all sorts of wonderful words
- they made up words to describe the noises in the beast's stomach – an introduction to the alien words of the phonic screening check!
- [one morning when they arrived in school] they discovered a set of beast footprints and worked out that the beast must have been there in the night. The footprints had numbers on them and so by following the order of the numbers they worked out where the beast had been.

It was all really exciting and the children were completely engaged throughout. At the end of those two weeks they were still a lively class who were learning how to learn but they were drawn into the story and gained from it.

Friday

I am Henry Finch

I am going to Fly in the Sky.

Figure 8.2   Using Henry Finch as a model for their own aspirations

Boom Bangepacss

Figure 8.3   Writing down the noises made by the beast

Comment

Notice how in all these activities the teacher was relating what was happening in the book to the children and their own experiences.

When Henry Finch realised he could think, it was an exciting moment and the children were encouraged to think about what they could do and this became a source of celebration. They composed sentences and shared them with each other, reflecting on each other's sentences and the responses they engendered. Nothing was transcribed and yet these children were behaving as writers, composing and editing their sentences in the light of the readers' response.

These conversations enabled the children to reflect on their own desires and dreams and, through the focus of *Henry Finch*, to write about what they would like to do.

In drawing the beast and describing him, the children were carefully choosing words and relating their words to the pictures. In this instance they did not have to put their writing into a sentence but were focusing on finding the best possible words to convey what their beast was like.

Finally, in making up funny sounds which came from the beast's stomach, the children were concentrating on their transcriptional skills – listening to sounds in their heads and drawing on their phonic knowledge to work out how to write it down.

Each activity drew on a different aspect of being a writer – composition, choosing the correct words and spelling – and yet all were within the context of an engaging story. In addition, these very young children could focus on different elements of being a writer within a story which had a powerful emotional effect on them.

Read

Myhill, D. and Jones, S. (2010) 'How talk becomes text: investigating the concept of oral rehearsal in early years' classrooms', *British Journal of Educational Studies*, 57(3): 265–84.

As Pie Corbett argues, it is true that all stories have the same basic structure, and familiarity with that structure helps children in their own writing. When planning a unit of work in literacy it is important that children first have lots of experience of the type of text they are going to write and have spent time talking about it and looking at specific texts to draw out key features. The process can be described as a series of over-lapping circles, which you will see if you look at the *Talk for Writing* publication (DCSF 2008).

The essential stages of the writing process which need to be taken into account when planning a unit of work are:

- familiarisation with text type
- capturing ideas
- teacher demonstration
- independent writing.

These stages build upon each other and so it is important that each one is given enough time before moving on to the next. The following observation shows how this works in practice.

OBSERVATION: Unit of work on adventure stories with Year 3 class (ages 7 and 8)

The unit of work described here lasted for five sessions, taking place on consecutive days over a week. It was the precursor of work the following week where the children wrote their own adventure stories.

Lesson 1

The first lesson began with the teacher asking the children what 'adventure' means. They suggested words such as exciting, funny, scary, unusual, which she recorded on the whiteboard. She then reminded them of books they had read recently, both as a class and as individuals, and related those words and ideas to the books the children knew. This led to some more words being added to the list.

Comment

The teacher was starting this unit with the children's own ideas and understandings. This activity was a way for the teacher to review the children's existing knowledge and understanding and so establish a firm basis for future work.

The teacher then showed the children the cover of the book *Gorilla* by Anthony Browne. They knew this book well as they had done some focused work on it in Year 2 and it was also a popular text for independent reading.

Comment

A well-known text was chosen because that allowed the teacher to direct the children's attention to selected features of the text. They had already made their own personal affective responses to the text and were familiar with the outline of the plot. This enabled the teacher to move them on into analysis of the text.

The teacher read the story to the class and, with her encouragement, they joined in and became involved. The teacher then explained that many stories have the same structure and showed them a visual way of describing this structure using the analogy of a mountain. The structure starts at the bottom of one side of the mountain with the 'opening', setting the scene and introducing the characters. Moving up the slope of the mountain, the 'build-up' creates the possibility of tension or a problem. At the top of the mountain the 'dilemma' manifests itself and as we descend the other side we move towards a 'resolution'. Reaching the flat land on the other side of the mountain the story comes to a satisfactory 'ending'.

The class were told to work with a talking partner and decide what the problem in this story was. There was much animated discussion and when each pair had come to a decision ideas were shared with the whole class. Not all had come to the same conclusion; some thought it was that Hannah was lonely, some thought that it was the fact that her father was too busy and spent too much time at work and others thought it was that the Gorilla gift was not what she wanted. All ideas were listened to and accepted but each group was required to justify their answers by referring to the text.

Comment

The teacher was showing here that all ideas are valid but that it is important to be able to justify an answer by referring to the text. This meant that the children were engaged in really close reading of the text – reading what was actually said not only through words but also in the illustrations, using the skills of inference and deduction.

The children were then given a task to complete in pairs. They had to use the story mountain structure and decide which parts of the story fitted into the different stages. Each pair had a copy of the text and had to put sticky notes where they thought each stage was. They had to agree as a pair and be able to justify their decisions. The teacher emphasised that there was no one correct answer and so it was important for each pair to be able to explain to others how they had come to their answer. They then came together in groups of six (three pairs) to compare and explain their decision.

Comment

This activity emphasises the importance of talk. At the end of the lesson there was no written work but the evidence of learning was in the explanations and justifications that the children shared with the class. This activity required them to become immersed in the text and to articulate their own personal understanding of it to others who might hold a different view.

After the class had compared their views each group was given a section of the story to demonstrate through freeze frame.

Comment

Freeze frame is a drama technique in which children take a particular scene or incident in a book and form a freeze frame or 'tableau' of the situation. This requires the children to think about the relationship of the characters to each other, body language and facial expression. A further development is that the teacher will ask different characters in the frame to say what they are thinking at that moment in time.

Read

Baldwin, P. and Fleming, K. (2003) *Teaching Literacy Through Drama: Creative Approaches*. London: Routledge.

The lesson ended by referring back to the list of words describing adventure stories. These were read as a class and the children were asked to relate them to the text of *Gorilla*. Some extra words were added and the lesson finished with the teacher telling the children that they would look at the book again in more detail in the next lesson.

Reflect

How do you think this lesson had begun to prepare the children for writing adventure stories?

Lesson 2

The second lesson began with a recap of the stages of a story:

- an opening which introduces the characters and setting
- a problem or a dilemma
- resolution of the dilemma
- an ending.

The teacher then returned to the text of *Gorilla* and asked the children to name the characters in the book. The focus moved to Hannah and the children were told they were going to act as detectives and find out what kind of person Hannah was. They would have to hunt through the text for clues. This was done as a shared reading activity.

Comment

By setting this up as a problem-solving activity the children were immediately engaged. The teacher could have said, 'I want you to write a description of Hannah and support what you say by examples from the text'. What difference would this make to how the children tackled the text?

The teacher then modelled the activity by looking at the first page together. The first sentence on the page said, 'Hannah loved gorillas'. The teacher explained how it was easy to discover something about Hannah from that sentence and the children nodded wisely. She then asked if they could discover anything more about Hannah from the first page. A few children commented that she was lonely. When asked to justify this most of the children referred to the illustration which shows Hannah sitting on her own reading a book and looking rather sad. The children commented on the fact that she was by herself and that her facial expression was sad. The teacher then asked the children to read the second paragraph on the page. This says, 'Her father didn't have time to take her to see one at the zoo. He didn't have time for anything'.

The teacher explained that hunting for clues in the text means also looking for what we can guess from what people say. The children then discussed how Hannah might be lonely because her father was so busy.

Comment

When we read, our understanding of a text often comes through what is implied rather than what is directly said; in other words we are often reading 'between the lines'. This is known as inferential reading and relates to the ability to deduce ideas which are not in the text explicitly. It is an important aspect of learning to become a reader. Teachers can teach this skill by the questions they ask.

Read

Zucker, T.A., Justice, S.B. and Piasta, S.B. (2010) 'Preschool teachers' literal and inferential questions and children's responses during whole-class shared reading', *Early Childhood Research Quarterly*, 25(1): 65–83.

The class then went through the book looking for clues about Hannah and how she was feeling. By her questions, the teacher encouraged them to read inferentially and to look at both the words and the illustrations for clues.

The next task required the children to work in pairs, looking at copies of the text. They had to think about the father and list adjectives describing him on their individual whiteboards. Each pair came up with a good list of adjectives, having used both the words and the illustrations. The teacher then sent the children off to work independently. The core and lower ability groups were asked to create a list of adjectives describing the gorilla and then to use these adjectives to write a character description of the gorilla. The higher ability groups were asked to create a list of adjectives for both the gorilla and the father and then to write a comparison of the two characters. The children were asked to share their ideas as they worked.

Comment

Look at how the teacher initially supports the children. First, she was structuring the reading very closely by directing their attention to particular parts of the text and by her questioning focusing their thinking.

Secondly, she gave them a framework for writing a character description: read the text closely, identify key words and then write the description. Lastly, she asked them to do the same thing independently, challenging the more able by introducing the idea of comparison.

Lesson 3

The third lesson continued to focus on the aspect of character within story structure, but the learning objective was to introduce the idea of empathy or seeing things through the eyes of somebody else. The lesson began with the class sitting on the carpet and the teacher gave examples of real-life situations, asking the children if they could understand how people were feeling. The examples started with Theo Walcott not being selected to play for England and this immediately got the boys engaged and talking energetically about how he must have felt. A variety of examples were given which involved the whole class and after much talk the teacher introduced the word 'empathy', explaining that this is what happens when we understand what somebody is feeling.

Comment

Notice how the teacher started with examples that were relevant and meaningful to the children. She gave them the opportunity to talk about events which were important to them first and that allowed them to experience empathy first hand. She then gave them the term to describe what they had already felt and discussed, and so the new word was useful to them and so more likely to be remembered and used.

The teacher then turned to another book by Anthony Browne called *The Tunnel*. She read the story to the children up to the point where Rose has to decide whether or not to go through the tunnel. If you do not know this book already, go and read it before you carry on reading this observation. It is an established children's text and should be in your repertoire.

Read

Browne, A. (1997) *The Tunnel*. London: Walker Books.

The teacher stopped and said to the class, 'Rose faces a dilemma here. What is it?' There followed a discussion about Rose's situation. The teacher asked questions such as:

- What choices does Rose have?
- What thoughts do you think might be going through her head?
- Can you empathise with her?

The children worked in talk partners and came up with many different suggestions of what Rose might be thinking. The class then came together to share ideas. Children were asked to share what their talk partner had said rather than their own ideas.

Comment

Why do you think the teacher asked the children to report back on their partner's ideas and not their own? It is much easier to report on what somebody else has said in a public domain than to risk exposing one's own ideas. It also means that the children have to actively listen to what their partner is saying in order to be able to repeat it. It is often a good idea while they are learning to do this to get the children to repeat back to their talk partner what they are going to say.

The ideas shared by the children varied from 'There might be something dangerous in there' to 'What if my brother needs help?' After hearing all the thoughts the teacher asked each person to decide if the thought they had expressed would lead Rose to go into the tunnel or stay outside. Again, they discussed this with their talk partner. The children were then asked to stand in two lines facing each other; on one side were those who were for going into the tunnel and on the other were those who were against going into the tunnel. The teacher was then Rose and walked between the two lines while the children whispered their comments to her, acting as her conscience.

Comment

'Conscience alley' is sometimes known as 'decision alley' or 'thought tunnel' and is a way of exploring the dilemma faced by a character. Those on one side of the tunnel give the opposing point of view from those on the other. It can be used in any area of the curriculum. On a practical note, it is a good idea to make sure the tunnel is quite wide; the children can sometimes become too enthusiastic and overpower the person walking through the tunnel. This is especially important if that person is a child. Note also that the children whispered their views. The children need to be reminded that it is not a case of who can shout the loudest in order to convince, but rather that this is a demonstration of the debate which is going on in the mind. Drama can be a very powerful teaching tool as it allows children to experience the feelings of protagonists in any situation and so understand them more deeply.

This was a moving experience for the children and served to enhance their understanding both of what a dilemma was and also what it felt like to experience a dilemma. The teacher emphasised that having walked through the tunnel and listened to all the different points of view, Rose could now make a decision. She informed the class that Rose had decided not to go through the tunnel. Some of the children were clearly and vocally disappointed, an indication that they were fully engaged and empathised with Rose's dilemma. They were told that Rose was going to write a note to Jack and leave it under a stone outside the tunnel, explaining why she did not follow him. The children were given roughly torn scraps of paper on which to write their notes.

Comment

Why do you think the teacher gave them paper like that on which to write? How would it increase the quality of their writing? It certainly would have continued the sense of being in role; Rose would not have had an English exercise book with her and in such a situation would not have written the date and title neatly underlined! The teacher was consciously giving the children an authentic writing experience and this is an important thing to remember when planning.

When the writing was completed the children folded up their notes and placed them under large stones put around the classroom. The role play was continuing and it was the experience of the whole context of the lesson which enabled the children to achieve the learning objective of understanding what empathy is and being able to empathise with a character in a story.

The class then gathered for the plenary and one child was chosen to be Rose; another child was chosen to be a police officer. The teacher explained that Jack had never reappeared and Rose was being questioned later in her home about what had happened. This worked really well; the police officer was a little self-conscious at first but soon became more comfortable in his role and was quite perceptive and scary in his questioning. The girl in role as Rose answered the questions well, showing that she fully understood Rose's position.

Comment

The plenary was not used as a show-and-tell activity where children can easily get very bored by looking at lots of examples of the same thing. Instead the teacher went back to the learning objective and devised another activity which explored the children's understanding. All the children were involved as they began by suggesting what the police officer might ask and evaluated the responses given by Rose. Right to the very end of the lesson, the class was engaged and enthusiastic.

Lesson 4

This lesson began with the teacher finishing reading *The Tunnel* to the class. After the reading, she referred back to the story structure which she had introduced to the class through the use of the 'story mountain' in the first lesson. Through fairly direct questioning, she asked the children to identify the characters, the problem and the adventure in the story. The first two questions were answered quickly and without debate as they were reviewing prior learning but the third led to more debate. The question asked was, 'Where do you think the adventure began in the story?'

Comment

Note how the teacher was asking for the children's opinion. There was no sense that there was only one correct answer, and the children were required to draw on their generic knowledge of adventure stories and their specific knowledge of this text to answer. This type of questioning continued right through the first part of the lesson.

There was a debate about whether the adventure began when Jack entered the tunnel or when Rose did, and the discussion involved lots of debate about what constituted an adventure. The children were then asked how they thought Jack got turned into stone. Again, there were lots of ideas – ghosts, ice, evil spirits. The teacher referred the children back to the illustration for clues and they all felt that he looked as though he was running away from something or someone. Suggestions were made as to what that might be.

The children were then put into mixed-ability groups and asked to tell the story of what happened to Jack when he went through the tunnel by creating three freeze frames. The last of these was to be Jack being turned into stone; the first one was to be Jack emerging from the tunnel, showing what he saw and the middle one was completely up to the children. Before going off to work, the children were again shown the illustration in the book which showed Jack turned to stone. They were reminded that probably their final freeze frames would be quite similar but the first two could be very different.

Comment

Why do you think the groups for this activity were mixed ability? What would be the advantage of this? A 'freeze frame' is like a still image from a drama, when the characters freeze. It enables exploration of relative positioning, body language and expression to help understanding what is happening in a text at a particular moment of time. This is sometimes known as 'thought tracking'.

The children then watched each other's freeze frames and discussed the different viewpoints.

Lesson 5

The fifth lesson was a shorter lesson at the end of the first week which summed up what the children had learned about adventure stories during the week, before they began to start planning their own adventure stories. It began with a recap of the two books by Anthony Browne that the class had worked on. The teacher used the discussion to draw up a list of the features of an adventure story, taking suggestions from the children. The focus in this lesson had gradually shifted from looking at setting, character and plot to considering how language was used to convey a sense of adventure. The final list contained the following features:

- written in first or third person
- written in past tense with occasional switch to the present tense
- the main characters tend to be human
- the setting is linked to the adventure – being lost, at night, in a nightmare
- use of time connectives – early that morning, later on
- connectives to gain attention used – meanwhile, at that very moment
- connectives to establish suspense used – suddenly, without warning
- speech and dialogue used
- verbs used to describe actions, thoughts and feelings
- vocabulary was chosen to give impact – adverbs, adjectives, expressive verbs, precise nouns, metaphors and similes.

Comment

All the items on this list were from suggestions by the children. Are you confident in your own subject knowledge that you could identify and discuss these features, giving examples from texts? The teacher used this list as the basis for a checklist for evaluating the children's writing.

The children were then sent to sit at their tables on which were placed a selection of different adventure stories; some were known to them and some were not. They spent time looking through them and searching for examples of the features identified above. In the plenary they were asked to identify these examples and told that next week they would begin to write their own adventure stories.

Comment

The five lessons which began this unit were designed to help children understand the features of a particular story type. If you look back at the lessons you will see that there was not much writing – this is not what the lessons were about. Go back to the beginning of the chapter and reflect on how the children had learned about story.

In this chapter on story we have seen how story-making is an essential characteristic of our humanity and that putting things into the framework of a story can greatly enhance the learning potential. Stories have been used for centuries to teach and convey cultural values and beliefs.

Read

Barrs, M. and Cork, V. (2002) *The Reader in the Writer*. London: Centre for Language in Primary Education.

The last two observations have been concerned with children preparing to write stories. It is important to remember that this need not, indeed should not, always be the case. Story-making and storytelling can take place through a variety of media. We began by claiming that one value of story is that it helps us to see the world through somebody else's eyes, and this is what the next observation illustrates.

OBSERVATION: Year 5 children (ages 9 and 10) writing stories about Vikings

The class had been studying the Vikings in History and the class teacher wanted to give them an opportunity to demonstrate their understanding through story writing. He told them the story of the Viking raid on Danby. There was a lot of talk about what it was like for both the Vikings and the Saxons and how it felt for both sides to experience this raid first hand. Role play, talk and drama were among the teaching strategies used to help the children do this. The class first wrote stories about the raid as though they were a Saxon. This is Chris's story:

> In the mist there was a large figure appearing from the sea. As it got closer and closer I could see a Viking boat! As it came closer I heard CHARGE! And they came towards us. The huge boat had a gigantic dragon face on the front, with the biggest sails I have ever seen! As I ran I saw fierce and tuff [sic] terrifying Vikings sprinting after me, Their faces were red with rage. I ran as fast as I could go. As I got home, I told my family, 'We have to run. Follow me!' We got to the point where we couldn't run any more and stopped but we were away from the Vikings.

Comment

Look carefully at Chris's story and consider how writing it had given the teacher an insight into Chris's understanding of this Viking raid that writing a non-chronological account might not have done.

The next day the children were asked to write about the raid from the perspective of the Vikings. This is what Chris wrote:

> I bellowed 'Charge!' We started to attack the Saxons. We were shocked at how many Saxons there were. They shouted, 'Ambush!' when I started to run at them. I knew they had been waiting anxiously for this day. There were metal swords flying up in the air and it felt terrifying. Red warm blood was spluttering out of cut and bruised bodies.

Comment

Look carefully at both these stories and consider what they tell us about Chris and his understanding of story. He has written well from the different perspectives. Why do you think he talks about killing and death as a Viking but not as a Saxon? Why has he described the Viking boat as a Saxon but not as a Viking?

What we have not seen in this final observation is the preparation and work that went on before these stories were written. Chris could only write stories about this Viking invasion because he was familiar with the facts but also he had discussed what it would be like and had experienced it through drama. The story element of the work brought the history to life and deepened the children's understanding.

Booker (2004) argues that there are just seven basic plots to stories:

- overcoming the monster
- rags to riches
- the quest
- voyage and return
- comedy
- tragedy
- rebirth.

In looking at these plots we can see that, if Booker is correct, the whole gamut of human experience and emotion can be found and expressed in story. Bruner (2003) argues that we are all engaged in a self-making narrative through which we define and understand ourselves as we tell stories about our experiences. He argues that story gives us a particular kind of knowing; we can 'know how' and 'know what' but we can only 'know what it is like' through story, and that knowing enhances both understanding and our notion of self.

Summary

The observations in this chapter have, I hope, shown the importance and centrality of story in the learning process and how it can be included both in plans for teaching and in unplanned activities. In order to ensure that work on story is as effective as possible, the following need to be part of our provision:

- providing access to a wide range of quality literature in all formats – oral, visual and written storytelling
- creating attractive displays that focus children's interests on story
- focusing on a writer or storyteller of the week or month
- selecting stories to record for other classes to develop children's storytelling skills
- working with writers and storytellers
- providing author boxes of books and lists of stories
- spreading enthusiasm by giving recommendations and encouraging children to share their favourites
- developing stories through drama and play.

It is through story that many children can find their way into learning and so we need to ensure that stories are at the heart of every subject on the curriculum.

Further reading

Daniel, K. (2011) *Storytelling Across the Primary Curriculum*. London: Routledge.

Ginnis, S. and Ginnis, P. (2006) *Covering the Curriculum with Stories: Six Cross-curricular Projects that Teach Literacy and Thinking through Dramatic Play*. Carmarthen: Crown House Publishing.

Teaching primary literacy

9

This concluding chapter considers all that has gone before in the journey towards becoming a teacher. What happens on that journey and how can we make it as smooth as possible?

There comes a time when the observing becomes less frequent and the teaching starts. Having said that, however, it is important to keep observing as much as possible. I have been teaching for a very long time but I still learn something every time I observe. Reflecting on what has been learned is essential, but that learning will have no value if it does not impact on practice. This concluding chapter draws together all the key features from previous chapters and puts them into the context of effective primary teaching.

Before looking at the different elements, it is important to remind ourselves of what we are teaching when we are teaching children to be readers and writers. It is quite old now but I think nothing has beaten Luke and Freebody's (1999) *Four Resources Model*. This says that in order to be fully literate children need to be taught to be code breakers, meaning makers, text users and text critics. All are equal and their development is not sequential or hierarchical. Fashions come and go and different emphases come on to the scene with schemes and resources to support them. The effective teacher of literacy ensures that all aspects of being literate are taught and that the texts through which they are taught reflect the social and cultural contexts of the time and place.

Understanding texts

Our teaching must reflect the wide variety of texts that exist in society

Effective teaching of literacy means that we are enabling children both to read and create texts in a variety of different modes. Literacy as it is used in the twenty-first century is very different from even 20 years ago. I used to find it very difficult to compose directly onto a screen and still prefer to read from a book rather than an e-reader. I have just upgraded my mobile phone and needed my son to explain to me the different options. However, I have started writing a blog and am beginning to understand how to make podcasts! My experiences do not count in teaching literacy; the world takes electronic communication in its stride and new developments happen daily. How is that reflected in the primary classroom?

It must mean that we use a range of texts in our teaching and we recognise the impact this will have on how we talk about texts. Electronic texts are often, but not always, predominantly visual and are rarely linear in construction. How do we teach children to read and create texts like that? It means that in our shared reading and writing, texts like this are as usual as traditional paper-based texts and we are able to model and demonstrate the reading and writing process using these texts.

Texts must be at the heart of our planning

Teaching literacy is about teaching children to use different modes of communication to communicate and so they must be given experience of these texts in the classroom. There has been an unfortunate tendency to use only extracts in teaching and this cannot effectively show children how texts work. I have known classes which have spent days reading lots of openings of books and stories and then writing several openings themselves without ever going on to read or write the continuation. I commend the children for their patience – I would find that experience very frustrating.

It is difficult, if planning is focused on skills, not to make your teaching very atomistic. If I am learning to write recipes, the best way is by reading lots of recipes and trying them out to see if they work. If they do work, consider why they work – what are the common features of successful recipes? I then need to write recipes and the test of my recipes will be if somebody can follow them and cook successfully what the recipe describes. The test of a good cake recipe is the end product of an edible cake and a calm cook. It is not how many time connectives or imperative verbs are used. The whole text is what is important.

The purposes of texts must be made clear and authentic texts used for genuine purposes

Unsworth argues that,

> In order to become effective participants in emerging multiliteracies, students need to understand how the resources of language, image and digital rhetorics can be deployed independently and interactively to construct different kinds of meanings. This means developing knowledge *about* linguistic, visual and digital meaning-making systems (2001: 9).

This means that literacy teaching must involve genuine experiences so that children understand the purposes of texts and can see how this works in practice. Letters and emails will be sent and responded to; notices will be put up to inform; instructions will be placed by the relevant object; and stories will be shared and responded to. This means that discussions will be held about when it is more appropriate to write a letter than send an email, about whether a poster or a web page will reach more people with the information, about how the younger children will be most easily able to access the story.

Reading aloud to children

It is this element of literacy teaching that too frequently falls off the edge and it is easy to forget that reading aloud to children is actually a reading lesson and is a vitally important part of the curriculum. Make time to read to your children at least once every day and read them a variety of different types of texts. Try out new authors and new types of texts and reflect on them together. Use every spare moment to read a poem or a notice on the notice board. Make it a priority in your classroom.

Knowing texts

As a teacher of literacy it is imperative that you know about developments in texts. You need to know about children's authors and literature and you need to know about other forms of texts too. Make it your business to know what the children in your class are reading and watching, and read and watch it yourself. Know what texts you can recommend to them; as you get to know the children in your class and know their hobbies and interests, get to know books which you can recommend to them and which will develop them as readers.

Use expert knowledge

There are many resources out there to help you and you must take advantage of them as no teacher can expect to be familiar with everything. Below are just some of them:

Centre for Language in Primary Education: www.clpe.org.uk

Literacy Shed: www.literacyshed.com

Schools Library Association: www.sla.org.uk

United Kingdom Literacy Association: www.ukla.org

National Association for the Teaching of English: www.nate.org.uk

Books for Keeps: www.booksforkeeps.co.uk

Carousel Guide to Children's Books: www.carouselguide.co.uk

Book Trust: www.booktrust.org.uk

National Literacy Trust: www.literacytrust.org.uk

Talk

There is an abundance of evidence to show that talk is a key factor in the learning process and so it needs to be a central feature in literacy teaching. Do not feel pressurised into thinking that every lesson must have a written outcome but consider how you are going to monitor the learning. Early years practitioners are often recognisable because they carry around with them a notebook or pad of sticky notes and pencil with which they record not only the interesting things they see children doing but also the interesting things they hear children say. It would be good if every primary teacher emulated this practice.

However, an implication of this is that you create opportunities for all kinds of different talk. Use Alexander's (2008) characteristics of dialogic teaching to ensure that the opportunities you create are conducive to talk with the potential for learning:

- *Collectivity* – plan for you as the teacher and the children to address learning tasks together both as part of groups or in whole-class circumstances. This will mean that you will create genuine problem-solving or enquiry-based lessons.

- *Reciprocity* – create an ethos within your classroom of teacher and children listening to each other, sharing ideas and learning to consider alternative viewpoints. Do not feel you need to give the impression that you are always correct.
- *Cumulation* – plan for opportunities which build on each other so that knowledge and understanding are created as teachers and children build on their own and others' ideas, chaining them into coherent lines of thinking and enquiry.
- *Support* – be sure that in your classroom children feel secure enough to express their ideas freely and without embarrassment
- *Purposefulness* – identify clear and specific learning outcomes and make those apparent to the children.

You will see that all of these characteristics require the teacher to relinquish some control and this can be challenging. Do not be afraid of silence when children can think; allow children to think aloud and do so yourself, and make sure any question you ask opens up thinking and learning rather than closing it down.

Recognise the importance of talk and plan for it specifically. It is not just a few minutes on a plan labelled 'discussion' which you use to test knowledge or draw the class together.

Teaching reading and writing

Unsworth (2001) outlines three types of literacy learning and teaching which can be found in classrooms:

- *Recognition* is when children recognise and can reproduce the different codes that are used to construct and communicate meanings.
- *Reproduction* is when they understand and can produce different texts in appropriate ways and formats.
- *Reflection* is when they understand that texts are socially constructed and can stand back and reflect on the nature of texts and the implicit values and understandings contained in them.

How is this evident in what happens on a day-to-day basis? How do teachers plan to ensure that children not only recognise but can reproduce and reflect? I want to propose that these are not hierarchical or linear but that each type of literacy teaching and learning can take place in every classroom – a Foundation Stage 1 classroom and a Year 6 classroom. What does it look like?

In primary classrooms children are taught 'how to' read and write. They take part in shared reading and writing, guided reading and writing, and independent reading and writing. They have daily discrete phonics teaching. Their environment is full of print used for genuine purposes and responded to. They are read to several times every day. What moves all those activities from the recognition to the reproduction and the reflection are the interactions that take place between the children and an informed teacher. While reading a notice the teacher will discuss who put the notice up and what message they want to convey; when sharing a book the teacher will encourage the children to relate what they read to their own experiences and evaluate its authenticity; when writing a letter the recipient will be considered and their perceived needs and understandings will determine what is put into the letter and how it is expressed.

Talk is the central element and it is what can change a mundane lesson instructing in skills to an exciting and powerful reflection on the use of literacy.

Literacy across the curriculum

I have a strongly held belief that literacy is at the heart of the curriculum and accept Langer's (1986) claim that it is a 'way of thinking'. This means that in every lesson teachers should be aware of the literacy demands that are being placed on children and plan accordingly. Whether you are teaching in a cross-subject way, a creative way or a subject-based way, children will need to use literacy in the lessons. Teachers need to ensure that they have the skills which are required.

This emphasises the fact that the first and most important thing a teacher must do when planning is to identify the learning objective, that is, you need to be absolutely clear in your own mind what it is you want children to gain from this lesson. If it is a history lesson and you want them either to learn that things were different in the past or what it felt like to be an evacuee in the Second World War, you need to be sure that nothing in the lesson will distract from that learning intention. For example, if you ask them to read a text that is too challenging or to write in an unknown format all energies will be focused on that and the thing you wanted them to learn will fade into the background. You need always to be aware of literacy within every lesson.

It also means, however, that literacy learning can be a focus of a lesson and any content can be used. In the history lesson about evacuees you can use drama techniques, critically read accounts from different perspectives or look for emotive words and phrases within a text. This would make it a literacy lesson but with the bonus of developing knowledge about the history curriculum.

Planning and assessment

The role of a teacher is to ensure that every child in the class is learning. It is relatively easy to keep children busy and amused but if you have not made a difference to their understanding, knowledge or skills it is a waste of time. This means that teachers are continually monitoring the learning and adjusting their plans accordingly. We have seen in observations how plans were changed and modified to address the needs of the class, of groups and of individuals.

The observations have also shown how it is possible to over-plan. This is very difficult for an inexperienced teacher, especially when you are reminded of the importance of detailed planning at every opportunity during your training! There are several key points:

- Know what the purpose of a lesson or a unit of work is -- what do you want to achieve at the end of this time of teaching?
- What do the children know now? What do they understand? What can they do? That is your starting point.
- How does understanding in the subject develop from the starting point to where I want to go? As teacher, I need to know what the next step is – it might be the next set of phonemes to teach, it might be a more challenging text to read, it might be challenging assumptions.
- What teaching strategies will help me to address this development? What degree of scaffolding do the children need – shared, guided or independent?
- How will I know if the children have reached my hoped-for end point? What will tell me that they know, understand or can do? What evidence can I look for and how will I look for it and record it?

What does effective teaching in literacy look like?

When discussing the stages of planning above, most trainees have wanted to know what good or outstanding teaching looks like. In the introduction to this book I compared effective teachers to swans gliding over the water.

They look beautiful; there is scarcely a ripple in the water and they are progressing purposefully towards their destination. Under the water, however, they are busy paddling, without which nothing would happen. I hope that the chapters in this book have enabled you to look under the water and to begin to understand the nature of what lies beneath and enables effective literacy teaching to take place.

At the risk of mixing images, I often compare learning to teach with learning to drive. At first you are very aware of all the component actions required: you turn on the ignition, check the mirrors, let in the clutch, go into, hopefully, first gear, let out the clutch, trying hard to recognise what is described as the 'bite', and then lurch off down the road. At the time it all seemed so difficult and complex and, if you were like me, you wondered if you would ever be able to do it. However, as an experienced driver you probably now do all those things without even thinking about them and, if asked, would find it difficult to articulate all that is involved in safely driving a car.

Teaching is exactly the same. Experienced teachers do all those things under the surface which make life in the classroom smooth and purposeful but often do not consciously think about it or articulate why they are doing it. That makes life difficult for trainee teachers. They need to understand what is happening and why it is happening because learning to teach is not just about copying what you see. I hope this book has helped you to see and understand the paddling of the feet under the water and to know the questions you need to ask about what you see in classrooms.

Effective teaching of literacy

Hall and Harding (2003) did a review of the literature on effective literacy teaching. They attempted to identify key teaching strategies which were effective but found that this was not straightforward. Some key features which seemed to emerge from all the studies were:

- a balance of direct skills instruction and more contextually grounded literacy activities
- integration of literacy modes, and linking with other curricular areas
- pupil engagement, on-task behaviour and pupil self-regulation
- teaching style involving differentiated instruction (incorporating extensive use of scaffolding and coaching and careful and frequent monitoring of pupil progress)
- links with parents and local community.

Look back over all the observations in this book and you will see that these features were present in many, if not all, of them. There is no one way to teach literacy and anyone who tries to tell you otherwise is misguided. As professionals, teachers are continually making judgements about children and the appropriate next steps. Often these judgements are immediate and are based on a solid basis of subject knowledge for teaching. 'Effective teachers of literacy … are alert to children's progress and can step in and use the appropriate method to meet the child's instructional needs. The "effective" teacher uses an eclectic collection of methods' (Hall and Harding 2003: 3).

It is challenging for trainee teachers to make sense of this process and to come to a position where they are able to make those judgements and decisions themselves. The report goes on to say that it is through observation and reflection that trainees will gain the required experience:

> Students in training will not only need to be exposed to this wide and varied array of teaching practices but will also need experience in blending these practices in different ways for different children. They will also need opportunities to reflect on their own and others' practice in the light of the research base. Case study and exemplification material would be useful supports for teacher educators in promoting this learning and reflection. (Hall and Harding 2003: 4)

This book aims to provide those exemplifications and to model the process of reflection which leads to deep learning.

Becoming a teacher

The process of teacher training is extremely demanding and stressful. Hobson and Malderez (2005) identified some key themes which are shared by all trainee teachers:

- *The language and the terminology* – teaching is as full of jargon as any other profession. Do not be afraid to challenge your tutors, mentors and teachers to explain to you what they mean when you cannot understand the language.
- *Relationships* – the relationship you have with your school-based mentor is crucial to your growth as a teacher. If there is a problem here you must talk with your tutor or the headteacher.
- *Relevance* – trainees often want to know 'how to do it' and become impatient with theory lectures. The distinction between the two is not

as obvious as it may first seem. Becoming a teacher is all about making sense of what is going on in the classroom and to do this meaningfully a framework of established knowledge and understanding is needed. That framework is often what is called theory. The research found that those who had had more experience in school prior to training appreciated the need for understanding the 'why' (theory) more.

- *Emotions* – Hobson and Malderez found that:

  > the process of becoming a teacher is a highly emotional experience for most trainees. Many trainees use highly emotive language, such as excitement, love, panic, shock and overwhelmed to describe aspects of their early experiences as trainees, and many trainees refer to experiences which have boosted their confidence on the one hand, and undermined their confidence on the other. (2005: 139)

  It is comforting to know that you are not the only one who experiences vulnerability and varying degrees of confidence. I am feeling both those emotions as I prepare to send this manuscript to the publishers! In teaching, we are making ourselves vulnerable because teaching is, among other things, sharing ourselves with our pupils. It is as we grow in experience that our confidence also grows.

- *Being a teacher* – it is an exciting and challenging thing to be a teacher and it is significant that we always talk about *being* a teacher rather than *doing* teaching. One trainee I worked with wrote in his reflective journal about two-thirds of the way through his training, 'At last I am beginning to feel like a teacher rather than just behave like one'.

Being a teacher is also about being a learner and all that that involves – asking questions, taking risks and collaborating with others.

Being a teacher of literacy is even more exciting because it means entering different worlds with your pupils and creating different worlds with them; it means discovering the power of language and different means of communicating with all sorts of people for all sorts of reasons; it means giving children the opportunity to become effective citizens of the future and to share in and contribute to the development of humanity. The stakes are high but the rewards are great.

Further reading

Grigg, R. (2015) *Becoming an Outstanding Primary School Teacher*, 2nd edn. Abingdon: Routledge.
Pollard, A. (2014) *Reflective Teaching in Schools*, 4th edn. London: Bloomsbury Academic.

References

Alexander, R. (2002) 'The curriculum in successful primary schools: a response', keynote address given to HMI invitation conference, 14 October 2002.

Alexander, R. (2005) 'Culture, dialogue and learning: notes on an emerging pedagogy', keynote address given to the conference of the International Association for Cognitive Education and Psychology, University of Durham, July. Available at: www.learnlab.org/research/wiki/images/c/cf/Robinalexander_IACEP_2005.pdf

Alexander, R. (2008) *Towards Dialogic Teaching: Rethinking Classroom Talk*, 4th edn. Thirsk: Dialogos.

Almond, D. (2016) *The Great Tester.* Available at: www.tes.com/news/school-news/breaking-news/top-author-and-childrens-laureate-publish-illustrated-poem-dangers

Andrews, R.C., Torgerson, S., Beverton, A., Freeman, T., Lock, G., Low, G., Robinson, A. and Zhu, D. (2006) 'The effect of grammar teaching on writing development', *British Education Research Journal*, 32(1): 39–55.

Andrews, R., Torgerson, C., Low, G. and McGuinn, N. (2009) 'Teaching argument writing to 7 to 14 year olds: an international review of the evidence of successful practice', *Cambridge Journal of Education*, 39(3): 291–310.

Armstrong, M. (2006) *Children Writing Stories*. Maidenhead: Open University Press.

Bakhtin, M.M. (1981) *The Dialogic Imagination*. Austin and London: University of Texas Press.

Baldwin, P. and Fleming, K. (2003) *Teaching Literacy Through Drama: Creative Approaches*. London: Routledge.

Barnes, J. (2015) *Cross-curricular Learning 3–14*, 3rd edn. London: SAGE.

Barnes, D. and Todd, F. (1977) *Communication and Learning in Small Groups*. London: Routledge and Kegan Paul.

Barrett, L. (2010) 'Effective school libraries: evidence of impact on student achievement', *The School Librarian*, 58(3): 136–9.

Barrs, M. and Cork, V. (2002) *The Reader in the Writer*. London: Centre for Language in Primary Education (CLPE).

Bennett, N. and Desforges, C. (1984) *The Quality of Pupil Learning Experiences*. Hove: Psychology Press.

Billingsley, B. (2016) 'Ways to prepare future teachers to teach Science in multicultural classrooms', *Cultural Studies of Science Education*, 11(2): 283–91.

Black, P. and Wiliam, D. (1998) 'Inside the black box: raising standards through classroom assessment', *Phi Delta Kappan*, 80(2): 139–48.

Black, P., McCormick, R., James, M. and Pedder, D. (2006) 'Learning how to learn and assessment for learning: a theoretical inquiry', *Research Papers in Education*, 21(2): 119–32.

Booker, C. (2004) *The Seven Basic Plots*. London: Continuum.

Booth, D. (2006) *Reading Doesn't Matter Anymore …: Shattering the Myths of Literacy*. Markham, Ontario: Pembroke.

Bruner, J. (1996) *The Culture of Education*. Cambridge, MA: Harvard University Press.

Bruner, J.S. (1966) *Toward a Theory of Instruction*. Cambridge, MA: Belknap.

Bruner, J.S. (2003) *Making Stories: Law, Literature, Life*. Cambridge, MA: Harvard University Press.

Cambourne, B. (2000) 'Observing literacy learning in elementary classrooms: nine years of classroom anthropology', *The Reading Teacher*, 53(6): 512–15.

CLPE (1985) *The Primary Language Record*. London: CLPE.

CLPE (2016) *Reading and Writing Scales*. Available at: www.clpe.org.uk

Chamberlain, L. (2015) *Inspiring Writing in Primary Schools*. London: SAGE.

Chambers, A. (2011) *Tell Me (Children, Reading and Talk)* with *The Reading Environment*. Stroud: Thimble Press.

Clark, C. (2013) *Children and Young People's Reading in 2013*. London: National Literacy Trust.

Clarke, S. (2008) *Active Learning Through Formative Assessment*. London: Hodder Education.

Clay, M.M. (1991) *Becoming Literate: The Construction of Inner Control*. London: Heinemann Education.

Corbett, P. (2008a) *Book-Talk*. Available at: http://nationalstrategies.standards.dcsf.gov.uk/node/154871

Corbett, P. (2008b) *Talk for Writing*. London: Crown.

Craft, A. (1999) *Creativity across the Primary Curriculum: Framing and Developing Practice*. London: Routledge.

Cremin, T. and Myhill, D. (2011) *Thinking Critically About Writing: Writers' Voices in the Classroom*. London: Routledge.

Cremin, T., Mottram, M., Bearne, E. and Goodwin, P. (2008) 'Exploring teachers' knowledge of children's literature', *Cambridge Journal of Education*, 38(4): 449–64.

Daniel, K. (2011) *Storytelling Across the Primary Curriculum*. London: Routledge.

Davis, A. (2012) 'A monstrous regime of synthetic phonics: fantasies of research-based teaching "methods" versus real teaching', *Journal of Philosophy of Education*, 46(4): 212–25.

Dawes, L. (2001) 'Interthinking – the power of productive talk', in P. Goodwin (ed.), *The Articulate Classroom*. London: David Fulton.

Dawes, L., Mercer, N. and Wegerif, R. (2000) *Thinking Together: Activities for Teachers and Children at Key Stage 2*. Birmingham: Questions Publishing.

DCSF (2008) *Talk for Writing: Primary National Strategies*. London: HMSO.

DCSF (2009) *Primary School Curriculum Omnibus Survey: Top Line Findings Report*. London: HMSO.

DfE (2010) *The Importance of Teaching: Schools*. White Paper. London: DfE.

DfE (2013) *The Primary National Curriculum in England*. London: Shurville Publishing.

DfE (2016) *Educational Excellence Everywhere*. London: DfE.

DfES (2001) *The National Literacy Strategy: Framework for Teaching*, 3rd edn. London: DfES.

DfES (2007) *Letters and Sounds*. London: DfES.

Dombey, H. (2010) *Teaching Reading: What the Evidence Says*. Leicester: United Kingdom Literacy Association.

Duff, F.J., Mengani, S.E., Bailey, A.M. and Snowling, M.J. (2015) 'Validity and sensitivity of the phonics screening check: implications for practice', *Journal of Research in Education*, 38(2): 109–23.

Dweck, C.S. (2006) *Mindset: The New Psychology of Success*. New York: Random House.

Ehri, L.C. (1995) 'Phases of development in learning to read words by sight', *Journal of Research in Reading*, 18(2): 116–25.

Eke, R. and Lee, J. (2009) *Using Talk Effectively in the Primary Classroom*. London: David Fulton.

Flynn, N. and Stainthorp, R. (2006) *The Learning and Teaching of Reading and Writing*. Oxford: Wiley Blackwell.

Galton, M. and Simon, B. (eds) (1980) *Progress and Performance in the Primary Classroom*. London: Routledge and Kegan Paul.

Gillies, D. (2006) 'Curriculum for Excellence: a question of values', *Scottish Educational Review*, 38: 25–36.

Ginnis, S. and Ginnis, P. (2006) *Covering the Curriculum with Stories: Six Cross-Curricular Projects that Teach Literacy and Thinking Through Dramatic Play*. Carmarthen: Crown House Publishing.

Goodman, K. (1992) 'Why whole language is today's agenda in education', *Language Arts*, 69: 354–63.

Goodwin, P. (ed.) (2001) *The Articulate Classroom: Talking and Learning in the Primary Classroom*. London: David Fulton.

Goodwin, P. (ed.) (2005) *Literacy Through Creativity*. London: David Fulton.

Goodwin, P. (ed.) (2008) *Understanding Children's Books: A Guide for Education Professionals*. London: SAGE.

Goodwin, P. (2011) 'Creating young readers: teachers and librarians at work', in J. Court (ed.), *Read to Succeed*. London: Facet.

Goodwin, P. and Perkins, M. (2009) 'Reading aloud in the primary school', paper presented at UKLA Conference 'Changing Horizons', University of Greenwich.

Goodwin, P. and Perkins, M. (2010) 'Teachers choosing books to read aloud in the primary school', paper presented at UKLA Conference, University of Winchester.

Goouch, K. and Lambirth, A. (2008) *Understanding Phonics and the Teaching of Reading: Critical Perspectives*. Maidenhead: McGraw-Hill/Open University Press.

Goswami, U. (2006) 'The brain in the classroom? The state of the art', *Developmental Science*, 8: 467–9.

Goswami, U. (2008) 'Reading, complexity and the brain', *Literacy*, 42(2): 67–74.

Gough, P.B. and Tunmer, W.E. (1986) 'Decoding, reading and reading disability', *Remedial and Special Education*, 7(1): 6–10.

Gove, M. (2009) Interview in the *Daily Telegraph*, 3 August.

Grainger, T. (1997) *Traditional Storytelling*. Leamington Spa: Scholastic.

Graves, D.H. (1983) *Writing: Teachers and Children at Work*. Portsmouth, NH: Heinemann Educational.

Grigg, R. (2010) *Becoming an Outstanding Primary School Teacher*. Harlow: Pearson.

Grugeon, E. and Gardner, P. (2000) *The Art of Storytelling for Teachers and Pupils: Using Story to Develop Literacy in the Primary Classroom*. London: David Fulton.

Hall, K. and Harding, A. (2003) 'A systematic review of effective literacy teaching in the 4 to 14 age range of mainstream schooling', in *Research Evidence in Education Library*. London: EPPI-Centre, Social Science Research Unit, Institute of Education, University of London.

Halliday, M. (1993) 'Towards a language-based theory of learning', *Linguistics and Education*, 5: 93–116.

Halliday, M.A.K. (1976) *Language as Social Semiotic*. London: Arnold.

Hardy, B. (1977) 'Narrative as a primary act of mind', in M. Meek, A. Warlow and G. Barton (eds), *The Cool Web: Pattern of Children's Reading*. London: Bodley Head.

Harrison, C. (2010) *Interdisciplinary Perspectives on Learning to Read*. London: Taylor and Francis.

Heath, S.B. (1983) *Ways with Words*. Cambridge: Cambridge University Press.

Hillocks, G. (1986) *Research on Written Composition: New Directions for Teaching*. Urbana, IL: National Council of Teachers of English.

Hobson, A.J. and Malderez, A. (eds) with Kerr, K., Tracey, L., Pell, R.G., Tomlinson, P.D and Roper, T. (2005) *Becoming a Teacher: Student Teachers' Motives and Preconceptions, and Early School-based Experiences During Initial Teacher Training* (ITT), DfES Research Report No. 673.

Howe, C. and Abedin, M. (2013) 'Classroom dialogue: a systematic review across four decades of research', *Cambridge Journal of Education*, 43(3): 325–56.

Jeffrey, B. (ed.) (2006) *Creative Learning Practices: European Experiences*. London: Tufnell Press.

Johnston, R. and Watson, J. (2007) *Teaching Synthetic Phonics*. Exeter: Learning Matters.

Joubert, M. (2001) 'The art of creative teaching', in A. Craft, B. Jeffrey and M. Leibling (eds), *Creativity in Education*. London: Continuum.

Kress, G. (1982) *Learning to Write*. London: Routledge and Kegan Paul.

Laevers, F. (ed.) (1994) *The Leuven Involvement Scale for Young Children* (Manual and Video). Experiential Education Series, No 1. Leuven: Centre for Experiential Education.

Langer, J.A. (1986) *Children Reading and Writing*. Norwood, NJ: Ablex.

Lockwood, M. (2008) *Promoting Reading for Pleasure in the Primary School*. London: SAGE.

Luke, A. and Freebody, P. (1999) 'Further notes on the 4 resources model', *Practically Primary*, 4(2): 5–8.

Maine, F. (2013) 'How children talk together to make meaning from texts: a dialogic perspective on reading comprehension strategies', *Literacy*, 47(3): 150–6.

Marsh, J. (2003) 'Connections between literacy practices at home and in the nursery', *British Education Research Journal*, 29(3): 369–82.

Marsh, J. and Millard, E. (2000) *Literacy and Popular Culture: Using Children's Culture in the Classroom*. London: Paul Chapman.

Maybin, J., Mercer, N. and Stierer, B. (1992) 'Scaffolding learning in the classroom', in K. Norman (ed.), *Thinking Voices: The Work of the National Oracy Project*. London: Hodder. pp. 186–95.

Medwell, J., Strand, S. and Wray, D. (2009) 'The links between handwriting and composing for Year 6 children', *Cambridge Journal of Education*, 39(3): 329–44.

Meek, M. (1988) *How Texts Teach What Readers Learn*. Stroud: Thimble Press.

Meek, M. (1991) *On Being Literate*. London: Bodley Head.

Mercer, N. (1995) *The Guided Construction of Knowledge: Talk Amongst Teachers and Learners*. Clevedon: Multilingual Matters.

Mercer, N., Hennessy, S. and Warwick, P. (2010) 'Using interactive whiteboards to orchestrate classroom dialogue', *Technology, Pedagogy and Education*, 19(2): 195–209.

Merchant, G. (2007) 'Writing the future in the digital age', *Literacy*, 41(3): 118–28.

Michener, J.A. (n.d.) www.brainyquote.com/quotes/authors/j/james_a_michener. html (accessed 6 June 2011).

Moon, J.E. (2004) *A Handbook of Reflective and Experiential Learning: Theory and Practice*. Abingdon: RoutledgeFalmer.

Morris, M. and Smith, S. (2010) *Thirty-Three Ways to Help with Spelling: Supporting Children Who Struggle with Basic Skills*. London: Routledge.

Mroz, M., Smith, F. and Harding, F. (2000) 'The discourse of the literacy hour', *Cambridge Journal of Education*, 30(3): 379–90.

Mullen, R. and Wedwick, L. (2008) 'Avoiding the digital abyss: getting started in the classroom with YouTube, digital stories and blogs', *The Clearing House*, 82(2): 66–9.

Myhill, D. (2000) 'Misconceptions and difficulties in the acquisition of metalinguistic knowledge', *Language and Education*, 14(3): 151–63.

Myhill, D. and Jones, S. (2010) 'How talk becomes text: investigating the concept of oral rehearsal in early years' classrooms', *British Journal of Educational Studies*, 57(3): 265–84.

Myhill, D., Jones, S., Lines, H. and Watson, A. (2012) 'Re-thinking grammar: the impact of embedded grammar teaching on students' writing and students' metalinguistic understanding', *Research Papers in Education*, 27(2): 139–66.

Nystrand, M. (1997) *Open Dialogue: Understanding the Dynamics of Language and Learning in English Classrooms*. New York: Teachers College Press.

Ofsted (2002) *The Curriculum in Successful Primary Schools*. London: Ofsted.

Ofsted (2005) *English 2000–05: A Review of Inspection Survey*. London: Ofsted.

Ofsted (2010) *Reading by Six: How the Best Schools Do It*. London: Ofsted.

O'Sullivan, O. and Thomas, A. (2007) *Understanding Spelling*. London: Routledge.

Pahl, K. and Roswell, J. (2005) *Literacy and Education: Understanding the New Literacy Studies in the Classroom*. London: SAGE.

Pang, E.S., Muaka, A., Bernhardt, E.B. and Kamil, M. (2003) *Teaching Reading*. Geneva: International Academy of Education.

Paratore, J.R. and McCormack, R.L. (eds) (2007) *Classroom Literacy Assessment: Making Sense of What Students Know and Do*. New York: Guilford Press.

Pascal, C. and Bertram, A.D. (eds) (1997) *Effective Early Learning: Case Studies of Improvement*. London: Hodder and Stoughton.

Peacock, A. (2016) *Assessment for Learning without Limits*. London: Open University Press.

Perkins, M. (2015) *Becoming a Teacher of Reading*. London: SAGE.

Pentimonti, J.M. and Justice, L.M. (2010) 'Teachers' use of scaffolding strategies during read alouds in the preschool classroom', *Early Childhood Education Journal*, 37(4): 241–8.

Pollard, A. (2008) *Reflective Teaching: Evidence-informed Professional Practice*, 3rd edn. London: Continuum.

Priestley, M. and Hughes, W. (2010) 'The development of Scotland's Curriculum for Excellence: amnesia and déjà vu', *Oxford Review of Education*, 36: 345–61.

Reedy, D. and Bearne, E. (2013) *Teaching Grammar Effectively in Primary Schools*. Leicester: UKLA.

Rose, J. (2006) *Independent Review of the Teaching of Early Reading*. Rose Review. London: DCSF.

Rose, J. (2009) *Independent Review of the Primary Curriculum: Final Report*. London: Crown Publications.

Rosen, H. (1984) *Stories and Meanings*. Sheffield: NATE.

Rosen, M. (2010) 'Foreword', in H. Dombey et al., *Teaching Reading: What the Evidence Says*. Leicester: United Kingdom Literacy Association.

Rutherford, G. (2016) *Wyche Way to Teach*. Gloucester: Little Inky Fingers.

Safford, K. (2016) 'Teaching grammar and testing grammar in the English primary school: the impact on teachers and their teaching of the grammar element of the statutory test in spelling, punctuation and grammar (SPaG)', *Changing English: Studies in Culture and Education*, 23(1): 3–21.

Schön, D. (1983) *The Reflective Practitioner: How Professionals Think in Action*. New York: Basic Books.

Scottish Executive (2004) *A Curriculum for Excellence*. Available at: www.educa tionscotland.gov.uk/learningandteaching/thecurriculum/whatiscurriculumfor excellence/keydocs/index.asp

Sinclair, J. and Coulthard, M. (1975) *Towards an Analysis of Discourse*. Oxford: Oxford University Press.

Smith, F., Hardman, F., Wall, K. and Mroz, M. (2004) 'Interactive whole class teaching in the National Literacy and Numeracy Strategies', *British Educational Research Journal*, 30(3): 403–19.

Smith, V. (2008) 'Learning to be a reader: promoting good textual health', in P. Goodwin (ed.), *Understanding Children's Books: A Guide for Education Professionals*. London: SAGE.

Stone, G. (2011) *The Digital Literacy Classroom*. Leicester: UKLA.

Taeschner, T. (1991) *A Developmental Psycholinguistic Approach to Second Language Teaching*. Norwood, NJ: Ablex.

Tennent, W. (2014) *Understanding Reading Comprehension: Processes and Practices*. London: SAGE.

Topping, K. (2016) *What Kids are Reading*. Renaissance Learning. Available at: http://whatkidsarereading.co.uk/

Truss, L. (2009) *Eats, Shoots and Leaves: The Zero Tolerance Approach to Punctuation*. London: Fourth Estate.

Unsworth, L. (2001) *Teaching Multiliteracies across the Curriculum*. Buckingham: Open University Press.

Vasquez, V. (2010) 'Critical literacy isn't just for books anymore', *The Reading Teacher*, 63(7): 614–16.

Verenikina, I. (2004) 'From theory to practice: what does the metaphor of scaffolding mean to educators today?' *Outlines: Critical Practice Studies*, no. 2.

Watson, A. (2012) 'Navigating the pit of doom: affective responses to teaching grammar', *English in Education*, 46(1): 22–37.

Watson, C. (2010) 'Educational policy in Scotland: inclusions and the control of society', *Discourse Studies in the Cultural Politics of Education*, 31: 93–104.

Watts, Z. and Gardner, P. (2013) 'Is systematic phonics enough? Examining the benefit of intensive teaching of high frequency words in a Y1 class', *Education 3–13*, 41(1): 100–10.

Waugh, D., Warner, C. and Waugh, R. (2016) *Teaching Grammar, Punctuation and Spelling in Primary Schools*, 2nd edn. London: SAGE.

Wells, G. (1999) *Dialogic Inquiry: Towards a Sociocultural Practice and Theory of Education*. Cambridge: Cambridge University Press.

Wolfe, C.S. (2015) 'Talking policy into practice: probing the debates around the effective teaching of early reading', *Education 3–13*, 43(5): 498–513.

Wood, D., Bruner, J.S. and Ross, G. (1976) 'The role of tutoring in problem solving', *Journal of Child Psychology and Psychiatry*, 17: 89–100.

Wray, D., Medwell, J., Fox, R. and Poulson, L. (2000) 'The teaching practices of effective teachers of literacy', *Educational Review*, 52(1): 75–84.

Wyse, D. and Ferrari, A. (2015) 'Creativity and education: comparing the national curricula of the states of the European Union and the United Kingdom', *British Educational Research Journal*, 41(4): 30–45.

Wyse, D. and Styles, M. (2007) 'Synthetic phonics and the teaching of reading: the debate surrounding England's "Rose Report"', *Literacy*, 47(1): 35–42.

Wyse, D. and Torrance, H. (2009) 'The development and consequences of national curriculum assessment for primary education in England', *Educational Research*, 51(2): 213–28.

Children's books referred to

Ahlberg, A. and Ahlberg, J. (1999) *The Jolly Postman*. London: Puffin.
Browne, A. (1997) *The Tunnel*. London: Walker Books.
Browne, A. (2008) *Gorilla*. London: Walker Books.
Cannon, J. (1993) *Stellaluna*. Oxford: Harcourt Children's Books.
Cronin, D. (2003) *Click, Clack, Moo: Cows that Type*. London: Simon and Schuster.
Deacon, A. and Schwarz, V. (2016) *I am Henry Finch*. London: Walker Books.
Geraghty, P. (1995) *Over the Steamy Swamp*. London: Voyager Books.
Geraghty, P. (2010) *Solo*. London: Anderson.
Hunt, R. (2003) *Getting Up*. Oxford: Oxford University Press.
Lobel, A. (1983) *Fables*. New York: Trophy Press.
Murphy, J. (2007) *Peace at Last*. London: Macmillan Children's Books.
Rosen, M. (1993) *We're Going on a Bear Hunt*. London: Walker Books.
Sheldon, D. and Blythe, G. (1993) *The Whale's Song*. London: Red Fox.
Tan, S. (2001) *The Red Tree*. Sydney: Lothian Children's Books.
Waddell, M. (1994) *Owl Babies*. London: Walker Books.
Walliams, D. (2013) *The Boy in the Dress*. London: HarperCollins.
Willems, M. (2004) *Don't Let the Pigeon Drive the Bus*. London: Walker Books.

Index